# Languages in Africa

# LANGUAGES IN AFRICA
## Multilingualism, Language Policy, and Education

Edited by Elizabeth C. Zsiga, One Tlale Boyer, and Ruth Kramer

GEORGETOWN UNIVERSITY PRESS
Washington, DC

Cover design by James Keller (jim@creationrebel.com).
Cover photograph courtesy of iStockphoto: Portrait of South African girls studying in a rural classroom.

Library of Congress Cataloging-in-Publication Data

Georgetown University Round Table on Languages and Linguistics
(2013 : Washington, D.C.)
Languages in Africa : multilingualism, language policy, and education / edited by Elizabeth C. Zsiga, One Tlale Boyer, and Ruth Kramer.
    pages cm.— (Georgetown University round table on languages and linguistics series)
    "Contributors to this volume came together to discuss the problems and promise of African multilingualism at a joint meeting of the Annual Conference on African Linguistics and the Georgetown University Round Table on Languages and Linguistics in Washington, D.C., in March 2013. As part of that joint conference, a workshop on language and education in Africa was organized by Carolyn Adger of the Center for Applied Linguistics. That workshop became the inspiration for this volume."—Introduction.
    Includes bibliographical references and index.
    ISBN 978-1-62616-152-8 (pbk. : alk. paper)—ISBN 978-1-62616-153-5 (ebook)
    1. Multilingualism—Africa.—Congresses.    2. Native language and education—Africa—Congresses.    3. Language policy—Africa—Congresses.    4. African languages—Social aspects—Congresses.    I. Zsiga, Elizabeth C.    II. Tlale Boyer, One.    III. Kramer, Ruth (Ruth T.).    IV. Title.    V. Series: Georgetown University round table on languages and linguistics series (2004).
P115.5.A35G46    2014
306.44'6096—dc23

                                                                        2014014514

15  14  13        9  8  7  6  5  4  3  2
First printing

Printed in the United States of America

Cover design by James Keller. Cover photo courtesy of iStockphoto: Portrait of South African girls studying in a rural classroom.

*We dedicate this volume, on the occasion of his retirement,*
*to our colleague and friend*
Dr. James E. Alatis

Professor of Linguistics,
Dean Emeritus of the Georgetown University
School of Languages and Linguistics,
ardent supporter of the Georgetown University
Round Table on Languages and Linguistics,
prolific scholar and beloved teacher, and strong advocate
for the importance of bringing linguistic science to bear on
issues of education and language policy around the world.

# Contents

# Figures and Tables

## Tables

# Introduction: Layers of Language—Some Bad News and Some Good News on Multilingualism, Language Policy, and Education in Africa

ELIZABETH C. ZSIGA, ONE TLALE BOYER, AND RUTH KRAMER
*Georgetown University*

THE CHAPTERS IN THIS VOLUME examine the phenomenon of multilingualism in Africa as it affects individuals, communities, ethnic groups, nations, and the larger interconnected world. The perspectives and case studies presented here cover the whole of the continent, from Morocco to South Africa, from Côte d'Ivoire to Kenya. Some chapters present a discouraging picture; others, a more hopeful one. There is both bad and good news to report.

The contributors to this volume came together to discuss the problems and promise of African multilingualism at a joint meeting of the Annual Conference on African Linguistics and the Georgetown University Round Table on Languages and Linguistics in Washington in March 2013. As part of that joint conference, a workshop on language and education in Africa was organized by Carolyn Adger of the Center for Applied Linguistics. That workshop became the inspiration for this volume. (The general proceedings of the conference, containing papers on all aspects of the linguistics of African languages, is being published by Cascadilla Press.) For the present, more focused volume, we invited participants to submit papers that addressed multilingualism in Africa as it interacts with education and language policy.

## Layers of Language

In so many African communities, languages are layered, or nested, in concentric circles. Commonly, a speaker's mother-tongue language, the language that is spoken in the home, is known and used only by a small group. Often the language is not written, it is not used in school, and it is not known or used outside the local community (or sometimes, when a community of speakers is dispersed or intermingled, it is not even used by the family next door). This mother-tongue language may be critically endangered.

Surrounding this home and community language is a national or vehicular language, an indigenous language that is more widely used and is probably spoken by the majority in that particular country. Examples include Akan in Ghana, Swahili in Kenya, and Setswana in Botswana. This language will have a written literature and media presence, may have official status, and may be used in school, especially in the primary grades.

Surrounding the national language will be an international language, such as English or French, a legacy of colonialism. The international languages carry high prestige, are the languages of instruction for all higher education, and are widely believed to be the means of greater social and economic opportunity. Yet not many people will know these languages well.

Thus we see layers of language:

- Small/medium/large,
- My language/our language/their language, and
- Language that expresses my ethnic identity/language that expresses my national identity/language that expresses my connection to the world.

Or is it "language that reminds me every day of past injustice"? "Language that reinforces my powerlessness"? How easy is it for the speaker to come to believe that the relationship is not intimate/public/international, but inferior/neutral/superior? Is it possible for individuals and communities to embrace the local mother-tongue language as an asset and means of empowerment rather than as a liability and means of disenfranchisement?

The specific countries and languages described by the contributors to this volume are listed in table 1 (depending on the focus of the chapter, not all cells will be filled, of course). For some contributors, the focus is on the concentric circles surrounding a small rural community. Others look at language juxtaposition and intermixing in urban settings, or at national trends. Many concentrate on the classroom setting; others consider multilingualism as it is expressed in other domains of life, including politics, advertising, music, movies, and figurative language. In chapter 2 Bokamba sets African multilingualism in the context of the theoretical and sociolinguistic literature, providing an explicit definition of multilingualism as opposed to bilingualism, and discussing how studies of multilingual individuals and societies benefit linguistic science. All the contributors ask how language policies and language attitudes affect and are affected by the facts of living in a world of multi-layered languages.

Across the different countries, languages, and settings, common questions emerge:

- *At the level of the individual:* What do I think of my own language, and what does that say about me? Is language crucial to identity? How do individuals leverage the languages available to them to increase their own social, educational, and economic potential?
- *In the home:* How are parents passing the mother-tongue language and cultural values on to their children?
- *In the local school:* What language or languages should be used in school? At what point should a national or international language be introduced? How can communities best educate their children?

Table 1
**Layers of Languages**

| Chapter | Author | Country | Local Language | Majority Language | International Language | Focus |
|---------|--------|---------|----------------|-------------------|----------------------|-------|
| 1 | Trudell and Adger | Kenya | Maasai and others | Swahili | English | School |
| 2 | Bokamba | Morocco, DR Congo, and others | Multiple | Multiple | Arabic, English | Linguistic theory |
| 3 | Kiramba | Kenya | Multiple | Swahili | English | School |
| 4 | Walter | Cameroon | Kom | | English | School |
| 5 | Arkorful | Ghana | Multiple | Multiple | English | School |
| 6 | Beyogle | Ghana; Burkina Faso | Dagara | Akan | English; French | Community |
| 7 | Boyer and Zsiga | Botswana | Sebirwa | Setswana | English | Community |
| 8 | Seid | Ethiopia | Nao | Kefinoono, Amharic | | Community |
| 9 | Shah | South Africa | Gujarati | Afrikaans | English | Community |
| 10 | Njwe | Cameroon | Multiple | | | Figurative language |
| 11 | Odebunmi | Nigeria | | Yorùbá | English | Music |
| 12 | Muaka | Tanzania; Kenya | Swahinglish; Sheng | Swahili | English | Advertisement |
| 13 | Muaka | Kenya | Luo | Swahili | | Politics |
| 14 | Pandey | Multiple | Multiple | | English | Movies |

*In the local community:* How does language define a community or minority ethnic group? What is the local "linguistic landscape" (the languages we hear and see around us), and in what ways does that matter? When the community and ethnic identity is threatened, what can be done about it? What kinds of language teaching, preservation, and revitalization can be carried out at the community level? What if it is too late?

*At the national level:* Are laws and policies enacted at the national level helping or hurting? What languages should have official status, and what does that really mean? How does multilingualism affect the interplay between national identity and ethnic pride? How does multilingualism play out in politics?

*Internationally:* How does the multilingualism of Africa affect its presence on the world stage?

*And finally*, in all this, what role can linguists play?

In investigating the answers to these questions, the contributors to this book find that the news is mixed. First the bad news.

## The Bad News
### *Languages Are Dying*
Seid (in chapter 8) and Boyer and Zsiga (in chapter 7) document the critically endangered status of the languages Nao in Ethiopia and Sebirwa in Botswana. Although the general fact of minority-language endangerment should come as no surprise, the critical status of these two languages has not been previously reported. In fact, recent census data shows many thousands of speakers for both languages. Nonetheless, research into the lives of the Nao and Bobirwa people finds that their mother-tongue languages are being used in increasingly restricted spheres (either ceremonially or just among elderly people) and are not being learned by children. Without revitalization, both will soon be extinct. Boyer and Zsiga suggest that the census data may be unreliable because they are self-reported. A person may identify as a speaker of a language as an expression of ethnic affiliation rather than linguistic ability.

For these communities, language and ethnic identity are closely intertwined. For both Nao and Sebirwa, the language and culture are dying by assimilation. Similarity to the surrounding majority language and culture has hastened the loss of the native language and culture, new ways and new words are gradually adopted, almost without being noticed. As Seid reports, "Nowadays the Nao people are suffering and losing their cultural values and ethnic identity due to the influence of the surrounding community. . . . As a result [of language shift], Nao as an ethnic identity is loosely attached or insignificant among the Nao, who are already intermixed with the groups of Kefinoono speakers through intermarriage and other social practices." A similar point is made in chapter 2 by Bokamba, who argues that the biggest threat to African minority languages in general is not English or any other international language, but the African majority languages surrounding the minority communities.

Seid sees little hope for Nao revitalization, but the situation with Sebirwa is a bit more hopeful. The Bobirwa people maintain a strong ethnic identity. Yet they need help with revitalization efforts, and so far are not receiving any. They would like to see Sebirwa receive some sort of official recognition from the government of Botswana, but requests have been turned down on the basis of a need for national unity. What would happen to national unity if every minority language were granted official status? So Sebirwa continues to decline.

In an interesting comparison with Nao and Sebirwa, in chapter 9 Shah reports that the Gujarati community in South Africa is also losing its language. Not that the Gujarati language as a whole is in any danger, being spoken by 46 million people in India alone. But Shah reports that the children of expatriate Gujarati in South Africa have lost interest in the Gujarati language. The youth in this community prefer to use Afrikaans and English in all spheres, including both home and school, because of the perceived "international outlook" of these languages. Gujarati, conversely, "was regarded as rather useless." Nonetheless, the young people in this community continue to feel strong pride in and connection to their ethnic identity. Shah finds, however, that the youth believe that they can maintain a Gujarati identity without Gujarati language, through religion, food, marriage within the community, and other cultural practices. Shah writes: "This study has highlighted how young South African Gujaratis increasingly view Gujarati as unimportant in defining their ethnic identity. Conversely, ethnic culture and religion are viewed as integral aspects of their Gujarati identity and are successfully maintained at home, at school, and through various community organizations. Although most South Africans are already displaying extremely low levels of proficiency in Gujarati and though this pattern is likely to continue among future generations, this study has shown that the loss of proficiency in the heritage language does not necessarily entail the loss of ethnic identity."

It may be that a separate Gujarati identity is easier to maintain without the Gujarati language because Gujarati culture (religion, food, etc.) is so different from the surrounding South African culture. The possibility of assimilation, however, is never absent.

The examples of Nao, Sebirwa, and Gujarati illustrate the importance of language attitudes in language death or revitalization. If the people do not value their mother-tongue language, they will make no effort to preserve it. This leads to our second piece of bad news.

### Even Healthy Indigenous Languages Are Devalued

The contributors to this book report that many African people are valuing English and other international languages over their mother tongues, and that national policies, school policies, and the media are not helping. In chapter 6 Beyogle's report on Dagara makes this point very starkly. Beyogle asked speakers of Dagara in Ghana (where English is the national language) and Burkina Faso (where French is the national language) to talk about their attitudes toward their native language. Although strong majorities supported giving Dagara some official status, they were also very strongly opposed to using Dagara in school, even at the elementary level. Beyogle reports a "general attitudinal misconception by Africans that the 'implanted European languages and cultures' are more apt for education, whereas the African indigenous languages are inferior and not fit for education." Using Dagara rather than English in the classroom, they believe, would "shut the proverbial window on the world" for their children. Outside school, the use of English or French rather than Dagara, even among a group of native Dagara speakers, is a sign of high social status. Speakers report, "We mix Dagara with English just to show our superiority."

In chapter 14 Pandey takes a different perspective on language devaluation, stepping outside the concentric circles of African multilingualism to ask how African languages are portrayed by the international media, specifically Hollywood movies. The answer is disturbing. Pandey examines twenty-first-century popular movies that portray scenes of Africa, from comedies like *Night at the Museum* to thrillers such as *Blood Diamond* (set in Sierra Leone), to docudramas such as *Invictus* (which depicts the life of Nelson Mandela). Pandey finds that in movie after movie, African languages are both "invisibilized" and "pathologized." Rather than portraying the

value of individual languages and cultures, Hollywood movies present Africa as a
"monolithic mass" where people speak "chaotic, indecipherable" languages and do
uncivilized, unspeakable things. For example, when a character speaks a European-
based language (including Afrikaans), the language is named and straightforwardly
translated in subtitles, but when a minority indigenous language is spoken, the subtitles will simply report "speaking [or, more often, 'shouting'] in native language," most
often paired with an image of violence. Pandey presents "generous visual evidence of
the extent to which cinematic accounts persist in conflating African polyglossia with
pathologized indecipherability, linguistic cacophony, and unintelligibility." The result of
such media imaging, she argues, is not just that Americans and Europeans devalue
African languages but also that Africans devalue their own languages: "If nothing else,
it has led the African elite to despise everything African, their languages being the
clearest example." Pandey further wonders, provocatively, if such cinematic devaluation
has a bald economic motive, because a monolingual society (preferably one where
everybody speaks English) would be better from a marketing perspective.

In chapter 12 Muaka examines marketing strategies directly, describing the billboards in different languages that make up the "linguistic landscapes" of cities in
Kenya and Tanzania. He notes that though Swahili may be used in advertising to
grab attention or to create an emotional connection, billboards that advertise items
connected with high status or with technology inevitably use English. One billboard
goes so far as to proclaim that "smart people" read the English-language newspaper.
"This means," Muaka notes, "that knowledge can only be gained through the English language. It would be rare to see a billboard that says smart people read *Taifa
Leo* or *Mwananchi* Swahili newspapers."

Devaluation of the indigenous language is the flip side of the high value placed on
English and other international languages. If English is the "language of opportunity,"
then any time spent speaking and studying other languages is opportunity lost. Unfortunately, an exclusive focus on English in education is bad news for the local school.

### Schools Are Failing

In her introduction to the 2013 workshop on language in African education at the
joint meeting of the Annual Conference on African Linguistics and the Georgetown
University Round Table on Languages and Linguistics, Adger wrote:

> African governments and international stakeholders are looking beyond
> issues of children's access to schooling, to focus on education quality. In this
> context, literacy learning becomes central, and with it, unresolved issues of
> language choice for schooling in multilingual situations. In the sixty years
> since UNESCO published *The Use of Vernacular Languages in Education*,
> the various declarations, conferences, monitoring reports, and publications
> have not led to consensus on language of instruction at the country level. At
> issue is how to accommodate the need to build knowledge and skills out of
> what children already know—especially their language resources—along with
> the demand for children to learn the country's international language, which
> opens doors to economic and educational opportunities.

That is, it is not enough to make sure that children are in school. Educators and parents also need to make sure that schools are providing students the education they need to succeed. In chapter 1 of the present volume, Trudell and Adger go on to argue that in order for African schools to be successful, curricula, especially those for teaching reading, need to be African-centered, not unthinkingly based on English. And a big part of that is figuring out what language of instruction to use.

In chapters 3 and 4, respectively, Kiramba and Walter document the painful fact that children who are taught in a language they do not know do not learn. They end up being competent in neither the language nor the content area. Kiramba reports on scenes in Kenyan classrooms of passive students unable to pose a question or respond with more than a single-word answer, because they cannot understand the material that is presented to them in English. In order to get any response at all, teachers must break from the official English-only policy and speak to the children in Swahili, a language they know. Kiramba reviews the educational literature that argues against introducing a second language (L2) in school until after children have learned to read in their first language (L1) and argues that "the compelling conclusion is that Kenyan children fail in school mainly due to language failure."

Walter presents data from Cameroon and from the Philippines. For both countries, he finds that ineffective teacher training, in both the content area and in the language of instruction (English), leads to poor classroom performance. He also notes (as do other contributors to this volume) that even when the official policy is to begin elementary education in an African language, parents and politicians pressure the teachers to begin English earlier and earlier. But how can you learn to read in a language you do not speak? And if the African language of instruction is the national language rather than the local language, children who are speakers of minority languages are not helped. Further, because the English-only policy does not work, as the contributors document, teachers revert to the local language anyway, but only on an ad hoc basis. If policies and lesson plans are consistently followed, the children are lost; but as the teachers improvise and code-switch, the consistency and coherence of the lesson are lost.

Thus far, the picture of multilingualism, language policy, and education in Africa presented in this volume has been discouraging. Minority languages are dying out, and even those that are numerically strong may be devalued by their speakers and by the world at large. English is valued as conferring high prestige and economic opportunity, but a push to teach English in the schools as early as possible is hurting rather than helping students.

The news, however, is not all bad. The contributors to this book also describe policies and programs that are working and present hopeful practical proposals for the future.

## The Good News
### Communities Want to Preserve Their Culture and
### Language, and Are Taking Steps to Do So
In the face of minority-language endangerment, and working against the devaluation of their languages by governments, schools, and the media, communities are taking

steps to preserve and promote their mother-tongue language. Recall that Beyogle found that the speakers of Dagara strongly identified with their language and wanted it to be officially recognized (even though they wanted English or French taught in school). Boyer and Zsiga report similar linguistic pride among speakers of Sebirwa.

Trudell and Adger report a success story on the development of a new Maasai orthography. Reading and writing in the traditional orthography, which was developed by missionaries, was very difficult for Maasai speakers. Because of an over-dependence on English as a model, the traditional orthography did not mark tone and only indicated half the vowel distinctions, so words were underdifferentiated. The local community formed a committee to address the problem and, with help from linguist consultants, worked out a new orthography that balanced explicitness and complication, usability and respect for tradition, to most clearly represent the words of Maasai, not English.

Boyer and Zsiga report on language revitalization projects in Botswana for Naro, Ikalanga, and Shayeyi. They write: "Work on the Naro Project involved documenting the Naro language, grammar, and stories as well as developing literacy programs with educational materials developed for children and adults. Preschools in the area teach the language, and many youth have joined the literacy classes. These have all been community efforts with very little, if any, involvement from the Botswana government. The project is credited with developing a sense of pride among the speakers of the language and also with attracting interest from other marginalized groups in the area." They propose a similar program for Sebirwa.

As these programs illustrate, action at the community level, based in the local culture and tailored to local needs, can work to promote and preserve the local language. The same success can be found in community-based education.

### Local Education Programs Work

In chapter 5 Arkorful reports on a successful community-based "complementary education" program in Ghana named the "School for Life." These are local schools in small communities that are designed for young children who, due to family circumstances, cannot attend the government school full time. These schools use mother-tongue instruction, with lessons at times and in places that work for local families. The lessons are closely linked to the lives of the children. One sample lesson is about cows, for example: The children learn about caring for cattle, learn to spell the word "cow" (in their own language), and practice phonics based on the vowels and consonants in the word. Community elders are recruited to tell stories and teach about local history and culture.

Arkorful finds that in the Schools for Life, use of the local language "created a real community of learning" between children and teachers. Further, consistent with the educational research cited by Arkorful (as well as by Kiramba and other contributors to this volume), children who transition from a School for Life to the government schools in the fourth grade do better in mathematics and other content areas than children who have received English-only education, and the School for Life students quickly catch up in English as well. They quickly learn to read in the L2 after they have mastered learning to read in the L1.

Arkorful and the other contributors to this volume who advocate for mother-tongue education in the early grades are not suggesting that the teaching of English be abandoned. But they do advocate for policies that allow local languages and international languages to be studied together. In all kinds of classrooms, rote repetition of English fails. What succeeds is a solid foundation of phonics and reading in the L1, upon which nuanced, linguistically informed teaching of English or another international language can be layered.

### Policies Can Change

Education policies can and must change. Parents and educators want children to be able to access the opportunities that learning an international language like English affords. But present policies, which insist on English-only from the earliest grades, do not foster better English speakers. Rather, they result in students who are losing respect for their local language, are not learning the international language, and are also falling behind in the content areas. The good news is that African-centered, not English-centered, policies can be developed and can work, as the contributors to this book attest. Every child has the right not only to be in school but also to be educated in a language that he or she understands. As Boyer and Zsiga write: "To merely state that communities have the linguistic right to freely use their language in any context is not enough, however. The government needs to take steps to ensure that these linguistic rights are asserted through the inclusion of other languages in the country's language and education policies." Language policies can be created to both preserve local languages and provide access to international languages as well.

### Linguists Can Help

In all these areas—language revitalization, curriculum and school development, and issues of national language policy—linguists can help. Linguists *are* helping. Outside experts cannot substitute for community initiative and community action, but as many of the contributors point out, linguistically trained experts can provide services to local people who want to work for language revitalization and education reform but are not sure where to begin. Linguists are providing phonetic, phonological, and grammatical expertise for language documentation. They are providing educational research for curriculum development. They can advise policymakers on language strategies that do and do not work, although, as Trudell and Adger remind us, their input must be sought.

### Creativity Thrives

The best news of all is that in a multilingual society, creativity thrives. As Bokamba states in chapter 2, "Multilingualism represents diversity, richness of cultural heritages, centuries of accumulated wisdoms, and opportunities to learn to live harmoniously with people of other or related cultures through sustained cross-language contacts." Several of the contributors to this volume point to the importance of poetry and figurative language for the preservation of culture and for language revitalization. Njwe, writing in chapter 10, makes this point most clearly, where she presents a collection of proverbs from a number of different endangered languages of Cameroon, many of which have not previously appeared in any print form, but were collected from the oral traditions of family elders. Such proverbs are first of all an uplifting force: this kind of poetic expression pithily preserves the values and cultures of endangered languages in Cameroon. They work directly against the forces of "invisibilization" and "pathologization" that Pandey finds in the popular media, by presenting unique and beautiful aspects of the culture, and by showcasing its wisdom, generosity, and community spirit. Proverbs and other oral traditions can be used in school as part of teaching the local language, fostering a sense of pride that counters language devaluation.

At the same time, by presenting similar proverbs from different languages side by side, Njwe emphasizes values that are shared among neighboring languages. The tension between ethnic pride and shared values is also at the center of chapter 13, in which Muaka examines the use of metaphorical language in political speeches. Muaka focuses on the speeches of one Luo politician who, in running for the presidency of Kenya, must rally supporters from his own ethnic group, distance and diminish his political enemies, and reach out to other ethnic groups to form a coalition. Figurative language, in the hands of this skilled orator, can unite those who share in the story's meaning, can be used to indirectly but very effectively paint enemies in a bad light (as thieves or as voracious perch), and can appeal to a very wide audience: Who would not want to cheer for the player who scores the winning goal in a soccer game?

Muaka also documents, in chapter 12, how creativity thrives on the billboards of Kenya and Tanzania. We noted above that these billboards do privilege English in associating the international language with "smart" people and high-status goods. Yet Muaka also shows how private advertising, free of official policies on language use, is mixing English and Swahili in creative ways and showcasing new varieties of language—Sheng in Kenya and Swahinglish in Tanzania—as part of the linguistic landscape.

The creativity that multilingualism affords is most clearly presented by Odebunmi in chapter 11 on hip-hop music in Nigeria. Odebunmi notes that some criticize African musicians for adopting Western music styles such as rap and hip-hop, and some argue that "uses of loan words and borrowed syntax are signs of a helpless acquiescence in language loss." He argues, however, that this is not a case of English taking over but of local artists reinventing Western influences for themselves, in a combination of global and local termed "glocal." Nigerian musicians mix English, Yorùbá, and other local languages, purposely using language in new and different ways for social and artistic effect, for example, by rhyming English and Yorùbá words with each other in code-switched lines, by using English words in Yorùbá poetic forms, and by inventing new proverbs more or less on the spot: "They do not search for one language to elevate above all others, but rather throw all into the same mixilingual pool, including the English language." For Nigerian hip-hop musicians, multilingualism is a blessing to be celebrated rather than a curse to be overcome.

In summary, then, the fourteen chapters of this volume look at multilingualism, at layers of language, in a variety of African-language communities. The chapters ask the question: What does it mean for Africa when, across the continent, the home language of the individual does not match the larger national, or vehicular, language, which itself does not match the international language used in school, business, government, and international communication? There is both bad and good news in the answers. The bad news is that minority languages are dying, that indigenous languages are being devalued even by their own speakers, and that many schools are failing to effectively teach the children who attend them. The good news, however, is that community members care about their languages, that language revitalization programs are under way, and that local education programs that emphasize education in the mother tongue can work. Language policies and practices can be informed by linguistic expertise, and they can change. And most encouragingly, across the continent—in music, in the linguistic landscape, and in figurative language—creativity thrives.

# 1

# Early Reading Success in Africa: The Language Factor

BARBARA TRUDELL AND CAROLYN TEMPLE ADGER

*SIL Africa and Center for Applied Linguistics*

**TO THE CASUAL EYE,** the two domains of literacy and linguistics may not seem closely linked. In fact, however, concerns about reading and writing competencies do intersect with the field of linguistics, particularly where unwritten or recently written languages are being developed for written use in learning and communication. This situation is particularly common in the language-rich regions of Africa, Latin America, Asia, and the Pacific. For this reason, understanding the role of linguistics in developing written-language competencies is becoming increasingly critical to successful reading and writing acquisition across the two-thirds (or developing) world.

Reading competencies have become central in discussions of international education and development. In the last decade of Education for All and the Millennium Development Goals, attention has focused increasingly on the *quality* of education rather than solely on *access* to education (EFA Global Monitoring Report Team 2005). In this environment the ability to accurately assess the quality of education has taken on new importance, and user-friendly mechanisms for measuring learning are being sought. An increasingly popular means of assessing the quality of learning in developing-world classrooms is the assessment of students' ability to read. The rationale here is that if a child is not reading, he or she is probably not learning other content either—at least not to the degree desired.[1] Thus, literacy learning in early primary grades becomes central to the assessment of learning in general.

A related issue arises in environments where the language of instruction in the primary classroom is not one that the students have mastered. This is typical in countries that are former colonies, where the colonial language has been designated the official language despite limited national-level proficiency in that language. In such an environment, reading—which is arguably centered on the comprehension of, and on interaction with, a written text—becomes a difficult goal to reach. This linguistic challenge is not always recognized by those responsible for ensuring student learning. Even when the challenge is recognized, it is difficult to accommodate the need to build new knowledge and skills out of what children already know—especially their language resources—as well as the demand for children to learn an official language, which opens doors to economic and educational choices and opportunities.

At present, a degree of support exists in some quarters for mother-tongue-based bilingual education that involves teaching reading skills first in the child's language rather than in an international language that the child is unlikely to speak. Large donor agencies such as the US Agency for International Development (USAID), the World Bank, and others that together constitute the Global Partnership for Education are demonstrating varying degrees of resourcing support for country plans to develop mother-tongue-based early literacy programs and to ensure that they thrive (USAID 2011; Global Partnership for Education 2012).

Certainly in Africa the demands of improving education, the current centrality of reading instruction to this undertaking, and the large number of African languages that are unwritten or recently written are opening a space for linguistic expertise to contribute to success in reading and in education generally. Deep knowledge of language structure is crucial to the processes involved in developing reading and writing programs, assessing students' reading performance, and reforming the systems that support the teaching of reading and writing. Linguistic expertise constitutes a significant resource for a range of activities related to literacy learning: engaging with the development of phonemic awareness and phonics skills in the primary school reading curriculum, the revision of language courses so that they are directly relevant to children's literacy learning, and testing pupil performance. Linguistic input is in fact essential for the entire range of language development activities that support literacy in African languages—including the standardization and development of orthographies, dictionaries, and grammar descriptions.

## Reading Research and Program Development in Africa: Where Are the Linguists?

Given the role of African linguists over the years in advocating on behalf of African languages in African education (e.g., Bamgboṣe 1991; Ouane 2003), it is reasonable to expect that linguists would also be central to the wave of early grade literacy education reform sweeping across Africa. And indeed, African linguists have been at the heart of some landmark African-language education initiatives, including the distinguished scholars Aliu Babs Fafunwa in Nigeria (Fafunwa, Macauley, and Funnso Sokoya 1989), Neville Alexander in South Africa (Alexander 2005), and Maurice Tadadjeu and his colleagues at the University of Yaoundé (Tadadjeu 1990). However, the development and management of education curricula have not typically been seen to need linguistic input. This is equally true in the teacher training institutions, which should ideally serve as the preparation grounds for effective multilingual education. If linguists do have a role in training or curriculum development, that role is often limited to teaching language structure, which is more relevant to teaching language arts than to teaching reading (Akyeampong et al. 2011).

In the United States involvement by theoretical linguists and sociolinguists in reading research and program development for children has been more visible. Linguists have been involved in research on reading and vernacular dialects (e.g., Labov and Baker 2010), a domain in which language structure is foregrounded in explaining reading difficulties. Psycholinguistics has contributed to theories of reading, as has the field of orthography studies (e.g., Templeton and Bear 1992; Snowling and

Hulme 2005; Smith 2011). Such linguistic research has contributed to the design and implementation of reading instructional programs in the formal education curriculum over a number of years.

In fact, reading research in the United States has been extensive—so much so that in the late 1990s, the National Reading Panel was commissioned to review the enormous body of research on reading instruction. The panel's report has been widely accepted as an authoritative account of the implications of this research for reading instruction (National Institute of Child Health and Human Development 2000). The panel focused on five elements that have been found to be key for learning to read, at least in the language contexts studied:

- Phonemic awareness: the ability to focus on the phonemic structure of words;
- Phonics: the alphabetic principle and knowledge of the correspondence between the sounds of a language and print;
- Reading fluency: the ability to read a text with speed, accuracy, and appropriate prosody;
- Vocabulary: knowledge of the words in a text and their meanings; and
- Reading comprehension: the ability to process a text and interpret its meaning.

These five skills have become the touchstone for designing reading programs in the United States, and reading program implementers from the United States have brought these principles to bear on African-language reading instruction programs as well.

In African countries where relatively little research is taking place on reading in African languages, the research base for informing and reforming literacy acquisition has largely been imported from Europe and the United States. However, its appropriateness for designing reading programs and assessments in African contexts and African languages is questionable (Trudell and Schroeder 2007). The research reviewed by the National Reading Panel pertained to children who are learning to read in their first language, English. However, the many structural differences between English, an Indo-European language, and the African languages, which belong to many other language families, raise questions about how the elements of reading that have been examined through research in the United States might best be addressed in the curriculum, instruction, and assessment in African schools.

Thus, with regard to linguistics and reading in African languages, a few points seem clear. First, linguistics has informed some reading research to date, but the language environment of this research has in general been English or another European language. Second, the research that is informing reading instructional programs in African nations tends not to be indigenous, and so is not shaped by African linguistic realities. It is the contention of this chapter that these two conditions could and should be changed through the addition of a distinctly African and distinctly linguistic perspective on reading methodology in Africa. The remainder of the chapter presents examples of the possibilities for such contributions.

## The Impact of Various Linguistic Features on Reading Methodology

The goal of reading instruction is to promote reading for meaning. Ready processing of word parts, whole words, and larger chunks of text as well is a matter of the reader gaining automatic recognition of the most relevant and productive sequences of symbols (letters, characters, character combinations and strings, suprasegmentals, etc.). However, the most relevant and productive symbols vary from language to language, as do a range of other orthographic features.

One distinctive characteristic of many African languages is a high degree of orthographic transparency. Reading such languages can be productively taught through a focus on syllables, sound–symbol relationships, and blending. In contrast, a language featuring greater orthographic depth lends itself to a reading method that emphasizes sight words and morpheme recognition as well as sound–symbol correspondence. Morpheme recognition skills, including the recognition of infixes, are also very important for being able to fluently read agglutinative languages.

Another orthographic feature of many African languages is underdifferentiation. Tone, vowels, vowel length, and other phonological and grammatical features that are not typically marked in European languages have tended to be ignored as these languages have been reduced to writing. This has tended to occur particularly where linguistic expertise has not contributed significantly to the process.

Other features of a language that affect reading methodology include syllable complexity and morphological complexity. An important aspect of building reading fluency involves focusing on morpheme shape as conditioned by the various noun classes and on the fact that the different morpheme shapes maintain the same meaning.

One other example of the linguistic dimension of reading instruction has to do with the various types of scripts in which African languages are written: Latin, Arabic, and Ethiopic, as well as indigenous scripts in some West African languages. The unique features of each of these scripts have different implications for reading instruction. A bias in favor of Latin script may lead Western-trained educators to assume that it is the easiest script for learning to read; however, evidence from research in Ethiopia (Piper and Van Ginkel 2013) indicates that the Ethiopic script may actually be more effective than Latin script in facilitating the application of symbol recognition skills to word reading.

The larger lesson, then, is that effective reading pedagogy in a language other than English requires an understanding of the unique linguistic characteristics of the language. It cannot be assumed that teaching reading is best done the same way in African languages as it is in English. Linguistic input into the development and implementation of reading methodology can make the difference between a student learning to read easily and that same student struggling to gain reading capability.

## The Relevance of Linguistics to Reading Assessment

Reading assessment—in both international languages and African languages—has become a regular component of educational interventions in Africa. In particular, assessment tools based on the Early Grade Reading Assessment (EGRA) (Gove and Wetterberg 2011) are being included in donor-funded education projects across the continent. The EGRA tool and other tools based on this kind of rapid assessment of reading skills are being used to evaluate overall literacy program effectiveness—and individual classrooms as well. However, as these tools are being developed and applied in African-language-medium classrooms, the linguistic components of such testing are not always given due attention.

As an example, oral reading fluency is one dimension of the EGRA; the links between oral reading fluency and comprehension (National Institute of Child Health and Human Development 2000) make it a particularly productive skill to measure. Reading fluency is typically measured in terms of words per minute (WPM); in the United States the general expectation is that, by the end of first grade, children should be reading in English at an average rate of 50 WPM (Hasbrouck and Tindal 2006). As with other aspects of reading research and practice, this notion of a target WPM rate has also made its way into the curriculum and testing expectations of some African nations.

Three language-related challenges present themselves here, however. One has to do with the child's proficiency in the language of testing. Where a child is being tested in a language that he or she has not mastered (which is frequently the case in African classrooms), the test results will not distinguish between the child who cannot read well and the child who has not mastered the language in which he or she is being tested. Conversely, if the child is tested in a language in which he or she has not been taught to read (which occurs where testing is done in a language that the child does speak but that has not actually been used as the medium of reading instruction), the results are again difficult to interpret. Thus, it is important to establish the degree of each child's oral proficiency in the language(s) of testing.

A second linguistic challenge has to do with the establishment of a universal WPM target for measuring fluency. It is well known among linguists that word length varies from language to language, due to both the linguistic structures and the writing conventions of languages around the world. The following brief example of Kiswahili and English demonstrates that one morphologically "loaded" word in a given language may carry as much meaning as several English words:

Walinipatia saa jana.

(They-got-for-me a watch yesterday.)

Because word length does not transfer between languages, it follows that a WPM fluency measurement does not transfer across languages either. To attempt to apply a universal WPM metric to reading in all languages is to ignore this fundamental fact about language; using a WPM metric based on English-language reading speeds for this purpose demonstrates an unconscionable lack of sensitivity to linguistic realities across Africa and around the world. What is needed is some way to calibrate oral reading fluency rates to the target language. A few informal means of doing so have been attempted, but a more formalized and better-researched model is needed.

A third linguistic challenge to the focus on reading fluency has to do with the varying links between decoding and comprehension, as demonstrated by the fact that transparent orthographies facilitate oral reading fluency more than do opaque orthographies, regardless of the degree of text comprehension. For example, the Spanish sentence *Esta es la casa de mi abuela* (this is my grandmother's house) can be easily pronounced by anyone who reads Kiswahili without any understanding of the Spanish meaning. A language with a deeper orthography, such as English, is much more difficult for attaining oral reading fluency; for example, the sentence *You might thoroughly enjoy this movie* can only be read with fluency by someone who has mastered a number of the spelling irregularities of the English language. The nature of the links between the language and oral reading fluency is rather different in these two languages. This fact makes it extremely important that oral reading fluency assessment includes careful attention to naturalness, the interpretation of punctuation, and other indications that the child is reading for meaning.

Thus, the morphological and orthographic characters of a given language are highly relevant to the development of effective reading assessment measures. Particularly where African languages that have not been researched thoroughly are being considered for use in schools, the contribution of linguistic expertise is crucial.

## Orthography Choices: An Example from Maasai

As is apparent in English reading, orthographic issues are a major influence on both the choice of reading method and the ease of learning to read in a given language. As noted above, underdifferentiation can become a real obstacle to effective reading acquisition. This is one aspect in which linguistic input can be highly significant to an African-language reading program.

A current example of this fact can be found in the Opportunity Schools project, which focuses on local-language reading and writing and on teacher capacity development in twenty Maasai-speaking primary schools in southern Kenya (Trudell, forthcoming). The development of reading and writing instructional materials in Maasai language for grades 1 through 3 is part of this project. The materials are based on an inventory of letters and sounds in the language and are sensitive to its grammatical features; they also feature significant attention to phonological awareness, sight–sound correspondence, reading fluency, vocabulary building, comprehension, and writing.

In the early stages of the materials' development process, concerns arose among language stakeholders regarding the adequacy of the current Maasai orthography for teaching reading and writing to children in early primary school. The Maasai language was first recorded in written form in the mid-1800s; the full Bible was published by the Bible Society of Kenya in 1991.[2] Other materials published in Maa languages include collections of folktales and hymns, as well as easy readers.[3] However, Maasai-language text is reported to be difficult to read, even for native speakers of the language. The principal problem seems to be that the orthography marks neither tone nor four of the nine Maasai vowels. The concern in the Opportunity Schools project was that, even with Maasai as their mother tongue, the children could encounter significant obstacles to fluent reading due to the challenging features of Maasai orthography.

As a result, a multiphase, community-based orthography review component has been added to the project. This process of engaging community thinking on orthography reform—along with the engagement of linguists, teachers, and school authorities in the training and implementation processes—has provided insights into how education myths and realities are perceived and dealt with in this language community. The work of Payne and her colleagues at the University of Oregon on Maasai orthography has served as the primary linguistic resource for this phase of the project.[4]

The general sense in both of the orthography review meetings held in the context of the Opportunity Schools project was that this discussion of the adequacy of Maasai orthography is long overdue. Two of the Maasai participants commented as follows: "We are the people who have been called at this very time to be involved in transforming the writing system of our language. It will not be easy—sometimes we will be accused of messing up our language, but we are improving the language for the next generation. Something is happening in Kenya; there is a renaissance of local language interest. The Maasai are also being affected: young people, elites. They could take up this new orthography and use it."

At the same time, there was a general concern that the new Maasai orthography should feature as few new markings as possible; the motivations here had to do both with the desire that Maasai should not look "strange" (i.e., unlike written English or Swahili) and with the great reverence accorded to the current Maasai Bible. Acceptance as a "normal" Kenyan community seems to be a strong value.

In addition, both review groups expressed a strong desire that the new orthography should serve "all": children and adults, fluent readers, and new readers alike. Such inclusiveness made the task of orthography reform much more difficult, because each of these four target audiences has different implications for orthography choice. However, even knowing that this was the case, both groups demonstrated a determination to maintain a community-inclusive approach to the orthography review process.

Eventually, the choice was made to mark high and falling tone, but to mark only five of the nine phonemic vowels. These decisions were not as linguistically thorough as they might have been. However, they were momentous and even risky for the Maasai speakers involved. Locally important criteria for the orthography took precedence over the advice of academic experts, leading to an experimental orthography that is strong on inclusion and perceived national acceptability. These decisions speak to the speakers' determination that written Maasai must serve the community well, even in the changing sociocultural environment brought on by globalization.

## Conclusion

In general, public education in Africa has come late to explicit literacy instruction in children's home languages, and assumptions are being made about language and reading that have not been tested in African-language contexts. Addressing these challenges to successful reading instruction in African languages requires linguists and educators to work together, each with their complementary knowledge of how language and reading actually work.

This is not only true, but in fact the arena for this professional collaboration between linguists and educators is even larger than what has been mentioned here. It also includes the development and implementation of language policy that can lead to real learning. It includes program design and materials development for teaching the national languages, based on the assumption that children will transition to the use of these languages *after* they have built initial literacy skills in their own language and oral language skills in the national language. It includes a focus on building the capacity of teachers to effectively teach both language and literacy and on orienting education administrators to the critical importance of teaching both of these subjects.

For linguists to be able to take their rightful place in the arena of language and reading, they will need to market their contributions to meeting the pedagogical needs that are recognized by program implementers and educators in Africa. Linguists will need to negotiate the sociolinguistic realities that present themselves and proactively offer their expertise as a solution to the linguistic challenges facing those who seek to integrate African languages into reading and writing instruction in African schools. Doing so could revolutionize the effectiveness of African-language literacy and thus provide a significant boost to the learning achieved in African classrooms.

## Notes

1. This perspective itself has some real challenges, however, particularly in cultural contexts where oral learning is seen as a primary means of knowledge acquisition.
2. See www.masaikenya.org; and www.worldscriptures.org/pages/maasai.html.
3. Maasai is a member of the Maa language family, which also includes languages such as Samburu and Ilchamus (Lewis, Simons, and Fennig 2013).
4. See http://pages.uoregon.edu/maasai/.

## References

Akyeampong, Kwame, John Pryor, Jo Westbrook, and Kattie Lussier. 2011. *Teacher Preparation and Continuing Professional Development in Africa: Learning to Teach Early Reading and Mathematics.* Brighton: University of Sussex Centre for International Education.

Alexander, Neville, ed. 2005. *Mother-Tongue-Based Bilingual Education in Southern Africa: The Dynamics of Implementation.* Cape Town: PRAESA.

Bamgboṣe, Ayo. 1991. *Language and the Nation.* Edinburgh: Edinburgh University Press.

EFA Global Monitoring Report Team. 2005. *Literacy for Life: EFA Global Monitoring Report, 2006.* Paris: UNESCO.

Fafunwa, Aliu Babs, Juliet Iyabode Macauley, and J. A. Funnso Sokoya. 1989. *Education in Mother Tongue: The Ife Primary Education Research Project (1970–1978).* Ibadan: University Press Limited.

Global Partnership for Education. 2012. *Strategic Plan 2012–2015.* www.globalpartnership.org/media/docs/library/GPE_Stategic_Plan_2012-2015_English.pdf.

Gove, Amber, and Anna Wetterberg, eds. 2011. *The Early-Grade Reading Assessment: Applications and Interventions to Improve Basic Literacy.* Research Triangle Park NC: RTI Press.

Hasbrouck, Jan, and Gerald A. Tindal. 2006. "Oral Reading Fluency Norms: A Valuable Assessment Tool for Reading Teachers." *Reading Teacher* 59:636–44.

Labov, William, and Bettina Baker. 2010. "What Is a Reading Error?" *Applied Psycholingustics* 31:735–57.

Lewis, M. Paul, Gary F. Simons, and Charles D. Fennig, eds. 2013. *Ethnologue: Languages of the World,* 17th ed. Dallas: SIL International. Online version available at www.ethnologue.com.

National Institute of Child Health and Human Development. 2000. *Teaching Children to Read: An Evidence-Based Assessment of the Scientific Research Literature on Reading and Its Implications for Instruction.* Report of National Reading Panel. Washington DC: US Government Printing Office.

Ouane, Adama, ed. 2003. *Towards a Multilingual Culture of Education*, trans. Colin Shearmur. Hamburg: UNESCO Institute for Education.

Piper, B., and A. Van Ginkel. 2013. "Reading the Script: Ethiopian Language Scripts and Writing Systems' Impact on Letter and Word Identification." Unpublished manuscript.

Smith, Frank. 2011. *Understanding Reading: A Psycholinguistic Analysis of Reading and Learning to Read*, 6th ed. London: Routledge.

Snowling, Margaret J., and Charles Hulme, eds. 2005. *The Science of Reading: A Handbook.* Oxford: Blackwell.

Tadadjeu, Maurice. 1990. *Le Defi de Babel au Cameroun.* Yaoundé: PROPELCA.

Templeton, Shane, and Donald R. Bear, eds. 1992. *Development of Orthographic Knowledge and the Foundations of Literacy.* Hillsdale NJ: Lawrence Erlbaum.

Trudell, Barbara. Forthcoming. "Education and Global Culture: Shaping and Being Shaped in the Maasai Community of Kenya." *Linguistics and Education.*

Trudell, Barbara, and Leila Schroeder. 2007. "Reading Methodologies for African Languages: Avoiding Linguistic and Pedagogical Imperialism." *Language, Culture and Curriculum* 20:165–80.

US Agency for International Development. 2011. *USAID Education Strategy, 2011–2015.* Washington DC: US Agency for International Development. http://pdf.usaid.gov/pdf_docs/pdacq946.pdf.

2

# Multilingualism as a Sociolinguistic Phenomenon: Evidence from Africa

EYAMBA G. BOKAMBA
*University of Illinois at Urbana-Champaign*

## Introduction

There are 6,909 spoken languages in the world (*Ethnologue* 2009), but there are only approximately 196 to 200 countries. In spite of the realization in the twenty-first century that societal and individual multilingualism must therefore be common, rather than exotic, phenomena, multilingualism remains grossly understudied and is therefore highly misunderstood.

### The Problem

This misunderstanding ranges from incorrect answers to the fundamental question of "what constitutes multilingualism" to flawed evaluations and characterizations of multilingual competence and practices. Except for a few recent studies published since the beginning of the last decade—including those by Cook (2009); Cenoz, Hufeisen, and Jessner (2001); Aronin and Hufeisen (2009); Grosjean (2010); and Aronin and Singleton (2012)—much of the research on multilingualism has been characterized by confusion, even at the level of the basic distinction between *bilingualism* and *multilingualism*. Often, the latter is erroneously defined as a covariant of the former, thus exacerbating the perpetuation of flawed theories of second language acquisition (SLA) that are predominantly informed by monolingualism in much of the West at the disregard of other world regions (i.e., Africa, Asia, Pacific, South America, and parts of Western Europe), where individual and societal multilingualism are pervasive phenomena (Broeder, Extra, and Maartens 1998; Laitin 2001; Simpson 2007, 2008; Grosjean 2010; Aronin and Singleton 2012; Anchimbe 2013).

### Objectives of This Study

This chapter aims to provide, on the basis of African-language ecologies, an empirically informed characterization of individual and societal *multilingualism* in contradistinction to *bilingualism*. It is argued and demonstrated that bilingualism and multilingualism are related but independent phenomena, and that the characterization of the latter must take into consideration not only the level of competence demonstrated in the speakers' linguistic repertoires, but also the various functions and domains that such speakers and their societies or speech communities allocate to these repertoires. That is, the description of multilingualism must be informed by the linguistic practices of multilingual societies and speakers.

To address these questions, this chapter is structured as follows to offer an empirically balanced and argued analysis. After this introduction, the chapter reviews the literature on multilingualism, with subsections devoted to a critical review of the research on the phenomenon in the general literature and in African sociolinguistics. One subsection discusses the multilingual discursive practices in Africa as an attempt to demonstrate the realities of the phenomenon contra the imagined ones criticized in another subsection. The chapter then draws on this examination to provide and argue for redefinitions of bilingualism and multilingualism as substantiated by selected data on language demographics and functional allocation from twenty-three African nations. This analysis is followed by a discussion of the social and cognitive effects of multilingualism. The last section summarizes the study with a focus on the theoretical implications of the findings for general and applied linguistics, especially for SLA, and it suggests potentially profitable directions for future research.

### *The Importance of Research on Multilingualism*
Research on multilingualism is both fascinating and frustrating. What is most fascinating about it are its complexity and the extent to which it offers fertile grounds upon which linguistic research can provide empirically valid and comprehensive answers to fundamental questions, such as the following:

1. What constitutes knowledge of language?
2. How is knowledge of language acquired?
3. How is knowledge of language put to use?
4. What are the psychological and social consequences of multilingualism?
5. What determines language choice/selection in communicative events?

The first three questions are articulated specifically by Chomsky (1986, 3), but they represent broad questions that are raised in different fashions in applied linguistic subfields (e.g., psycholinguistics; acquisition of a second, additional, or foreign language; and sociolinguistics). Questions 4 and 5 are typically raised in research on language acquisition and sociolinguistics.

The counterpart to the fascination aspect of the research on multilingualism, however, is that it is both frustrating and challenging in that there has been comparatively very little work done on it, although this picture appears to be changing rapidly as a result of research undertaken in Europe by scholars such as Cook, Grosjean, Aronin, Cenoz, Singleton, and their collaborators on the cognitive dimensions of the phenomenon. The momentum for this type of research effort appears to have begun in the early 2000s, and it recognizes multilingualism as a common occurrence. This counters the dominant paradigm in the studies that appeared from the 1970s until the late 1990s that viewed multilingualism as an exotic phenomenon, hence perhaps justifying the lack of serious attention given to it. Those earlier studies were superficial and yet influential to the extent that in the 1980s they perpetuated the flawed characterization of multilinguals as two monolinguals in one brain that was later decried by Grosjean (1989, 2001). They continue to dominate the study of additional languages that are viewed as SLA, in which, among others, theories such as the Critical Period Hypothesis, interlanguage, and language knowledge transfer (i.e., facilitation versus interference) have been produced and maintained (e.g., Lenneberg 1967; Gass and Selinker 1992) against increasing counterevidence. As Grosjean (2010, xv) points out: "That said [about the dearth of publications], even though the phenomenon is widespread, bilingualism as a topic is still unfamiliar to most people. In addition, bilingualism is surrounded by a number of myths: Bilinguals are rare and have equal and perfect knowledge of their languages; real bilinguals have acquired their two or more languages in childhood and have no accent in either of them; bilinguals are born translators." (It needs to be noted here that Grosjean uses "bilingualism" as a cover term for both bilingualism strictly defined and multilingualism. However, he acknowledges the difference in his analysis, which is discussed below.)

The veracity of what constitutes multilingualism can be ascertained correctly only by examining pervasively multilingual societies where the phenomenon is a daily reality. Africa is one such region. So let us now turn our attention to what is known regarding the characterization of multilingualism—first, in the general literature, and then in African linguistics—to demonstrate in part the pervasiveness of the misunderstanding referenced by Grosjean, as noted below, and to ascertain the reality of the phenomenon through the prism of Africanist scholarship before offering a better characterization of it below.

## Overview of the Literature on Multilingualism
Contrary to what had been the dominant perception in the West until recently, societal multilingualism, which presupposes individual multilingualism, is a common phenomenon, not an exotic one. Yet multilingualism has not been given the attention it deserves in the linguistic literature.

### Facts and Fictions
The data given in table 2.1 demonstrate the prevalence of multilingualism.

**Table 2.1**
**Distribution of Languages by World Region**

| Region | Living Languages | | Speakers |
| --- | --- | --- | --- |
| | Count/Number | Percentage of World Totals | |
| Africa | 2,110 | 30.5 | 1.033 billion |
| Americas | 993 | 14.4 | 953.7 million |
| Asia | 2,322 | 33.6 | 4.3 billion |
| Europe | 234 | 3.4 | 733 million |
| Pacific | 1,250 | 18.1 | 6,429,788 |
| Total | 6,909 | 100 | 7,026,129,788 |

*Sources:* The number of languages, percentages, and the population of the Pacific are extracted from *Ethnologue* (2009); those of speakers are from World Population Statistics, www.worldpopulationstatistics .com/asia-population-2013/.

What the facts presented in table 2.1 clearly indicate—allowing, possibly, for some errors in the definition of "language" versus "dialect of a language"—is that multilingualism is a dominant world phenomenon. And as such, it deserves serious attention in the most relevant subfields of linguistics, including language acquisition (i.e., psycholinguistics, SLA, and foreign-language acquisition), neurolinguistics, pragmatics, and sociolinguistics.

A cursory survey of the general literature shows that this has not been the case, even in books devoted entirely to or bearing the title of the phenomenon (e.g., Edwards 1994; Blackledge and Creese 2010). Instead, the preponderance of the discussion on the topic has largely been devoted to bilingualism (i.e., the existence of two languages as media of communication in a given nation, state, or an individual) with anecdotal references to actual multilingualism in society or education (Edwards 1994; Mesthrie et al. 2000; Blackledge and Creese 2010).

### The General Literature

At least three major questions arise at this juncture. First, given the prevalence of multilingualism in the world, why has it not been the subject of more research than bilingualism—because of its lower interface? Second, what has made bilingualism the leading topic for the study of additional language knowledge—acquisition, processing, and function? And, third, how much research has been conducted on multilingualism, and what are its findings? We turn to an examination of these questions in this subsection to establish a foundation upon which the discussion and analysis below can be built. I begin with an overview of the general literature and then proceed to its African linguistics counterpart.

#### General Overview

As a number of most recent studies acknowledge and lament, there is an abundance of studies on bilingualism from psycholinguistic and sociolinguistic perspectives, and a paucity of such research on multilingualism per se (e.g., Auer and Li Wei 2007; Cenoz, Hufeisen, and Jessner 2008; Aronin and Hufeisen 2009; Grosjean 2010; Aronin and Singleton 2012). A cursory survey of two recent general readers on sociolinguistics (Coupland and Jaworki 1997; Coulmas 1997) and four popular textbooks on sociolinguistics (Fasold 1990; Hudson 1996; Mesthrie et al. 2000; Wardhaugh 2006) evinces only a very limited treatment of multilingualism as a fundamental phenomenon under whose rubric many dimensions of language in society can be studied and understood. Hudson (1996), for example, discusses multilingualism in his first chapter, pointing out that contrary to the prevailing perception in the North, multilingualism is the norm rather than the exception in the world. Thereafter, he broaches the subject in a number of chapters dealing with "varieties of language," "language, culture and thought," and "linguistics and social inequality"; but he does not dedicate any chapter to a discussion of the topic. Coulmas (1997) devotes one chapter to the phenomenon per se and has two others on code-switching and language planning. Mesthrie and colleagues (2000), while providing an extensive discussion of key aspects of sociolinguistics, do not devote a single chapter or subsection to the characterization of multilingualism. This may have been an inadvertent omission, but it nonetheless reflects a general tendency in the linguistic literature. Although a large number of books have been published on the putative topic of "multilingualism" since the 1990s, most of them have been devoted to bilingualism and multilingualism in education rather than to the different facets of this phenomenon in linguistic practices. The fascination with bilingualism to the exclusion of multilingualism appears to have been motivated by "second language" acquisition in pervasively monolingual societies in the West, where learning an additional language after one's mother tongue, a common occurrence in stable multilingual societies, has been generally viewed as an extraordinary achievement. As a result, numerous extensive and highly informative publications address this topic from various cognitive perspectives: psycholinguistic, sociolinguistic, interaction, code-switching, bilingual brain, and speech processing (e.g., Grosjean 1982, 2010; Li Wei 2001a; Bhatia and Ritchie 2004). With respect to research on multilingualism, it needs to be pointed out that some of the studies assume knowledge of what it is and thus do not even explicitly define it (e.g., Blackledge and Creese 2010).

To my knowledge, the first and perhaps the most comprehensive study dedicated to multilingualism—notwithstanding the first part of its title—was by Grosjean (2010), *Bilingual: Life and Reality*. In very accessible language, Grosjean explores several major facets of bilingualism and multilingualism, including descriptions of its speakers, the functional allocations of their linguistic repertoires, language choices in communicative events, the psychological reality of such individuals over "a life span," and the debunking of many myths concerning bilinguals and multilinguals. A subsequent publication of a similar depth, except with a focus principally on the sociolinguistics of multilingualism, is Aronin and Singleton's (2012) *Multilingualism*, which presents a cross-cultural and linguistic description of the knowledge and utilization of multiple languages while gently deconstructing myths concerning multilingualism in Western societies, including on language processing by learners. Just like Grosjean (2010), Aronin and Singleton (2012) succeed in demystifying this common phenomenon for the predominently monolingual speakers in the West by documenting how it functions cross-culturally and linguistically, and by arguing forcefully why the phenomenon merits serious investigation in today's globalized world. One of their conclusions, which is not surprising for scholars of multilingualism, is that monolingualism, not multilingualism, is the aberation. This conclusion is supported by the existence, as noted above, of 6,909 languages in a maximum of 200 countries (see table 2.1) and by the sample data from selected African nation-states presented in table 2.2.

This movement from the essentialist assumptions of the dominant monolingual ideologies of one language, one nation and monolingualism as the norm, as Weber (2007) correctly observes in his critique of some of the studies done by Auer and Li Wei (2007), has not been easy or smooth. In this regard Weber shows that some of these early adopters of the new prism still retain, albeit implicitly, such assumptions while they argue for the abandonment of the long-established ideologies resulting from them.

Table 2.2
Distribution of African Languages in Selected Countries

| Row | Country | No. of Speakers | Total No. of Languages | Official Language | Principal/National Languages |
|---|---|---|---|---|---|
| 1 | Algeria | 37,367,226 | 21 | Arabic | French, Berber/Tamazight |
| 2 | Angola | 18,056,072 | 38 | Portuguese | Cokwe, Kikongo, Kimbundu, Lingala |
| 3 | Burkina Faso | 17,275,115 | 70 | French | Mooré, Bamanakan, Dioula, Fulfulde, Dagara |
| 4 | Burundi | 10,557,259 | 4 | French | Kirundi, English |
| 5 | Cameroon | 20,129,878 | 281 | English, French | Cameroon Pidgin English, Fulfulde |
| 6 | Chad | 10,975,648 | 133 | French | Classical Arabic, Chadian Arabic |
| 7 | Côte d'Ivoire | 21,952,093 | 96 | French | Agni/Baoulé, Bété, Dioula, Malinke, Sénoufo |
| 8 | D.R. Congo | 73,599,190 | 215 | French | Kikongo, Kiswahili, Lingála, Tshiluba |
| 9 | Egypt | 83,688,164 | 28 | Arabic | Egyptian Arabic, English |
| 10 | Ethiopia | 91,195,675 | 90 | Amharic | English, Oromo, Tigrinya |
| 11 | Ghana | 24,652,402 | 86 | English | Akan, Ewe, Dagara, Dagbani, Gã, Gonja |
| 12 | Kenya | 43,013,341 | 72 | English, Kiswahili | Gikuyu, Kikamba, Luo, KiLuyia, Kalenjin |
| 13 | Madagascar | 22,005,222 | 20 | French, Malagasy | — |
| 14 | Morocco | 32,309,239 | 14 | Standard Arabic (MSA) | Berber, Classical Arabic, English, French, MSA, Moroccan Arabic |
| 15 | Mozambique | 23,515,934 | 49 | Portuguese | Chinyanja, Changana |
| 16 | Nigeria | 170,123,740 | 529 | English | Hausa, Igbo, Yorùbá, Kanuri, Ijo, Tiv |
| 17 | Senegal | 12,969,606 | 47 | French | Diola, Malinke, Peul, Serer, Soninke, Wolof |
| 18 | South Africa | 48,810,427 | 44 | Afrikaans, English, isiNdebele, isiXhosa, isiZulu, Sepedi, Sesotho, Setswana, siSwati, Tshivenda, Xitsonga | Same as in row 5, plus Portuguese, Gujarati, Tamil |
| 19 | Sudan | 34,206,710 | 75 | Arabic | English |
| 20 | Tanzania | 46,912,768 | 127 | Kiswahili, English | Kisukuma, KiHa, KiGogo, Maasai, KiHaya, KiNyamwezi, KiMakonde |
| 21 | Uganda | 33,640,833 | 45 | English | Ateso, Kiswahili, Luganda, Luo, Lunyoro, Lugbara |
| 22 | Zambia | 13,817,479 | 53 | English | Chibemba, Chinyanja, Chitonga, Chilozi, Lunda, Luvale |
| 23 | Zimbabwe | 12,619,600 | 23 | English | Chishona, isiNdebele, Kalanga |

Sources: Albaugh (2012); Lewis (2009); Wikimedia Foundation (2014); Bokamba (2007).

### The Characterization of Multilingualism

Before reviewing the current state of knowledge regarding multilingualism, it is imperative to point out briefly here how it arises. What we know from sociolinguistic and historical research about the emergence of multilingualism is that it arises from a variety of sociopolitical developments, which include (1) migration, (2) military conquests, (3) colonization, (4) federation, (5) evangelization, (6) education, (7) interethnic marriage practices, (8) trade, (9) music, and (10) urbanization (Brosnahan 1963; Fasold 1990; Laitin 2001). Each of these factors constitutes an agent of not only the development, but also the spread and possible maintenance, of the phenomenon.

In the general linguistic literature, multilingualism is treated essentially from two perspectives. First, it is seen as a phenomenon that is synonymous with bilingualism, or the existence of two languages as media of communication in the same society or individual. And second, it is seen as multiculturalism (Richards, Platt, and Weber 1985; Crystal 1991, 1997; Clyne 1997; Baker and Jones 1998). The definitions presented here concerning *societal* and *individual multilingualism* that I have extracted from various studies since the late 1980s exemplify what is found in the literature and show the confusion that prevails therein, thereby indicating the level of our knowledge of the phenomenon.

In particular, in response to the question of who is a multilingual, Richards, Platt, and Weber (1985, 28) offer the following definition:

> Bilingual: a person who knows and uses *two* languages. In everyday use, the word *bilingual* usually means a person who speaks, reads, or understands *two languages* equally well (*balanced bilingual*), but a *bilingual* person usually has a better knowledge of one language than of the other. For example, he/she may:
>
> a. Be able to read and write in only one language.
> b. Use each language in different types of situations (domains), e.g., one language at home and the other at work.
> c. Use each language for different communicative purposes, e.g., one language for talking about school life and the other for talking about personal feelings. (emphasis added)

According to Richards, Platt, and Weber (1985), a bilingual person is characterizable from three dimensions: (1) the ability to know and use two languages and (2) the ability to demonstrate equal competence in speaking, reading, and understanding both languages "equally well," presumably as a native speaker; but (3), in reality, his or her mastery cannot be balanced in both languages. The reasons for the differential linguistic competence in the two languages, according to the elaborations of the definitions given here, is that his or her level of proficiency is domain-specific. There is some merit in this characterization, as is discussed below, but it is not only for the reasons advanced above.

Their definition of "multilingual" (1985, 185) is essentially the same, except that a multilingual "knows and uses three or more languages" and "usually, a mulitlingual does not know all the languages equally well." The main conclusion to be drawn from Richards, Platt, and Weber (1985) is that a multilingual is a bilingual with one extra language in which the person has limited competence.

Crystal's (1991) characterization of multilingualism represents a dramatic improvement over that of Richards, Platt, and Weber (1985) in terms of the clarity of its definition, the appropriateness of the example cases, and the restraint on the levels of proficiency. For Crystal (1991, 259), "[multilingualism is a] situation where a speech community (or an individual) makes use of several languages, as in Switzerland or Belgium; sometimes called pluralingualism or polyglottism. The term *may subsume bilingualism* (strictly, the use of two languages), but is often contrasted with it, by emphasizing the use of more than two languages (as is the case with the everyday word polyglot)" (emphasis added). It is to be noted here also that Crystal recognizes the confusion between bilingualism and multilingualism that has been perpetuated in the literature by pointing out what it subsumes under the term and indicating that the correlation is inaccurate.

The clarity offered by Crystal (1991), however, was later lost, as a subsequent study by him appears to succumb to the dominant monolingual ideology that permits the conflation of bilingualism and multilingualism. Thus, according to Crystal (1997, 42),

> [multilingualism is a] term used in sociolinguistics to refer in the first instance, to a speech community which makes use of *two or more languages*, and the *two* [sic] individual speakers who have multilingual ability. *"Multilingualism" (or pluralingualism) in this sense subsumes bilingualism, but it is often contrasted with it (i.e., a community or individual in command of more than two languages).* A further distinction is sometimes made between multilingualism which is internal to a speech community (i.e., *an additional language being used to facilitate communication with other nations,* as in the case of a lingua franca). Sociolinguists have emphasized both the frequency and complexity of the phenomenon; on the one hand, there are very few speech communities which are totally monolingual (because of the existence of linguistic minority groups within their boundaries); on the other hand, *the multilingual abilities demonstrated are of several levels of proficiency,* and raise different kinds of political, educational, and social problems, depending on the numbers, social standing, and national feeling of the groups concerned. (emphasis added)

The confusion in the definition given above, which essentially reflects Richards, Platt, and Weber (1985), is at two levels: (1) the conflation of bilingualism and multilingualism by stating that the latter references "two or more languages" and that "'multilingualism' (or pluralingualism) in this sense subsumes bilingualism, but it is often contrasted with it (i.e., a community or individual in command of more than two languages"; and (2) acceptance of the unspecified type of proficiency criterion proposed by sociolinguists as a necessary component of the definition. The relevance of such a degree of proficiency to being a multilingual is unclear. As suggested with regard to Richards, Platt, and Weber (1985), and as argued below, the conflation of the two phenomena is unwarranted and obscures important differences between them. Further, the inclusion of equal proficiency levels in their definitions is unnecessary. In fact, their inclusion amounts to a denial of the multilingual's abilities to function in his or her languages. Apart from the confusion observed above, however, Crystal's (1997) portrayal of bilingualism and multilingualism is instructive in that it reflects the lingering misunderstanding of the phenomena under consideration.

A similar but heightened degree of ignorance is found in a study published a year later by another scholar, Clyne (1997), as can be seen in the following description (301):

> The term "multilingualism" can refer to either the language use or the competence of an individual or to the language situation in an entire nation or society.
>
> However, at the individual level it is generally subsumed under "bilingualism." This may be because, *while there are probably more bilinguals in the world than monolinguals, there are not perceived to be so many people who use more than two languages habitually.* There are, of course, *many rich multilingual situations in the world. . . .*
>
> A common definition of "multilingualism" would then be—*"the use of more than one language"* or *"competence in more than one language."* This allows for further refinement in the actual description to cover different levels of command or use of the various languages. (emphasis added)

Clyne's description of multilingualism is relatively straightforward and does not require any comment. Similarly, his first sentence reiterates the flawed conflation commented upon above; the second clause of his second sentence in this statement— "while there are probably more bilinguals in the world than monolinguals"— demonstrates unwarranted speculation, because he does not even refer to any available or anecdotal statistics. It is clear from this clause that Clyne is unaware of the multilingual practices at least in regions such as India and Africa, where his assertion would be countered. Similarly, the claim that "there are not perceived to be so many people who use more than two languages habitually" is absolutely false from at least an African-language ecological perspective, as documented in part in this study. The statement given above is a reproduction of the misunderstanding observed earlier in this chapter.

It needs to be pointed out here that, though the previously cited studies clearly demonstrate their monolingual- to bilingualism-driven ideology, they appear to hesitate in making categorical statements regarding the multilingual's competence to function on a daily basis in his or her languages. Clyne (1997), however, not only reproduces the same misunderstanding of multilingualism but also denies the daily practice of multilingualism by speakers.

The confusion exemplified in the studies surveyed here represents what I indicated at the beginning of this chapter to be the frustrating aspect of research on multilingualism in the twentieth century: the fact that one can review so many studies and keep encountering persistent misunderstanding in spite of the preponderance of the phenomenon, as shown in table 2.1. It is very puzzling that such flawed descriptions of multilingual practices are reproduced ad nauseum in this era of quantum advances in sociolinguistics. It appears that these perspectives have moved from myths to stereotypes and thus are resistant to counterevidence (Hewstone and Giles 1997). (Note that there are numerous confusing definitions of bilingualism and multilingualism in the twentieth and twenty-first centuries, and they are not difficult to locate in the recent and current literature.)

The picture is not totally bleak, however; there are some proverbial bright spots in this pre-/pluri-/multilingualism movement, including McArthur (1992) and Baker and Jones (1998). Thus far, the clearest and most comprehensive definition of multilingual(ism) has been offered by McArthur (1992, 673), who is careful to point out the lack of general agreement on the qualifications for being multilingual, but proceeds to cite well-known examples of societal multilingualism and common ways in which multilinguals deploy their linguistic repertoires in such societies:

> Multilingualism [is] the ability to use *three or more languages*, either separately or in various degrees of code-mixing. There is no general agreement as to the degree of competence in each language necessary before someone can be considered multilingual; according to some, a native-like fluency is necessary in at least three languages; according to others, different languages are used for different purposes, competence in each varying according to such factors as register, occupation, and education. Where an individual has been exposed to *several languages*—as, for example, in India, Nigeria, or Singapore—*one language may be used in the home, another professionally, another passively for listening or reading, another spoken but not written or read, and so forth.* In a multilingual state, such as India, most individuals have *a knowledge of several languages*, but not uniformly nor in the same combinations across the nation: In Bombay, people may have a varying acquaintance with Marathi (the state language of Maharashtra), Hindi (the national associate official language), English (the national associate language and important language of business and culture in the city), and Gujurati (the language of two important minority groups, the Gujuratis and Parsis); *in such a setting, a few people are unilingual.* (emphasis added)

McArthur's description of societal and individual multilingualism captures the reality of this phenomenon without being categoric, as seen in several of the preceding definitions. Note, first, that in contrast to all the previously cited definitions, McArthur states clearly that multilingualism refers to knowleldge of *three or more languages*; he does not immerse himself into the "two or more" languages ambiguity that pervades much of the literature.

Second, McArthur's (1992) disjunctive statement, "one language may be used in the home, another professionally, another passively for listening or reading, another spoken but not written or read, and so forth," recognizes the commonly observed facts that multilinguals in pervasively multilingual societies allocate their code repertoires differentially, as determined by domains, and their competence in them may be oral or written (Fishman 1965; Grosjean 2001, 2010; Aronin and Singleton 2012). For example, in most postcolonial sub-Saharan African states, the continued exclusive use of the colonial languages (i.e., English, French, and Portuguese) has left the vast majority of the speakers of nonregional languages, the so-called minority or ethnic languages, illiterate in their mother tongues and subregional languages. African languages are not unique in this regard; similar situations exist in other regions throughout the multilingual world (Li Wei 2001b; Simpson 2007; Bokamba 2008b).

Third, McArthur points out that in such stable multilingual societies, monolinguals are "few"—that is, the exceptions. This refreshing description of multilingualism elucidates the phenomenon in contradistinction to bilingualism, and thus is one upon which we can build not only a much more accurate account but also a comprehensive and explanatorily adequate theory of the knowledge of languages.

As we proceed with our survey of research on the phenomenon into the late 1990s and up to the early 2000s, however, the sampled studies continue to exhibit the confusion described prior to McArthur's (1992) definition, suggesting that his was perhaps a fluke. This claim is demonstrated by Baker and Jones's (1998) definitions, which they begin with an acknowledgment of the difficulty of "defining who is and who is not a bilingual"; they then proceed to confuse completely bilingualism and multilingualism:

> Defining who is and who is not *bilingual* is a more difficult task than it appears. There will be a lack of agreement about the answers to the following section of questions (2).
>
> . . . The term *bilingualism* is usually reserved to describe *two languages* within an individual. When the focus is on two languages in society, the term *diglossia* is often used (5).
>
> Multilingualism: The word *bilingual* is used of an individual, [and] primarily describes the possession of *two languages*. However, *it can also be taken to include the many people in the world who have varying degrees of proficiency in three, four, or even more languages* (17).
>
> In many parts of Africa and Asia, *several languages* may coexist and large sections of the population may speak *two or more languages*. In such countries multilingualism is the result of a process of industrial development, political unification, modernization, urbanization, and greater contact between different local communities.
>
> Multilingualism can also be the possession of individuals who do not live within a multilingual speech community. Families can be *trilingual* when the husband and wife each speak a different language as well as the majority language of the country of residence (18). (emphasis added)

Baker and Jones's statement is puzzling in light of the one that correctly delimits bilingualism, but it is also deeply revealing with respect to the realities of bilingualism and multilingualism. If the authors had taken into consideration, or become aware of, bilingualism and multilingual practices in pervasive and stable bilingual and/or multilingual societies, they would not have had any difficulty describing and distinguishing the two phenomena.

The puzzlement continues. Although demonstrating a clear understanding and knowledge of multilingual practices, as indicated above, even scholars such as Li Wei (2001b, 7–8) apparently cannot avoid the trap of equating bilingualism with multilingualism, as her definition clearly shows:

> The word "bilingual" primarily describes someone with possession of two languages. *It* can, however, also be taken to include the many people in the world who have varying degrees of proficiency in and interchangeably use three, four or even more languages.
>
> In many countries of Africa and Asia, several languages coexist and *large sections of the population speak three or more languages. Individual multilingualism in these countries is a fact of life.* Many people speak one or more local or ethnic languages, as well as another indigenous language which has become the medium of communication between different ethnic groups or speech communities. *Such individuals may also speak a foreign language—* such as English, French, or Spanish—which has been introduced into the community during the process of colonisation. This latter language is often the language of education, bureaucracy, and privilege. (emphasis added)

Li Wei (2001b, 8), like McArthur (1992), however, leaves no doubts that she is well informed regarding multilingual practices: She points out forcefully and correctly that "it is important to recognize that a multilingual speaker *uses different languages for different purposes and does not typically possess the same level or type of proficiency in each language.* In Morocco, for instance, a native speaker of Berber may also be fluent in colloquial Moroccan Arabic, *but not literate in either of these languages.* This Berber speaker will be educated in Modern Standard Arabic and use that language for writing and formal purposes. Classical Arabic is the language of the mosque, used for prayers and reading the Qur'an. Many Moroccans also have some knowledge of French, the former colonial language" (emphasis added).

The claim made here by Li Wei is substantiated time and time again on the ground in innumerable multilingual societies around the world. In this respect, the domain-specific allocation of a multilingual's verbal repertoire and his or her illiteracy in one or more of the languages at his or her command debunk the myth of "balanced" bilingual or multilingual competence insisted upon by sociolinguists, such as those critiqued above. I return to these points below.

Although more confusing definitions of multilingualism can be cited from even the most recent publications, including Franceschini (2009, 33–34), it serves no further useful purpose to do so in this chapter. The studies sampled above have clearly demonstrated the depth of the inexplicable ignorance, in today's globalized societies, about the common phenomenon of multilingualism. It is this level of ingrained confusion, which is evidently informed by an ideology centered on monolingualism and bilingualism, that makes the recent movement to multilingual acquisition undertaken by a number of European scholars (e.g., Cenoz, Hufeisen, and Jessner 2008; Cook 2009; Aronin and Hufeisen 2009; Grosjean 2010; Aronin and Singleton 2012) exciting and exhilarating.

A number of these studies provide clear definitions of multilingualism in contradistinction to bilingualism, as exemplified in part by Kemp's (2009, 14–15) definitions and Aronin and Singleton's (2012) definitions. According to the former, who references other publications (i.e., McArthur 1992,), "'Bilinguals' are often described as persons who use two languages, and bilingualism is 'the ability to speak two languages' or 'the habitual use of two languages colloquially'" (Kemp 2009, 14, citing the *Oxford English Dictionary*; Fabbro 1999). Also, "a multilingual is a person who has 'the ability to use three or more languages, either separately or in various degrees of code-mixing. Different languages are used for different purposes, competence in each varying according to such factors as register, occupation, and education'" (Kemp 2009, 15, citing McArthur 1992).

Aronin and Singleton (2012, 6) concur with the definitions given here, after arguing that "bilingualism and multilingualism" must be distinguished not as "a matter of abstract terminological niceties" but because "there are qualitative distinctions between the [two] phenomena . . . involving language experience, use, and interactional strategies by bi- and multi-linguals." For them, "[societal] multilingualism [is] understood as *the phenomenon of the use of many languages in a given society*" (emphasis added).

As demonstrated by much of the research done from the 1990s to the early 2000s, it has taken the field of linguistics several decades to acknowledge the reality of multilingualism (documented in table 2.1) as a common and pervasive phenomenon, and to distinguish it from bilingualism. But this late and apparently reluctant recognition, as argued at least by Weber (2007) in his review of Auer and Li Wei (2007), continues to be influenced implicitly or subconsciously by empirically unwarranted "essentialist" and "ideologies," monolingual to bilingual. To see this, let us review what research on multilingualism in Africa, for example, has established.

## Research on Multilingualism in Africa

African scholars by and large have neglected the study of multilingualism from a comprehensive perspective; instead, they have focused mainly on its sociolinguistic, not cognitive, dimensions—including language planning and language policy, language variation, code-switching, varieties of English, and to a limited extent language spread and attitudes (e.g., Sey 1973; Bokamba 1976, 1984a, 1984b, 1991, 2007; Bamgbose 1991, 1992, 2000; Bamgbose, Banjo, and Thomas 1995; Singler 1991, 1997; Myers-Scotton 1993b, 1993c; Webb 2002; Bamiro 1994, 1995; Wolff 2001; Baldauf and Kaplan 2004; Kaplan and Baldauf 2007; Schmied 1991, 1997, 2006). Nonetheless, what the research on these facets of multilingualism has shown is absolutely clear: Africa is pervasively multilingual, at both the individual and societal levels, as shown partly in table 2.2, given that an estimated 2,035 to 2,100 languages are spoken in its fifty-five constituent nations.

In view of these facts, one would have expected Africanist linguists to have given serious attention to at least the social dimensions of multilingualism. This is indeed what we find, but the effort has been somewhat limited in light of the phenomenon's pervasiveness. The first study on aspects of multilingualism appears to be Alexandre's (1967) pioneering publication, titled *Langues et langages en Afrique noire*, which discusses issues of languages in African cultures and societies, with an emphasis on language policies during the colonial era. This study does not, however, deal with any other sociolinguistic aspects of multilingualism (e.g., language variation, spread, borrowing, nativization of loanwords, language shift and maintenance, and code-switching). The first in-depth study to address several major aspects of multilingualism is Heine's dissertation, which was published in 1970 under the title *The Status and Use of African Lingua Francas*. This book provides a relatively detailed discussion of both the historical development of the selected linguae francae (LFs) and some of the structural variation they exhibit. It also presents a sociolinguistic profile of each of these well-known and established African trade languages in about seven different countries, and discusses their importance as languages of wider communication in the target subregions.

From 1972 to 1978 the Ford Foundation's bureau in West Africa subsidized a series of country-specific language surveys that detailed the number of languages, the number of speakers, their histories, their de facto and de jure functional allocations, and their prospects vis-à-vis education and administration. This program produced four books on language in Uganda, Kenya, Ethiopia, and Zambia that were edited by different Africanist scholars. Unfortunately, however, the project was terminated when the Ford Foundation closed its West African bureau. Bamgbose (1991) presents the first continent-wide discussion of language planning in public domains (i.e., education and administration) by presenting an overview of the development of this planning in nation building and development and by demonstrating its failures and consequences.

These studies were followed fourteen years later by a study by Calvet (1992), *Les langues des marchés en Afrique*, in which selected African and non-African languages in six West African states and one Central African state are described almost exclusively with respect to their functional allocations as market/trade languages in urban centers. The book does not address any other aspect of multilingualism. Pütz (1995) provides a selection of invited papers on the same topic, with considerable emphasis on the Namibian experience in Southern Africa. In *The Power of Babel: Language and Governance in the African Experience*, Mazrui and Mazrui (1998) discuss several aspects of multilingualism, with a particular emphasis on the politics of language planning and language spread with special attention to English and Kiswahili in Eastern Africa. Even though one of the authors is a linguist, the book offers no discussion of language variation and code-switching, two characteristic phenomena of languages in any multilingual society.

In addition to these types of studies, there have been a few conference proceedings on some aspects of language planning vis-à-vis education, language spread, and language variation (Herbert 1992); but none of them, including doctoral dissertations, offers a comprehensive treatment of multilingualism, as described below. Myers-Scotton (1993a, 1993c) presents interesting analyses of code-switching and mixing based on African languages. She has proposed analytical models to account for aspects of the social motivations for code-switching generally, and for analyzing the grammar of code-mixed speech.

Simpson's (2008) edited book *Language and National Identity in Africa* provides a relatively comprehensive survey of the roles of African languages in language identity construction in the states covered. The book provides historical discussions of language policies and practices, and how they shape (sub)national identity and affect social developments. Although it does not address any other topics, the various surveys clearly demonstrate the extent of functional and stable multilingualism, along with the attendant issues of language policy practices in public domains. Two other recent publications that are similarly focused on a single dimension of multilingualism are Vigouroux and Mufwene's (2008) edited volume *Globalization and Language Vitality: Perspectives from Black Africa*, which addresses the issues of language competition and endangerment in multilingual Africa, and McLaughlin's (2009) edited volume *The Languages of Urban Africa*, which deals with the spread of selected linguae francae. Vigouroux and Mufwene (2008) address, on empirical grounds, the reality of language vitality and endangerment in Africa in the context of the ongoing debate on language endangerment and loss in developing nations that is reportedly caused by "globalizing" or "killer" languages such as English, French, and Spanish (Brenzinger 1998, 2008; Nettle and Romaine 2000). What the studies in this book show, among other things, is that African languages are not threatened or endangered by globalizing languages—as in the Americas, for example—but they face serious competition against African linguae francae, especially in urban centers.

Two of the recent publications dealing with Arabic-speaking North Africa are those by Moha (2005) and Bassiouney (2009). Moha's (2005) study is perhaps the first comprehensive attempt to address the language ecology in Morocco, and the historical developments that have occurred since the colonial era to shape the language practices and identity construction in education and the society in general, at times triggering contestations of language legitimacy between French and Arabic, on the one hand; and on the other, between Modern Standard Arabic, Moroccan Arabic, and Berber. In contrast, Bassiouney (2009) introduces the reader to the sociolinguistics of Arabic in Africa and in the Middle East, with a focus on issues such as diglossia, code-switching, language variation and change, Arabic and gender, and language planning.

The latest book-length publications dealing with language planning and practices in multilingual Africa are those by Koffi (2012) and Anchimbe (2013). Koffi's book, *Paradigm Shift in Language Planning and Policy: Game-Theoretic Solutions*, attempts to address the perennial question of language planning and policy implementation in Africa through a theoretical prism and in particular the failures of these efforts. It suggests a way out by applying the critical game theory discussed by Laitin (1992). In contrast, Anchimbe's book (2013), *Language Policy and Identity Construction: The Dynamics of Cameroon's Multilingualism*, presents the most comprehensive and incisive up-to-date analysis of not only functional multilingualism in an African country—Cameroon in this case—but also the blatant failure of the state's official bilingual policy in a country with an estimated 284 indigenous languages, plus two implanted ones, English and French (inherited from the colonial era).

Although it is abundantly clear from the research surveyed above that multilingualism in Africa is a daily reality, it should also be evident that there are major gaps in this research. These include the lack of studies on the variation in indigenous African languages as a result of long language contact and competition in certain contexts and domains (e.g., urbanization, trade, and music); the lack of studies on the cognitive aspects of the phenomenon, which include necessarily language acquisition from a multilingual, rather than monolingual, perspective, as well as the consequences of such a process for the learners; and the lack of studies on multilingual language acquisition research, and thereby its implications for language planning. The absence of research in these areas by Africanists can only perpetuate the misunderstanding of multilingualism illustrated above.

Space constraints here do not permit the pursuit of an extensive discussion and analysis of multilingualism; instead, in the interest of demystifying the phenomenon and advancing our understanding of its fundamentals, it is necessary to briefly survey how multilingualism functions in Africa to achieve two interrelated objectives: (1) to clarify the misunderstandings presented in most of the definitions cited here, and (2) to draw on this reality to propose an empirically informed characterization of multilinguals and multilingualism.

### Overview of the Functioning of Multilingualism in Africa
To offer an emperically based characterization of multilingualism as a societal and individual phenomenon, it is necessary to address at least two basic questions: (1) How does it manifest itself socially? (2) And how does it do so at the level of the (multilingual) speaker—that is, cognitively? Let us briefly consider each of these questions.

#### Social Manifestations of Mutilingualism
The evidence for societal multilingualism in Africa is overwhelming, as can be seen in part from the overview presented above. What is often less evident, but can be inferred from the language demographics from each of the continent's fifty-five nations, is how this phenomenon manifests itself at the level of social interactions. (1) What are the dominant or major languages in each country? (2) In what domains are they and the minority or ethnic languages used? That is, what are the discursive practices in such communities? (3) And what is the typical verbal or linguistic repertoire of the African multilingual?

Question 1 can be answered with the data in the last two columns of table 2.2, where a number of official languages (OL) and national languages (NL) are identified, ranging from a minimum of two to more than eleven. With respect to question 2, though it is unclear at this juncture to specify with any certainty which principal or national languages are used in which domains in all twenty-three states listed in table 2.2, the commonly established practices in this regard are as follows: (1) In most of the states the official languages—mostly English, French, and Portuguese, except for Arabic in North Africa—are used as the principal or exclusive medium of education, administration (including the executive, the judiciary, the legislative), international affairs, and other public domains (e.g., print and broadcast media, state parastatals, hospitals). (2) The principal/national languages in most, if not all, states are generally employed as transitional media of education in the lower cycle of primary education (i.e., kindergarten to third grade), where the official language(s) is taught as a subject. In contrast, the national languages compete with the official ones in the broadcast media, state parastatals, private companies (including postal services, hospitals/clinics, and transportation services), religious services, shopping centers, open marketplaces, lower-level administration in urban and rural communities, sport broadcasts, and mass political rallies. In certain states one of the national languages is used as the official language of the armed forces (e.g., Kiswahili in Kenya; Lingála in the Democratic Republic of Congo from 1932 to 1997 and Lingála and Kiswahili from 1997 to the present; and Setswana in Botswana). Further, the principal/national languages dominate intraregional and interregional trade, and serve as the link media for interethnic communication in urban centers, whereas the local/ethnic languages generally function as the intraethnic or family media of communication both in rural and urban centers.

## Cognitive Manifestations of Mutilingualism

At the individual level and in answer to question 3, it can be stated without hesitation whatsoever that the average African is minimally multilingual in that he or she speaks fluently at least three languages: a home language (HL), a community language (CL), and a (sub)regional language (RL) of some sort. This claim has been substantiated by several cross-national studies or reports that include those summarized above, as well as those by Berry (1971); Scotton (1975); Broeder, Extra, and Maartens (1998); Wolff (2001); and Anchimbe (2013).

Berry (1971, 324–25)—in perhaps the first systematic, empirical investigation of societal multilingualism in an African town back in 1966, which involved a two-part, house-to-house completion of a written questionnaire followed by interviews—came to six conclusions, of which the first three are most pertinent here:

The survey [of the two thousand plus residents of Madina, Ghana] clearly established that

1. Over 80 different languages are spoken natively by the residents of Madina.
2. There are very few monolinguals in Madina (less than 4 percent of all respondents admit to knowing only one language).
3. The majority (over 70 percent) of the respondents claim competence in three languages [Twi, English, and Hausa] or more languages. Respondents' claims of competence in second and third languages seem prima facie reasonably conservative. This statement, though purely impressionistic, is based, inter alia, on the evidence of the frequency of responses indicating a desire to improve knowledge of some language; . . . reluctance to speak a language for fear of ridicule by [its] native speakers; and responses indicating awareness that the mother tongue is the only one properly understood.

When all the factors given here are taken into consideration, the residents of Madina appear to know five languages with varying degrees of proficiency in communication. Scotton (1975), in a study conducted in Lagos, obtained similar results. She found that out of 187 respondents, only 5 percent spoke one language (viz., their mother tongue). Of the remaining 95 percent, 45 percent claim to speak two languages; 29 percent, three languages; and 4 percent, four languages. What is not stated explicitly by either Berry (1971) or Scotton (1975) but is well known in language practices in Africa is that many multilinguals acquire their verbal repertoires naturalistically, not only as prepubescent learners but also as grown adults through personal contact of one sort or another. These contacts include encounters with other language speakers on trade routes between regions within the same country or across national borders; among those migrating to urban centers for job opportunities, especially in the mining and farming sectors, and in the civil and military services.

Berry (1971) and Scotton (1975) are not isolated researchers; a similar degree of multilingualism is reported by Broeder, Extra, and Maartens (1998) for the city of Durban (which then had a population of more than 2.5 million), where at least three to five different languages are spoken or known by residents. More recently, Wolff (2001) cites a statement from a working document prepared for the Intergovernmental Conference on Language Policies in Africa, held in Harare in March 1997, that reported the average African speaks two to five languages in his or her daily interactions: "In a survey related to the case of Nigeria, the number of languages spoken by each of the subjects of the speech communities studied ranged from two to three as follows: 60 percent of the subjects spoke two languages; 30 percent three languages; and 10 percent over four languages. A similar observation could be made regarding many if not all the African countries, where there is a widespread tradition of handling multilingualism. Often there is a complementary distribution of this multilingualism across languages *by sectors of activities. The multilingualism is not only functional or commercial; it cuts across the social fabric. It forms a sociopolitical and sociolinguistic characteristic of most speech communities*" (316; emphasis added).

Anchimbe's (2013) study of Cameroon echoes this range of multilingualism without the statistical breakdown. He shows that the average Cameroonian speaks at least three languages—HL, CL, and Cameroon Pidgin English—and up to five languages (French and English, the two OLs) if he or she has a secondary education. For the youths, there is a sixth language, Camfranglais, a mixed French-English youth-speak.

If we take the "average speaker" to be a resident of either a rural or semi-urban community who has completed five years of primary education (PEduc), he or she will have a spoken repertoire of at least three languages—HL, CL, and RL—where the RL could also, but not necessarily, be the state or provincial LF (Broeder, Extra, and Maartens 1998; Bokamba 2008a; Anchimbe 2013). In contrast, if that speaker has completed six years of secondary education, he or she will likely acquire some degree of fluency in three additional languages—LF, NL, and OL—because of the educational requirements at this cycle of education. ("Some degree of fluency" corresponds to level 2+, "limited working proficiency plus," on the scale proposed by the American Council on the Teaching of Foreign Languages (ACTFL)/Interagency

Language Roundtable (ILR); see www.govtilr.org.) This amounts to a linguistic repertoire of six languages or more if a college education (ColEduc) is added, as is illustrated in the case of the Democratic Republic of Congo in table 2.3; an individual will possess different levels of proficiency that will permit him or her to communicate, at least orally, with sympathetic interlocutors of the same language.

Table 2.3
Illustration of a Multilingual Verbal Repertoire: Democratic Republic of Congo

| | Speaker | Languages[a] | | | | | | |
|---|---|---|---|---|---|---|---|---|
| | | HL | CL | RL | LF | NL | OL | FL |
| Rural | W/o PEduc (no formal schooling) | + | + | + | (±) | (±) | NA | NA |
| | W/PEduc (±5) (some primary education) | + | + | + | (±) | (±) | (±) | NA |
| | W/PEduc (6) (completed primary education) | + | + | + | + | + | + | NA |
| Semi-urban | W/o PEduc (no formal schooling) | + | + | + | + | + | NA | NA |
| | W/PEduc (±5) (some primary education) | + | + | + | + | + | + | NA |
| | W/PEduc (6) (completed primary education) | + | + | + | + | + | + | NA |
| | W/SEduc (±2) (some secondary education) | + | + | + | + | + | + | (±) |
| | W/SEduc (6) (completed secondary education) | + | + | + | + | + | + | (±) |
| Urban (major) | W/o PEduc (no formal schooling) | (±) | + | + | + | + | NA | NA |
| | W/PEduc (±5) (some primary education) | (±) | + | + | + | + | + | NA |
| | W/PEduc (6) (completed primary education) | (±) | + | + | + | + | + | NA |
| | W/SEduc (±2) (some secondary education) | (±) | + | + | + | + | + | NA |
| | W/SEduc (6) (completed secondary education) | (±) | + | + | + | + | + | (±) |
| | W/ColEduc (±3) (some college) | (±) | + | + | + | + | + | + |
| | W/ColEduc (5) (completed college) | (±) | + | + | + | + | + | + |
| | W/GradEduc (2) (graduate education) | (±) | + | + | + | + | + | + |

a. HL = home language; CL = community language; RL = regional language; LF = lingua franca; NL = national language; OL = official language; FL = foreign language; NA = option not available.

What this means socially is that this multilingual speaker will deploy the HL in the family domain with his or her children, spouse, and relatives; the CL at the marketplace or in interaction with nonspeakers of his or her HL; the RL at school in interacting with teachers in the school system and with speakers from other communities during his or her travels away from home but within his or her (sub)region; the LF whenever he or she travels away from his or her immediate subregion or across another region where the LF is spoken; the NL, if different from the LF, in interregional or national communication; and the OL for communication in public domains where such a language is required (e.g., in secondary and university education, in government offices in urban centers, with foreign nationals). As can be imagined, the speaker will likely be multidialectal in all these languages that he or she speaks fluently, thus adding to the complexity of his or her code repertoire.

### *Toward a Redefinition of Multilingualism*
In light of the characterization of the African multilingual presented above—and which can be replicated in India, the countries making up the former USSR, and Switzerland—we can now redefine multilingualism empirically by considering the primary criterion as *oral communication* at *the advanced level* (i.e., ACTFL/ILR, level 2) in *appropriate domains of interaction*. This approach excludes the literacy proficiency criteria, such as the speaker's capacities to write, read, and translate his or her languages with equal facility. Accordingly, and from a general perspective, multilingualism is the existence of three or more languages as media of daily (oral) communication for a given society or speaker.

In more specific terms, societal and individual multilingualism is the existence of three or more languages as media of daily (oral) communication, characterized by the de facto and/or de jure allocation of domains for the languages concerned, whereas at the individual level, within such societies, multilingualism refers to the speaker's ability to use the internalized languages at the advanced-plus level (i.e., ACTFL/ILR, level 2+) in oral communication in appropriate domains of interaction. That is, a multilingual speaker must be able to carry out and sustain conversations in any common life domains in any of his or her languages.

These definitions capture several key characteristics of and thus criteria for both societal and individual multilingualism: (1) the functionality criterion; (2) the implied context of situational criterion, that is, the ability to change language or language variety according to topic, context, and interlocutor; and (3) the competence or mastery criterion, which is not predicated on literacy. This third criterion is necessitated by the fact that the vast majority of speakers in the world are illiterate or semiliterate, and the vast majority of their languages are unwritten or undocumented.

We can now draw on these definitions to contrastively redefine *bilingualism* as follows: Bilingualism refers to the existence of two languages as media of daily (oral) communication in a given society or for a given speaker. At the societal level, bilingualism is characterized by the de facto and/or de jure allocation of domains for the two languages concerned, whereas at the individual level within such societies, bilingualism refers to a speaker's ability to use the two internalized languages at the advanced-plus level (i.e., ACTFL/ILR, level 2+) in oral communication in appropriate domains of interaction. It should be evident that these definitions provide a clearer characterization of the two phenomena than those published in the literature and critiqued above, and as such, these new definitions present a better basis for analyzing and advancing our understanding of these phenomena.

## The Impact of Multilingualism in Africa and Elsewhere

Let us now consider briefly the ways in which multilingualism constitutes both an opportunity and a challenge as a sociolinguistic phenomenon, with a focus on its consequences and implications on both the societal and individual levels.

### *The Social Perspective*

From a social perspective, societal bilingualism and multilingualism represent a potential linguistic capital that can become a liability if mismanaged. They constitute a benefit, or cultural capital, in different ways (including indigenous knowledge production) for the nation's inhabitants. Specifically, multilingualism represents diversity, richness of cultural heritages, centuries of accumulated wisdoms, and opportunities to learn to live harmoniously with people of other or related cultures through sustained cross-language contacts. Given that language is the quintessential medium of communication that defines groups of people as human societies, and thereby mediates all human relations, societal multilingualism is arguably linguistic capital in a diverse linguistic market, à la Bourdieu (1991). For social institutions engaged in nation building, for example, societal multilingualism facilitates and enhances their ability to reach the masses by packaging services and messages to them in the target languages. This is particularly crucial in areas such as public administration, education, the health care delivery system, the judiciary, agricultural extension services, and political mobilization for the effective implementation of nation-building objectives.

At the individual level, as is shown below, the ability of an individual to maintain his or her daily activities and a sense of identity in a multilingual society depends largely on his or her ability to interact with other citizens in the appropriate target languages. As Bamgbose (1991) observes, unlike in pervasively monolingual societies, it is very difficult to function fully as a monolingual person in stable multilingual societies. Knowledge of such societies' languages is an asset and a key that can be deployed to access a variety of life opportunities, including but not limited to education, employment, promotion, cultivation of interpersonal relationships, and creativity in one's chosen profession. Failure to be conversant in such languages, especially in a society that does not have a single common language, will have a number of negative consequences, including a sense of isolation, an inability to develop meaningful and lasting relationships, an inability to competently negotiate a variety of transactions requiring some of the languages, and an inability to access job or promotional opportunities necessitating them.

In contrast to these potential benefits, societal, but not individual, multilingualism constitutes a challenge that requires careful management of the society's linguistic diversity, including the necessity to carry out language planning and the adoption of language policies that are consistent with participatory democratic, educational, and socioeconomic goals. Failure to address these issues carefully can and often does result in ethnic conflicts that exploit linguistic diversity. These concerns are exemplified by the cases of Belgium in the 1960s through the late 1980s, when governments fell and were reconstituted several times (Karra 2007; Vogl and Hüning 2010); and of the strikes that characterized air traffic controllers in Canada in the 1970s and the subsequent attempts at secession by the province of Quebec (Martel and Pâquet 2012). Another example is the language conflict in India over the possible elevation of Hindi as the sole national and official language, to the exclusion of English, in 1965—fifteen years after the adoption of the January 1950 Constitution (Amritavalli and Jayaseelan 2007). And still another example is the Soweto massacre of 1976 over the imposition of Afrikaans as a second official language of instruction in African/black middle schools. There are also short- to medium-term costs associated with the implementation of multilingual policies, including expenses for teacher training, the publication of educational and administrative manuals, and the translation of government regulations.

Thus, multilingualism is a valuable asset that can benefit a nation in a number of respects, but if it is mishandled, it can also quickly turn into a liability. Perhaps the best way to deal with it effectively without fomenting linguistic-based conflicts and marginalizing some of the languages—especially in pervasively multilingual states such as those in the African, Asian, and Pacific regions—is to carefully plan the enactment of equitable language policies that will cost-effectively promote appropriately selected major languages (e.g., à la India's model of three languages and linguistic states) while protecting ethnic languages in their respective domains, and to then implement these policies accordingly.

### *The Linguistic/Cognitive Perspective*
From a linguistic perspective, multilingualism, whether societal or individual, offers an enormous panoply of benefits and challenges. On the positive side, it opens a window to linguistic competence in its general sense—not the decontextualized knowledge of the ideal, abstract speaker/listener in a homogenous speech community defined by Chomsky (1965), but the general cognitive ability of humans to use language in context. For example, at a psycholinguistic level, an examination of how the human brain functions vis-à-vis bilingual and multilingual activities is bound to provide critical and useful insights into the organization of language in the brain and into the processing and the acquisition mechanism for multiple languages. Fundamental questions to be investigated in this regard include:

1. Do the brains of bilingual and multilingual persons operate differently from that of a monolingual's with respect to language acquisition, processing, and use?
2. If so, how can this operation be characterized and explained?
3. What processing activities occur when a speaker switches and/or mixes two or more languages?
4. How can this process be described?
5. Does the Critical Period Hypothesis in language acquisition apply to bilingual and multilingual speakers?

6. If not, why not?

7. If it does, in what specific respects does it affect the acquisition of additional languages (e.g., at L3, L4, or L5)?

8. And what advantages or disadvantages, if any, do bilinguals and multilinguals have in the acquisition of additional languages over monolinguals?

Several of these questions have been and continue to be investigated with regard to language acquisition by the European scholars cited above, and they have offered very interesting preliminary results (Cenoz, Hufeisen, and Jessner 2008; Cook 2009; Aronin and Hufeisen 2009). Research on multilingualism in education is also having promising outcomes, as argued in at least in one recent study in Britain (Blackledge and Creese 2010).

From a structural/formal linguistic perspective, fruitful investigations could be conducted on the effects of multilingualism on the vowel quality of any of the internalized languages, lexical choices, semantic interpretations, syntactic constructions, and morpho-syntactic variations triggered by the cohabitation or internalization of several languages in the speaker's brain.

Sociolinguistically, multilingualism provides scholars with incomparable empirical data at both the individual and societal levels to study language function, form, and usage in vivo. For example, issues of language interaction, choice, attitudes, power, ideology, language and gender, language contact, variation and change, language vitality, and language planning and its implications can be studied with considerable profit and clarity from a multilingual, not monolingual-to-bilingual, perspective. Fundamental questions that could be studied systematically in some of these areas include:

1. The characteristics of the spread of one or more languages in stable multilingual environments;

2. The conditions that facilitate or impede the de facto allocation of functions to a language or more in given public domains;

3. The factors that condition language choice in face-to-face interactions;

4. The characteristics of language variation and change in multilingual contexts;

5. Borrowing between languages that have been in extended contact and the type of indigenization exhibited in such loanwords; and

6. The conditions that facilitate language vitality: maintenance, shift, attrition, revival, and intergenerational nontransmission (Fishman 1991; Brenzinger 1998; Nettle and Romaine 2000; Winford 2003; Bokamba 2008a, 2008b; Mufwene and Vigouroux 2008; Vigouroux and Mufwene 2008).

As argued and shown in a number of recent innovative studies in Europe on the acquisition of additional languages beyond the second language (L3 and L4), research on multilingualism offers a rich mine of data for the discovery of realistic, rather than restricted and imagined, insights regarding the spontaneous process of multilingual acquisition by children and even adults (Cenoz, Hufeisen, and Jessner 2001; Aronin and Hufeisen 2009; Grosjean 2010; Aronin and Singleton 2012;

Pawlak and Aronin 2013). This type of research effort would include examinations of how prepubescent children acquire the lexicon with respect to all the relevant grammatical components: phonetics, phonology, morphology, syntax, and semantics. Multilingual studies of these questions could be conducted from a comparative perspective with regard to monolingualism, and the findings would elucidate the similarities and differences between monolingual and multilingual communities and individuals. In so doing, we would gain unparalleled insights that would far better advance our knowledge of linguistic competence than our currently monolingually and monodialectally dominated approach. As long as linguistics remains an empirical science that aims to discover and formulate a theory of language knowledge, the study of multilingualism in its many manifestations is a necessity, not an option.

## Conclusion
This chapter has sought to demystify the phenomena of bilingualism and multilingualism, with an emphasis on the latter. Specifically, it has attempted to present an analysis of what constitutes multilingualism using an African database that shows the phenomenon to be not only a norm rather than an aberation, but also a necessity for daily interactions. The study has shown that African multilinguals use their verbal repertoires daily as dictated by contexts of situation: interlocutor, domain, and topic as a matter of necessity. This finding contradicts not only claims by scholars such as Clyne (1997) but also debunks the persistent myth of the necessity of equal or coordinated competence in speakers' repertoires as sine qua non criteria for the achievement of bilingual and multilingual status. The types of multilingual practices in Africa documented in this study—as McArthur (1992), Li Wei (2001a, b), and Grosjean (2010) correctly maintain, in general—reflect the differentiated requisite levels of proficiency, and facilitate the maintenance of stable multilingualism across generations. This first conclusion, by extension, also applies to the world's other multilingual regions. From the data and research reviews presented here, the most fundamental criterion of competence or proficiency in a bilingual or multilingual person's repertoire is his or her ability to function effectively in any of the languages in relevant domains of interaction for him or her. This is what the ACTFL/ILR terms "limited working [oral] proficiency, plus." This criterion is sufficient for a speaker to be considered as a bilingual or multilingual. Second, based on the survey of multilingualism and its functioning in Africa and on the implications of other research, the study has clearly characterized multilingualism, has defined it in contradistinction to bilingualism, and has thus demystified both phenomena. Third, and contrary to the dominant monolingual-to-bilingual paradigm perspective, multilingualim has been shown here to be a rich and rewarding linguistic phenomenon that is vastly challenging both socially and linguistically. Fourth, in these respects, per the linguistic knowledge and practices presented here, the systematic pursuit of multilingualim as an essential area of linguistic inquiry will very likely lead not only to the rejection or modification of monolingually based theories—such as the Critical Period Hypothesis; mother-tongue (L1) interference in language acquistion and interlanguage, as currently formulated in SLA—but also to the transformation of theories of SLA into ones of multilingual language acquisition in the

same manner that autosegmental phonology revolutionalized, in the 1970s, the classical linear phonology of Chomsky and Halle (1968). Fifth and finally, on the basis of the overview given here of multilingualism in Africa, the chapter has suggested that research on the phenomenon offers immense potential across linguistic fields, with equally enormous benefits, in that new insights, which are currently precluded given the dominance of the monolingualism-to-bilingualism paradigm, will be uncovered and far advance linguistic explanations and theorizing in all major subfields of linguistics.

## References

Albaugh, Ericka A. 2012. "Language Policies in African States." www.bowdoin.edu/faculty/e/ealbaugh /pdf/language-policies-in-african-states-albaugh.pdf.

Alexandre, Pierre. 1967. *Langues et langages en Afrique noire*. Paris: Payot.

Amritavalli, R., and K. A. Jayaseelan. 2007. "India." In *Language and National Identity*, ed. Andrew Simpson. Oxford: Oxford University Press.

Anchimbe, Eric A. 2013. *Language Policy and Identity Construction: The Dynamics of Cameroon's Multilingualism*. Philadelphia: John Benjamins.

Aronin, Larissa, and Britta Hufeisen, eds. 2009. *The Exploration of Multilingualism: Development of Research on L3, Multilingualism, and Multiple Language Acquisition*. Philadelphia: John Benjamins Publishing.

Aronin, Larissa, and David Singleton. 2012. *Multilingualism*. Philadelphia: John Benjamins.

Auer, Peter, and Li Wei, eds. 2007. *Handbook of Multilingualism and Multilingual Communication*. Berlin: Mouton de Gruyter.

Baker, Colin, and Sylvia Prys Jones, eds. 1998. *Encyclopedia of Bilingualism and Bilingual Education*. Clevedon, UK: Multilingual Matters.

Baldauf, Richard B., and Robert B. Kaplan, eds. 2004. *Language Planning and Policy in Africa. Vol. 1, Botswana, Malawi, Mozambique, and South Africa*. Clevedon, UK: Multilingual Matters.

Bamgbose, Ayo. 1991. *Language and the Nation: The Language Question in Sub-Saharan Africa*. Edinburgh: Edinburgh University Press.

———. 1992. "Standard Nigerian English: Issues of Identification." In *The Other Tongue: English across Cultures*, ed. Braj B. Kachru. Urbana-Champaign: University of Illinois Press.

———. 2000. *Language and Exclusion: The Consequences of Language Policies in Africa*. Hamburg: LIT.

Bamgbose, Ayo, Ayo Banjo, and Andrew Thomas, eds. 1995. *New Englishes: A West African Perspective*. Ibadan: Masuro.

Bamiro, Edmund O. 1994. "Lexico-Sematic Variation in Nigerian English." *World Englishes* 13, no. 1: 47–60.

———. 1995. "Syntactic Variation in West African English." *World Englishes* 14, no. 2: 189–204.

Bassiouney, Reem. 2009. *Arabic Linguistics*. Edinburgh: Edinburgh University Press.

Berry, Jack. 1971. "The Madina Project, Ghana." In *Language Use and Social Change: Problems of Multilingualism, with Special Reference to Eastern Africa*, ed. Wilford H. Whitely. Oxford: Oxford University Press.

Bhatia, Tek K., and William C. Ritchie, eds. 2004. *Handbook of Bilingualism*. Oxford: Blackwell.

Blackledge, Adrian, and Angela Creese. 2010. *Multilingualism: A Critical Perspective*. New York: Continuum.

Bokamba, Eyamba G. 1976. "Authenticity and the Choice of a National Language: The Case of Zaire." *Présence Africaine* 99–100:104–43.

———. 1984a. "French Colonial Language Policy and Its Legacies." *Studies in the Linguistic Sciences* 14, no. 2: 1–36. Reprinted in *Language Planning: Focusschrift in Honor of Joshua A. Fishman on the Occasion of His 65th Birthday*, ed. David F. Marshall. Philadelphia: John Benjamins, 1991.

———. 1984b. "Language and Literacy in West Africa." In *Annual Review of Applied Linguistics, 1983*, ed. Robert B. Kaplan. Rowley MA: Newbury House.

————. 1987. "Are There Syntactic Constraints on Code-Switching?" In *Variation in Language: NWAV-15 at Stanford*, ed. Keith M. Denning, Sharon Inkelas, Faye C. McNair-Knox, and John R. Rickford. Stanford CA: Department of Linguistics, Stanford University.

————. 1991. "[English in] West Africa." In *English Around the World: Sociolinguistic Perspectives*, ed. Jenny Cheshire. Cambridge: Cambridge University Press.

————. 1992. "The Africanization of English." In *The Other Tongue: English across Cultures*, ed. Braj B. Kachru. Urbana-Champaign: University of Illinois Press.

————. 2007. "Arguments for Multilingual Policies in Public Domains in Africa." In *Linguistic Identity in Postcolonial Multilingual Spaces*, ed. Eric A. Anchimbe. Newcastle, UK: Cambridge Scholars.

————. 2008a. "DR Congo: Language and 'Authentic Nationalism.'" In *Language and National Identity in Africa*, ed. Andrew Simpson. Oxford: Oxford University Press.

————. 2008b. "The Lives of Local and Regional Congolese Languages in Globalized Linguistic Markets." In *Globalization and Language Vitality: Perspectives from Africa*, ed. Cécile B. Vigouroux and Salikoko S. Mufwene. London: Continuum.

Bourdieu, Pierre. 1991. *Language and Symbolic Power.* Cambridge MA: Harvard University Press.

Brenzinger, Matthias, ed. 1998. *Endangered Languages in Africa*. Cologne: Rüdiger Köper.

————. 2008. "Language Endangerment in Southern and Eastern Africa." In *Language Diversity Endangered: Mouton Reader*, ed. Matthias Brenzinger. The Hague: Walter de Gruyter.

Broeder, Peter, Guus Extra, and Jeanne Maartens, eds. 1998. *Multilingualism in South Africa, with a Focus on KwaZulu-Natal and Metropolitan Durban*. PRAESA Occasional Paper 7. Cape Town: Project for the Study of Alternative Education in South Africa.

Brosnahan, Leger F. 1963. "Some Historical Cases of Language Imposition." In *Language in Africa*, ed. John Spencer. Cambridge: Cambridge University Press.

Calvet, Jean-Louis, ed. 1992. *Les langues des marchés en Afrique*. Montmagny, France: Marquis.

Cenoz, Jasone, Britta Hufeisen, and Ulrike Jessner. 2001. *Cross-Linguistic Influence in Third Language Acquisition: Psycholinguistic Perspective*. Clevedon, UK: Multilingual Matters.

————, eds. 2008. *Looking beyond Second Language Acquisition: Studies in Tri- and Multilingualism*. Tübingen: Stoeuffenberg.

Chomsky, Noam. 1965. *Aspects of the Theory of Syntax*. Cambridge MA: MIT Press.

————. 1986. *Knowledge of Language: Its Nature, Origin, and Use*. New York: Praeger.

Chomsky, Noam, and Morris Halle. 1968. *The Sound Pattern of English*. Cambridge MA: MIT Press.

Clyne, Michael. 1997. *Multilingualism*. In *The Handbook of Sociolinguistics*, ed. Florian Coulmas. Oxford: Blackwell.

Cook, Vivian. 2009. "Evidence for Multi-Competence." http://homepage.ntlworld.com/vivian.c/Writings/Papers/MCentry.htm.

Coulmas, Florian, ed. 1997. *The Handbook of Sociolinguistics*. Oxford: Blackwell.

Coupland, Nikolas, and Adam Jaworski, eds. 1997. *Sociolinguistics: A Reader and Coursebook*. Houndmills, UK: Palgrave.

Crystal, David. 1991. *The Cambridge Encyclopedia of Language*. Cambridge: Cambridge University Press.

————. 1997. *English as a Global Language*. Cambridge: Cambridge University Press.

Edwards, John. 1994. *Multilingualism*. London: Routledge.

*Ethnologue.* 2009. "Web Version: Statistical Summaries." Available at www.ethnologue.com.

Fabbro, Franco. 1999. *The Neurolinguistics of Bilingualism: An Introduction*. New York: Psychology Press.

Fasold, Ralph W. 1990. *The Sociolinguistics of Language*. Oxford: Blackwell.

Fishman, Joshua A. 1965. "Who Speaks What Language to Whom and When." *La Linguistics* 2:67–88. Reprinted in *The Bilingualism Reader*, ed. Li Wei. New York: Routledge, 2001.

————. 1991. *Reversing Language Shift*. Clevedon, UK: Multilingual Matters.

Franceschini, Rita. 2009. "The Genesis and Development of Research in Multilingualism: Perspectives for Future Research." In *The Exploration of Multilingualism: Development of Research on L3, Multilingualism, and Multiple Language Acquisition*, ed. Larissa Aronin and Britta Hufeisen. Philadelphia: John Benjamins.

Gass, Susan M., and Larry Selinker. 1992. *Language Transfer in Language Learning*, rev. ed. Philadelphia: John Benjamins.

Grosjean, François. 1982. *Life with Two Languages*. Cambridge MA: Harvard University Press.

———. 1989. "Neurolinguists, Beware! The Bilingual Is Not Two Monolinguals in One Person." *Brain and Language* 36:3–15.

———. 2001. "The Bilingual's Language Modes." In *One Mind, Two Languages: Bilingual Language Processing*, ed. Janet Nicol. Oxford: Blackwell.

———. 2010. *Bilingual: Life and Reality*. Cambridge MA: Harvard University Press.

Gumperz, John J. 1997. "Communicative Competence." In *Sociolinguistics: A Reader and Coursebook*, ed. Nikolas Coupland and Adam Jaworski. Houndmills, UK: Palgrave.

Heine, Bernd. 1970. *The Status and Use of African Lingua Francas*. Munich: Weltforum Verlag.

Herbert, Robert K., ed. 1992. *Language and Society in Africa: Theory and Practice of Sociolinguistics*. Johannesburg: Wits University Press.

Hewstone, Miles, and Howard Giles. 1997. "Social Groups and Social Stereotypes." In *Sociolinguistics: A Reader and Coursebook*, ed. Nikolas Coupland and Adam Jaworski. Houndmills, UK: Palgrave.

Hudson, Richard A. 1996. *Sociolinguistics*, 2nd ed. Cambridge: Cambridge University Press.

Kaplan, Robert B., and Baldauf, Richard B., eds. 2007. *Language Planning and Policy in Africa*. Vol. 2. *Algeria, Côte d'Ivoire, Nigeria, and Tunisia*. Clevedon, UK: Multilingual Matters.

Karra, Maria. 2007. "The Linguistic Conflict in Belgium." www.proz.com/translation-articles/articles /1250/1/.

Kemp, Charlotte. 2009. "Defining Multilingualism." In *The Exploration of Multilingualism: Development of Research on L3, Multilingualism, and Multiple Language Acquisition*, ed. Larissa Aronin and Britta Hufeisen. Philadelphia: John Benjamins.

Koffi, Ettien. 2012. *Paradigm Shift in Language Planning and Policy: Game-Theoretic Solutions*. Amsterdam: Mouton de Gruyter.

Laitin, David D. 1992. *Language Repertoires and State Construction in Africa: Cambridge Studies in Comparative Politics*. Cambridge: Cambridge University Press.

———. 2001. "Multilingual States." In *Concise Encyclopedia of Sociolinguistics*, ed. Rajend Mesthrie. Amsterdam: Elsevier.

Lenneberg, Eric H. 1967. *Biological Foundations of Language*. New York: Wiley.

Lewis, M. Paul, ed. 2009. *Ethnologue: Languages of the World*, 16th ed. Dallas: SIL International. www.ethnologue.com/16.

Li Wei, ed. 2001a. *The Bilingualism Reader*. New York: Routledge.

———. 2001b. "Dimensions of Bilingualism." In *The Bilingualism Reader*, ed. Li Wei. New York: Routledge.

Martel, Marcel, and Martin Pâquet. 2012. *Speaking Up: A History of Language and Politics in Canada and Quebec*. Montreal: Between the Lines.

Mazrui, Ali, and Alamin M. Mazrui. 1998. *The Power of Babel: Language and Governance in the African Experience*. Chicago: University of Chicago Press.

McArthur, Tom, ed. 1992. *The Oxford Companion to the English Language*. Oxford: Oxford University Press.

McLaughlin, Fiona. 2008. "The Accent of Wolof as an Urban Vernacular and National Lingua Franca in Senegal." In *Globalization and Language Vitality: Perspectives from Africa*, ed. Cécile B. Vigouroux and Salikoko S. Mufwene. London: Continuum.

———, ed. 2009. *The Languages of Urban Africa*. London: Continuum.

Mesthrie, Rajend, Joan Swann, Ana Deumert, and William L. Leap. 2000. *Introducing Sociolinguistics*. Philadelphia: John Benjamins.

Moha, Ennaji. 2005. *Multilingualism, Cultural Identity, and Education in Morocco*. New York: Springer.

Mufwene, Salikoko S., and Cécile B. Vigouroux. 2008. "Colonization: Globalization and Language Vitality in Africa—an Introduction." In In *Globalization and Language Vitality: Perspectives from Africa*, ed. Cécile B. Vigouroux and Salikoko S. Mufwene. London: Continuum.

Myers-Scotton, Carol. 1993a. *The Duelling Languages: Grammatical Structure in Code-Switching*. Oxford: Clarendon Press.

———. 1993b. "Elite Closure as a Powerful Language Strategy: The African Case." *International Journal of the Sociology of Language* 103:149–63.

———. 1993c. *Social Motivations for Code-Switching: Evidence from Africa*. Oxford: Oxford University Press.

Nettle, Daniel, and Suzanne Romaine. 2000. *Vanishing Voices: The Extinction of the World's Languages.* Oxford: Oxford University Press.

Pawlak, Miroslaw, and Larissa Aronin, eds. 2013. *Essential Topics in Applied Linguistics and Multilingualism: Studies in Honor of David Singleton.* Heidelberg: Springer International.

Pütz, Martin, ed. 1995. *Discrimination through Language in Africa? Perspectives on the Namibian Experience.* Amsterdam: Mouton de Gruyter.

Richards, Jack, John Platt, and Heidi Weber. 1985. *Longman Dictionary of Applied Linguistics.* London: Longman.

Schmied, Josef. 1991. *English in Africa: An Introduction.* London: Longman.

———. 1997. "Beyond Recipes, beyond Maks, beyond Africa: Texts, Text-Types, Text Collections, and African Realities." In *Englishes around the World 2: Caribbean, Africa, Asia, Australasia—Studies in Honor of Manfred Görlach*, ed. Edgar W. Schneider. Philadelphia: John Benjamins.

———. 2006. "East African Englishes." In *The Handbook of World Englishes*, ed. Braj B. Kachru, Yamuna Kachru, and Cecil L. Nelson. London: Blackwell.

Schneider, Edgar W., ed. 1997. *Englishes around the World 2: Caribbean, Africa, Asia, Australasia—Studies in Honor of Manfred Görlach.* Philadelphia: John Benjamins.

Scotton, Carol. 1975. "Multilingualism in Lagos: What It Means to the Social Scientist." In *Patterns in Language, Culture, and Society: Sub-Saharan Africa*, ed. Robert K. Herbert. Columbus: Department of Linguistics, Ohio State University.

Selinker, Larry. 1992. *Rediscovering Interlanguage.* Applied Linguistics and Language Study. London: Longman.

Sey, K. A. 1973. *Ghanaian English: An Exploratory Survey.* London: Macmillan.

Simpson, Andrew, ed. 2007. *Language and National Identity in Africa.* Oxford: Oxford University Press.

———. 2008. *Language and National Identity in Asia.* Oxford: Oxford University Press.

Singler, John Victor. 1991. "Social and Linguistic Constraints on Plural Marking in Liberian English." In *English around the World: Sociolinguistic Perspectives*, ed. Jenny Cheshire. Cambridge: Cambridge University Press.

———. 1997. "The Configuration of Liberia's Englishes." *World Englishes* 16, no. 2: 205–31.

Vigouroux, Cécile B., and Salikoko S. Mufwene, eds. 2008. *Globalization and Language Vitality: Perspectives from Black Africa.* London: Continuum.

Vogl, Ulrike, and Matthias Hüning. 2010. "One Nation, One Language? The Case of Belgium." *Dutch Crossing* 34, no. 3: 228–47.

Wardhaugh, Ronald. 2006. *An Introduction to Sociolinguistics*, 5th ed. Malden MA: Wiley-Blackwell.

Webb, Vic. 2002. *Language in South Africa: The Role of Language in National Transformation, Reconstruction, and Development.* Philadelphia: John Benjamins.

Weber, H. 2007. "Review [of] *Handbook of Multilingualism and Multilingual Communication.*" In *The Linguist List.* http://linguistlist.org/issues/18/18-3681.html.

Weinreich, Uriel. 1953. *Languages in Contact: Findings and Problems.* New York: Linguistic Circle of New York.

Wikimedia Foundation. 2014. *Wikipedia: The Free Encyclopedia.* http://wikimediafoundation.org/wiki/home.

Winford, Donald. 2003. *An Introduction to Contact Linguistics.* Oxford: Blackwell.

Wolff, H. Ekkehard. 2001. "Language and Society." In *African Languages: An Introduction*, ed. Bernd Heine and Derek Nurse. Cambridge: Cambridge University Press.

# 3

## Classroom Discourse in Bilingual and Multilingual Kenyan Primary Schools

LYDIAH KANANU KIRAMBA
*University of Illinois at Urbana-Champaign*

LANGUAGE PLAYS A MAJOR ROLE in education. It is a means of communication in the classroom and serves as an expression of identity and power. A need to connect the populations within different countries and around the globe has led to language policies being put in place in order to guide language practices in individual nation-states. These policies outline the use of languages and specify the national and official languages that the nation will adopt for education and general communication (Corson 1990). The central purpose of this chapter is to provide a critical review of studies of classroom discourse in Kenyan rural primary schools. Classroom-based research studies define classroom discourse as the oral interaction that takes place in a classroom context between teachers and their students and among students themselves. According to Cazden (2001), classroom discourse is the situated language use in a classroom setting, including the patterns of language use—who speaks, who receives thoughtful responses, and the verbal exchange or conversation in the classroom. In this sense, therefore, this chapter investigates how students and teachers make meaning of the literacy events in the classroom using a foreign language (FL), and how the literacy practices reflect students' acquisition of English in a multilingual and multicultural country, Kenya. The chapter begins by discussing the broader context of language in education practices in Africa and then narrows down to Kenyan primary schools.

### The African Context

Most African countries are multilingual. Despite the documented advantages accrued from well-implemented bilingual education, many postcolonial African countries have continued the use of FLs as languages of instruction (LOIs) from elementary school onward. Giving some reasons for the insistence on the use of FLs by the policymakers of African states, Qorro (2009) has pointed out that using English as an LOI requires an acceptable level of competence in English, and when teachers who are not sufficiently proficient in English are required to teach in English, the results are damaging to the subject and English-language learners.

Use of FLs as LOIs impedes learning for most schoolchildren. Students develop a feeling of inadequacy, and they resort to the memorization of phrases to pass their examinations. Alidou (2003) discusses the use of French as an LOI in Niger, arguing that children attending formal education in Niger in particular, and other francophone countries generally, experience exclusion in the classroom. Due to the lack of proficiency in French, they are silenced and spend most of their time listening to the teacher, memorizing lessons for the tests instead of trying to understand the relevance or the meaning of what they read. Alidou notes that most of the non-French-speaking students experience academic failure, owing in part to the lack of proficiency in the LOI and in part to the inappropriate language-teaching methods.

Although African children experience intellectual insecurity due to the use of an FL as a school language, there is substantial evidence that use of the first language (L1) in schools promotes learning. Studies by Brock-Utne (2007b) examined the effects of having a language unfamiliar to students as an LOI in Tanzania and Cape Town. The studies show that learners were struggling to write in English, and the stories the students wrote were largely incomprehensible, with several grammatical and spelling errors. The stories written in IsiXhosa and Kiswahili showed the opposite pattern. The learners were able to express what was happening in the pictures fairly accurately, and they wrote complex sentences. Brock-Utne concluded that the use of an LOI that is unfamiliar to most students is a recipe for increased inequality.

English and other colonial languages are rarely accessible to children in rural areas. Students access the colonial language only at school. Michieka's (2009) study explored the presence and accessibility of English in rural Kisii, Kenya, through a survey to 111 youths. The findings show that there was a limited presence of English in that rural context and that rural Kisii considered English to be a foreign language. These findings may also be true for most other African multilingual states.

## The Kenyan Context
Kenya is a multilingual state, with sixty-nine living languages (Lewis, Simons, and Fennig 2013). Of these, forty-two are indigenous languages. The current Kenyan language policy declares English the official language and Kiswahili the second official and national language. The other Kenyan languages are used mainly to perform interpersonal communication functions in the home and neighborhood. English is the LOI from fourth grade onward. From the policy, it is stipulated that "Transitional Bilingual Education Early Exit" (TBE Early Exit) is the education program by default.

## Bilingual Education
The available data show that in the classroom, both teachers and learners are more actively engaged in classroom interaction and that learners potentially learn more when lessons are taught through indigenous languages (Brock-Utne 2007a, 2007b; Jones 2008; Ogechi 2009). The use of English in Kenyan elementary and primary schools in general creates a dissonance between students' second language (L2) proficiency and the expected cognitive language practices.

Bilingual schooling has great potential to improve the quality of basic education in developing countries. Researchers worldwide (Baker 2006; Cummins 1978, 1979, 2000) have demonstrated that bilingual teaching offers clear pedagogical advantages over traditional programs. As mentioned above, content area instruction in the L1 can be understood, so that learning does not have to be postponed until children learn the L2. Further, initial literacy in the L1 means that children can make the connection between spoken and written communication, developing skills upon which they can build once they learn the L2, which is taught explicitly. Teachers and students can interact more naturally in the L1 and negotiate meanings together, which greatly facilitates participatory teaching and learning. It is unfortunate that native-language instruction is not validated in Kenyan schools beyond grade 3, yet most students use English only in school and native languages for all forms of communication out of school. It is therefore doubtful whether the TBE Early Exit program in Kenya helps students to reap the cognitive benefits of bilingualism.

L1 instruction is very important in education. According to Cummins's (2000) developmental interdependence hypothesis, a child's language competence in L2 is partly dependent on the level of competence already achieved in the first language. The more developed the first language, the easier it will be to develop the second language. When the first language is at an early stage of development, it is more difficult to achieve bilingualism. These assertions support first language instruction until it is fully developed.

L1 instruction in Kenya is designed to prepare students for academic language use. Although students may accrue some benefits of bilingualism, the limited use of English (in school only) means that students do not receive the full benefit. Additionally, the research studies cited above have shown that there are unwritten policies in most schools where English is used starting in kindergarten. It can be argued that by third grade, students only acquire social (not academic) language.

Cummins (1979) differentiates between social and academic language acquisition. According to him, basic interpersonal communication skills (BICS) are language skills needed in social interactions. With respect to Kenyan language-in-education policy practices, this means that English learners may employ BICS mainly to satisfy the English-only rule, because speaking other languages at school is punishable. And because social interactions between students usually occur in specific contexts and are not so demanding cognitively, the language proficiency required is not specialized. In contrast to this level of proficiency, Cummins (1981) proposes a separate consideration of cognitive academic language proficiency. He views this as the language for formal academic learning, which includes the four key skills of listening, speaking, reading, and writing about subject area content materials, as well as inferring, evaluating, and other demanding cognitive activities. This level of proficiency is essential for students to succeed in school.

Cummins (1979) found that everyday conversational language, or BICS, could be acquired in two years, whereas the more complex language abilities needed to cope with the full curriculum could take five to seven years or more to develop. He further posits that being exposed to more than one language during childhood can ease the transition from speaking and using the home language to acquiring a second language, usually English for school. And he argues that a child's language ability can easily be overestimated by looking at the BICS and not realizing the complexity and difficulty that second-language students have in acquiring cognitive academic language proficiency in the second language.

If L1 instruction is not provided, especially in the English-only schools in Kenya, what does it mean for student learning? According to Threshold Theory, which was first put forward by Skutnabb-Kangas and Toukamaa in 1976, a child has to reach a certain threshold (their "second" threshold) in order to experience possible positive benefits of bilingualism. This implies that not offering L1 instruction may lead to the children experiencing detrimental consequences from their bilingualism, especially where the child's language is insufficiently or inadequately developed. In the TBE Early Exit program in Kenya, most children begin school knowing no English at all. If their first language is not taught in the initial grades to reach the necessary second threshold level, then that bilingualism results in worse educational outcomes. It is doubtful whether within the three years of L1 instruction students are able to reach the second threshold level and reap the benefits of bilingualism, as well as receive comprehensible input in L2 for all instruction.

Skutnabb-Kangas (1981, 2000) has indicated the stresses of learning through undeveloped language. Skutnabb-Kangas notes that listening to a new language demands a high level of concentration. It is tiring, given the constant pressure to think about the form of language and less time to think about the curriculum content. This leads to a lack of self-confidence. Some students may drop out. The situation is quite challenging in the Kenyan context. How, then, do teachers ensure comprehensible input while at the same time making meaning of the literacy practices? How do literacy practices reflect students' acquisition of English?

## Goals of the Present Study

Kenyan education policy privileges the use of English as an LOI from the fourth grade onward. It assumed that by the fourth grade the student would have mastered enough English to understand content areas. The research on bilingual education cited above, however, casts serious doubts on this perspective. This chapter examines the apparent dissonance between Kenyan primary school students' L2 proficiency and their expected cognitive language practices. It is argued that the practice of TBE Early Exit in Kenya raises important issues about the acquisition of classroom literacy, including the obstruction, rather than the facilitation, of literacy practices of bilingual/multilingual classrooms in the country and the pedagogical strategies applied by teachers to ensure comprehensible input. Specifically, the chapter addresses the following questions:

1. How do students and the teachers make meaning of the literacy events in the classroom?
2. How do the literacy practices reflect students' acquisition of English?

## TBE Early Exit Realities in Kenya

The implementation of the TBE Early Exit program in Kenya has been inconsistent. Muthwii (2004) investigated the extent to which language policy and existing practices with regard to the LOI encourage or hamper the acquisition of desirable learning competencies. Muthwii notes that there is inconsistency between the policy of encouraging the mother tongue (MT) as an LOI and the reality. English dominates all other languages as a child progresses in school. MTs are essentially relegated to a less important role after lower school and are excluded from the national examinations that mark the end of primary education. Children are faced with the fact that their home language has no further use in education after the fourth grade. Similar findings have been reported by Ogechi (2009), who posits that the language practice in Kenyan primary schools does not reflect the policy. Ogechi (2003, 2009) found that there were schools that used only English from grade 1, and first languages were treated as a problem that needed to be eradicated for academic excellence in English. Ogechi concluded that the LOI in Kenyan schools remains a challenge for education even in the twenty-first century.

Jones (2008) investigated the place of the MT as a subject and as an LOI in the implementation of the Kenyan language-in-education policy. Jones reported that though the policy stipulates that MT should be taught as a subject on a daily basis in grades 1, 2, and 3, in Sumaneet School, Sabaot, it was taught as a subject only in grades 1 and 2. The teachers' aim was to transition pupils as quickly and as early as possible, first to Kiswahili and then to English. Jones (2008) advises that all education stakeholders need to be made aware of the importance of the MT, both at home and in school, to have their language flourish and their children succeed. Given the practical implementation of TBE Early Exit, how do teachers and students make meaning of literacy events in English?

## Meaning-Making Literacy Practices and English Acquisition

Brock-Utne (2001) has pointed out that studying a third language is a major barrier to children's learning. Many education specialists have lamented that the African child's major learning problem is linguistic, whereby teaching instruction is given in an unfamiliar language to students and even, to some extent, teachers. Some of the experiences of using an FL in instruction in Kenya have been documented through several research studies.

Ackers and Hardman (2001) studied classroom interactions in Kenyan primary schools by observing ninety lessons. In all the ninety lessons observed in mathematics, English, and science, they found that teacher recitation in the form of interrogation of the learners' knowledge and understanding was the most common form of teacher–learner interaction. Student-generated questions were very rare. Teacher presentation and teacher-directed questions and answers dominated most of the classroom discourse, accounting for 82 percent of total teaching exchanges. The discourse pattern reported in that study can in large part be attributed to the LOI. Students at the primary school level have not mastered English well enough to engage in academic discourse.

Ogechi (2009) investigated the use of English and other African languages in Kenyan primary schools to ascertain whether English as an LOI was practical and appropriate in grade 4 in three primary schools in three Kenyan provinces (Rift Valley,

Nyanza, and Western Provinces), in urban, peri-urban, and rural schools. The data were gathered for grade 4 mathematics and science lessons. Ogechi (2009) found that teachers did most of the talking, with learners making only minimal oral contributions; the learners mostly either gave brief responses or remained silent, and the few learners who did respond actively did so in ungrammatical English. He reports that learners in the peri-urban and rural schools appeared enthusiastic to answer questions when teachers translated or rephrased their questions in Kiswahili, that urban primary school learners also were not fully comfortable with English-only at the start of grade 4, and that teachers, especially those in rural and peri-urban schools, had difficulties using grammatical English. Teachers appeared to use code-switching between English and Kiswahili as an effective strategy across the three categories of schools. This study demonstrates the learning and pedagogical challenges that those teachers and students must experience in lessons taught in English. Learning in the area's catchment language would allow the students to develop a second threshold level in English, which would in turn aid in English acquisition.

Further, Ogechi (2009) assessed grade 4 essays and found that in English, pupils hardly wrote ten lines. In Kiswahili, pupils wrote a full-page essay expressing their ideas and there were few grammatical mistakes. Ogechi (2009) concluded that the use of English at the start of grade 4 is an infringement of both linguistic rights and the human right to education. Learners are not ready to use English, and some teachers are poor role models of both spoken and written English. Ogechi has pointed out that current English-language use in primary schools seems to be hindering students' participation and creative reasoning.

The classroom discourse in Kenyan primary schools further illustrates that there is very little meaning that students make of literacy events presented in English. The following excerpt from Ogechi (2009, 153) illustrates the difficulties pupils encounter in learning through English in a fourth grade classroom:

Teacher: How many knows a fruit?
   *No pupil raises a hand to respond*

Teacher: *Ninasema, ni wangapi wanajua matunda?* (I am saying, how many of you know what a fruit is?)
   *Entire class raises their hands*

Teacher: What does a root do?
   *Only one out of 54 learners raised a hand*

Teacher: *Mizizi inasaidia nini?* (What do roots do?)
   *More than half the class raised their hands*

Learner: *Inasaidia isianguke.* (It assists [the plants] not to fall).

This is a clear indication that students by the fourth grade do not know English well enough to allow classroom activities to take place only in English. Developing materials in students' languages and using these languages at school would not only produce better results in learning the content materials but would also enhance English-language acquisition.

Pontefract and Hardman (2005) studied the discourse styles of twenty-seven teachers—eighteen women and nine men—as they taught English (ten lessons in total), mathematics (nine lessons in total), and science (eight lessons in total) across grades 1 through 7 (students of ages five to thirteen years, approximately) in nine schools, five urban and four rural. The schools were selected to be as representative as possible geographically, economically, linguistically, and culturally. The lessons were audio-recorded, transcribed, and coded. Data were gathered on types of teacher explanations and questions, pupil responses, and the types of feedback given by the teacher. The findings revealed the dominance of teacher-led recitation, in which rote repetition dominated classroom discourse, which was made up of teacher explanation and question-and-answer sequences, with little attention being paid to securing pupil understanding. Choral responses to questions were common. Although direct repetition was observed in all three subjects, it was most prevalent in English lessons. Pontefract and Hardman (2005) explain that direct repetition constituted 66 percent of the teacher's input, that 99 percent of all teachers' questions across all three subjects were closed ended, and that 70 percent of those questions were factually narrow, requiring recall and the response of a single word. The analysis of the transcripts revealed that the classroom discourse was dominated by the initiation, response, and feedback structure made up of teacher explanations and question-and-answer sequences. Pontefract and Hardman further report that reasoning questions were extremely rare, such that in each subject fewer than 1 percent of the teacher questions could be classified as being open. Direct yes or no questions were asked, which elicited an affirmative response.

Such an emphasis on directive forms of teaching in Kenyan primary classrooms goes against the widely accepted socio-constructivist theory of learning (Vygotsky 1978). Research into the socio-constructivist function of dialogue and learning advocates for active participation of pupils for effective classroom discourse. Conversely, teachers may have adapted directive forms of teaching owing to the inability of students to use school language in the content classroom. These students may not have developed cognitive academic language proficiency to be able to engage with the academic content.

As the findings of Pontefract and Hardman (2005) show, pupils are mainly expected to be passive—to recall, when asked, what they have learned and to report other people's thinking. This passivity can be blamed on the English-only policy. The teacher adopts the strategy as a way of teaching students with low proficiency. Cazden (2001) discourages the initiation response evaluation strategy because teachers may be asking questions to which they already know the answers. The teacher may be simply testing the students' knowledge, or he or she may be inviting the students to participate in what could otherwise be a lecture. In this way the teacher is only transforming a monologue into a dialogue by eliciting short items of information at self-chosen points.

## Discussion

From the referenced research studies on Kenya and other multilingual countries, there is substantial evidence that students learn better in their first languages. The use of their familiar languages encourages critical thinking among students. The findings reported by Brock-Utne (2007a, 2007b), Ogechi (2009), and Muthwii (2004) show that using English as the LOI increases differences among students. It is unfortunate that recitation is the pedagogical style that is prevalent in most schools (Pontefract and Hardman 2005; Ogechi 2009). It seems the students are treated as passive learners and their participation is limited to choral responses and recall questions. Students do not have a chance to co-construct meaning in the classroom. Although this may be blamed on pedagogical styles, the styles may be informed by the language proficiency of the students, the teacher, and school language policy. The students have not acquired the cognitive academic language proficiency that is necessary for synthesizing, inferring, classifying, and other demanding cognitive activities. The literacy practices in the classroom, such as the repetition of words and choral affirmation of understanding, are cognitively undemanding and students are not engaging at a conceptual level. In the higher grades (e.g., grade 5 classrooms), it can be argued that there was a delay in acquiring English, that may have been due to an undeveloped L1. The students may not have reached the second threshold in the L1 that is necessary to facilitate acquisition of the L2.

In the examples presented, the teachers control knowledge production in the classroom. This reflects the hierarchical nature of the education system in Kenyan primary schools, which seems to render the children as passive recipients of educational knowledge. Halliday (1973) points out that educational failure is often a language failure. The child who does not succeed in the school system is undoubtedly the one who is not using language in the ways required by schools. An educationally relevant approach to language should take into account the child's own linguistic experience. From the literature reviewed, the compelling conclusion is that Kenyan children fail in school mainly due to language failure.

A common limitation in the cited studies is that they have not addressed the reasons for the prevalence of the recitation method of teaching in the classroom. An ethnographic study is necessary to investigate whether the teaching styles are informed by the training received by primary teachers or if they are coping strategies to observe language policy. Additionally, a research study into code-switching and its roles in multilingual classrooms is important to find out whether it is a strategy of communication or a way to ensure a comprehensible input.

## Conclusion and Implications

The use of English as an LOI has effects not only on the acquisition of the L2 but also on the teaching strategies that teachers employ in the classroom. Teachers have resorted to rote learning, and students are mostly passive and listeners. Students are less engaged in the meaning-making processes. This may be the result of unfamiliar LOIs, teachers' training, teachers' adaptation to deal with school policies that prohibit the use of the L1 in the classroom, or a combination of all these factors. It can be deduced from the research cited here that TBE Early Exit is not effective for Kenyan communities, considering that English is a foreign language for the majority of students. Additionally, the unwritten individual school policies worsen the situation by using English as the LOI starting in kindergarten.

In this chapter the first overall question addressed was how students and teachers make meaning of the literacy events in the classroom. It can be deduced that little meaning is made from the literacy events where the FL is solely used. This is well demonstrated by reports of choral responses and repetitions after the teacher. The students do not engage with the literacy to co-construct knowledge with the teacher, and this may be blamed on poor school language proficiency. And the second question was how literacy practices reflect English language acquisition. It can be argued that classroom interactions show that the students' level of acquisition of English is very low. For example, for Ogechi (2009), students remain silent after a question, but when the teacher translates it into Swahili, the whole class is excitedly ready to respond. Students' silence can be associated with their inadequate English-language skills. Kenya needs to consider its language-in-education policy and adopt proven research supporting bilingual education with a late exit, rather than an early exit, so as to enable Kenyan children to reap the cognitive benefits of bilingualism.

## References

Ackers, Jim, and Frank Hardman. 2001. "Classroom Interaction in Kenyan Primary Schools." *Compare* 31:245–61.

Alidou, Hassana. 2003. "Language Policies and Language Education in Francophone Africa: A Critique and a Call for Action." In *Black Linguistics: Language, Society, and Politics in Africa and the Americas*, edited by Sinfree Makoni. London: Routledge.

Baker, Colin. 2006. *Foundations of Bilingual Education and Bilingualism*. Bristol: Multilingual Matters.

Brock-Utne, Birgit. 2001. *Whose Education for All? Recolonization of the African Mind*. London: Garland.

———. 2007a. "Language of Instruction and Student Performance: New Insights from Research in Tanzania and South Africa." *International Review of Education* 53:5–6.

———. 2007b. "Learning through a Familiar Language versus Learning through a Foreign Language: A Look into Some Secondary School Classrooms in Tanzania." *International Journal of Educational Development* 27, no. 5: 487–98.

Cazden, Courtney B. 2001. *Classroom Discourse: The Language of Teaching and Learning*. Portsmouth NH: Heinemann.

Corson, David. 1990. *Language Policy across the Curriculum*. Clevedon, UK: Multilingual Matters.

Cummins, Jim. 1978. "Educational Implications of Mother Tongue Maintenance for Minority Language Groups." *Canadian Modern Language Review* 34:395–416.

———. 1979. *Linguistic Interdependence and the Educational Development of Bilingual Children*. Los Angeles: National Dissemination and Assessment Center, California State University.

———. 1981. *Bilingualism and Minority-Language Children*. Toronto: OISE Press.

———. 2000. *Language, Power, and Pedagogy: Bilingual Children in the Crossfire*. Clevedon, UK: Multilingual Matters.

Halliday, M. A. K. 1973. *Explorations in the Functions of Language*. London: Edward Arnold.

Jones, Jennifer M. 2008. "Teachers' Views and Practice: The Place of the Mother Tongue in the Implementation of the Kenyan Language-in-Education Policy." *New Zealand Studies in Applied Linguistics* 14, no. 2: 45–58.

Lewis, M. Paul, Gary F. Simons, and Charles D. Fennig, eds. 2013. *Ethnologue: Languages of the World*, 17th ed. Dallas: SIL International. Also available at www.ethnologue.com.

Michieka, Martha M. 2009. "A Second or Foreign Language? Unveiling the Realities of the Presence and Accessibility of English in Rural Kisii, Kenya." Paper presented at Annual Conference of African Linguists, University of Illinois, Urbana-Champaign, April.

Muthwii, Margaret Jepkirui. 2004. "Language of Instruction: A Qualitative Analysis of the Perceptions of Parents, Pupils, and Teachers among the Kalenjin in Kenya." *Language, Culture and Curriculum* 17, no. 1: 15–32.

Ogechi, Nathan Oyori. 2003. "On Language Rights in Kenya." *Nordic Journal of African Studies* 12, no. 3: 277–95.

———. 2009. "The Role of Foreign and Indigenous Languages in Primary Schools: The Case of Kenya." *Stellenbosch Papers in Linguistics PLUS* 38:143–58.

Pontefract, Caroline, and Frank Hardman. 2005. "The Discourse of Classroom Interaction in Kenyan Primary Schools." *Comparative Education* 41, no. 1: 87–106.

Qorro, Martha A. S. 2009. "Parents' and Policy Makers' Insistence on Foreign Languages as a Media of Education in Africa: Restricting Access to Quality Education—for Whose Benefit?" In *Language and Education in Africa: A Comparative and Transdisciplinary Analysis*, edited by Birgit Brock-Utne and Ingse Skattum. Oxford: Symposium Books.

Republic of Kenya. 1976. *Report of the National Committee on Educational Objectives and Policies.* Nairobi: Government Printer.

Skutnabb-Kangas, Tove. 1981. *Bilingualism or Not: The Education of Minorities.* Clevedon, UK: Multilingual Matters.

———. 2000. *Linguistic Genocide in Education—or Worldwide Diversity and Human Rights?* Mahwah NJ: Lawrence Erlbaum.

Skutnabb-Kangas, Tove, and Pertti Toukamaa. 1976. *Teaching Migrant Children's Mother Tongue and Learning the Language of the Host Country on the Context of the Socio-cultural Situation of the Migrant Family.* Tampere: Tampereen yliopiston sosiologian ja sosiaalipsykologian laitos.

Vygotsky, Lev. S. 1978. *Mind in Society: The Development of Higher Psychological Processes.* Cambridge MA: Harvard University Press.

# 4

# Investigating Teacher Effects in Mother-Tongue-Based Multilingual Education Programs

STEPHEN L. WALTER
*Graduate Institute of Applied Linguistics*

ALTHOUGH A LARGE CORPUS of research has accumulated documenting and investigating the existence of large teacher effects in education, especially in low-income countries (e.g., UNESCO 1998), there remains considerable uncertainty as to the specific nature of this effect. Much of the literature has focused on general issues, such as the training of pedagogues, compensation, certification, motivation and commitment, community support (or the lack thereof), and deployment. Fortunately, some researchers are beginning to explore the teacher effect issue in greater depth. For example, Mullens, Murnane, and Willett (1996) investigated teacher effectiveness in teaching mathematics concepts to grade 3 students in Belize. Teachers in Belize vary quite dramatically in terms of the level of education completed—from only primary to all the way through high school—and in knowledge of the subject matter (math). They found that having completed three years of pedagogical training to be a teacher had little impact on effectiveness, whereas tested mastery of "advanced" math concepts had a marked and statistically significant impact on student learning outcomes.

Shulman (1986, 1987) proposed that effective teaching depends not merely on a mastery of content but also on a domain-specific ability to teach that content— what he referred to as "pedagogical content knowledge." Ball, Thames, and Phelps (2008) proposed a number of refinements and extensions to Shulman's model using illustrations from the teaching of basic math concepts. These examples serve to emphasize the notion that teaching basic math requires not merely teaching or modeling standard procedures and algorithms but also recognizing and diagnosing systematic misapplication of these procedures by children and correcting them when necessary.

The introduction of multilingual education (MLE) instructional models adds further nuances to the issue of teacher effectiveness. For example, existing teacher-training institutions are typically committed to preparing teachers to teach in a second language, not in the mother tongue of the children. To date, research on MLE has given much more attention to model effects (e.g., does MLE improve learning outcomes?), in an effort to establish and defend the educational validity of the MLE model, than it has given to teacher effects (e.g., what is the effect of teacher experience?). As the research foundation of MLE grows and matures, the research agenda will inevitably expand to include more specific educational features of the MLE model. Attention to teacher effects is likely to be high on this agenda.

In this chapter teacher effects are explored in a preliminary way in two current MLE experiments—one in Cameroon, and one in the Philippines.[1] In both settings the primary introductory innovation was that of MLE, the use of the mother tongue as a language of instruction in early primary education. Also, in both cases, the analysis began with an investigation of model effects, but it quickly became apparent that these could not be adequately understood without also investigating teacher effects. Consider, for example, table 4.1, which sets forth program and school/teacher level results for year-end testing done in grade 3 in 2010 in the Cameroon example, which is known locally as the Kom Experimental Pilot Project (KEPP).

Although the model effect is quite evident when comparing schools across models, of more immediate interest is the observation that in both programs, the mean scores in schools also range quite dramatically *within* each program model. Because there was only one classroom or section in each school per grade, an initial hypothesis was made that the variation observed in table 4.1 was probably a teacher effect.[2] The size of this effect provoked curiosity from the onset of the research study and eventually led to an additional line of inquiry in the Cameroon research study described in the following sections.

Table 4.1

Comparative Performance of Schools (Actually, Individual Classrooms) in an MLE-versus-L2 Instructional Context in Cameroon

| Experimental Program (KEPP) | | Control Program (English-medium) | |
|---|---|---|---|
| School | Mean Score | School | Mean Score |
| GS Mboh | 58.55 | CS Kindoh | 33.88 |
| GS Ilung | 52.11 | GS Atondum | 30.46 |
| CBC Kikfuini | 50.96 | PS Ngwah | 30.13 |
| GS Muteff | 49.76 | GS Fundong Village | 29.11 |
| GS Laikom | 48.13 | GS Baichu | 23.08 |
| GS Ngwah Aloin | 41.11 | GS Meli | 20.19 |
| GS Ameng | 40.87 | CS Wombong Ikui | 18.70 |
| CBC Fujua | 39.36 | BS Fundeng | 16.58 |
| GS Kitchu | 38.69 | CBC Wainchia | 16.03 |
| GS Bolem | 31.59 | GS Mentang | 15.06 |
| CBC Belo | 30.97 | GS Yuwi | 8.47 |
| GS Wombong Ikui | 27.74 | GS Njinikejem | 7.28 |

## The Cameroon Study

KEPP was carried out in a rural part of Cameroon that is ethnically and linguistically homogenous (more than 96 percent of residents are members of the Kom people). There is also a teacher-training college in the area.[3] Most teachers in the area are graduates of this school, the Government Teacher Training College (GTTC) of Fundong, though some of the school's graduates do get posted to schools outside of the Kom area.

The director of the GTTC agreed to allow me to do some testing of the teacher trainees in this school to assess their knowledge and skill in English and mathematics. English is the default language of instruction in the schools of the region, and math is considered an important subject. Clearly, if there are deficiencies in English, they will affect instruction in all subjects, including English itself. Presumably, limitations in math will show up primarily in that subject, though there are also lesser implications for other subjects.

### Participants

One hundred and eighty-five students from the GTTC participated in the assessment, with 150 of these being only a couple of weeks away from graduating and beginning their work as teachers. The remaining 35 were at earlier points in their training to be teachers. Of the participants, 139 were female and 44 were male, with 2 missing data points. The average age was 24.15 years (23.9 for females and 24.9 for males).

### The Assessments

Two assessments were administered—one of English and English reading comprehension, and the other of mathematics. Both were designed to provide (1) a general assessment of knowledge and ability in English, and (2) some direct comparison with the knowledge and skills of students in the area's upper primary grades. The latter objective was accomplished by having points of overlap between the assessments taken by the teacher trainees and those administered to grade 5 children (in both experimental and control schools).

The English assessment had two parts. Part 1 measured reading comprehension of two English texts—one considered a grade 3–level text in the United States, and one considered a grade 9–level text. There was a total of twenty comprehension questions between the two texts. These twenty questions can be further subclassified as follows: Seven items probed knowledge of English, four items probed the ability to find factual information located in the texts, two items were on plot structure, and seven items required making inferences or drawing conclusions from the texts.

Part 2 of the English assessment probed knowledge of English via mastery of vocabulary. This part of the assessment included thirty probes, which were classified along two dimensions—grade level at mastery (US standard) and type of vocabulary (general versus academic).

The math assessment contained forty-two items, which can also be categorized along several dimensions. Twelve items required a free response from the subjects by supplying a math fact or doing a calculation. Thirty items used the multiple choice format, which did not obviate the need for analysis and computation but did give some feedback as to whether the subject's computations had been done properly. Twenty-two items were simple or directed computations (e.g., solve for $x$ in the equation $x + 5 = 12$). Twenty items were story problems requiring the respondent to read and understand a scenario and to apply appropriate operations to find the correct answer.

In terms of specific math skills, the test items can be categorized as follows:

- Basic operations, four items;
- Math facts (basic and advanced), four items;
- Operations with fractions, three items;
- Basic algebra, six items;
- Conversions and equivalences, two items;
- Probability and statistics, two items;
- Logical and applied analysis, seven items;
- Symbolic representation, six items;
- Problem solving with percentages, three items;
- Area and perimeter, three items (two of which were discarded because poor photocopy quality made the figures for the test items impossible to interpret);
- Graphical representation, one item; and
- Ratios, two items.

The difficulty level of the test items is mostly late primary and middle school, as per Cameroonian national curriculum standards. The algebra items would all be considered basic algebra 1 items. There was no Euclidian geometry, no trigonometry, no calculus or precalculus, and no plotting of equations in Cartesian space.

## Findings

The overall results of the two assessments are summarized in table 4.2. Study participants clearly performed much better on the English assessment than on the math assessment. In subsequent sections, I examine these results in greater detail.

### *The English Assessment*

The performance of the teacher trainees on the two reading comprehension tasks (ten questions each) is depicted in figure 4.1. Comprehension of the level 3 text was high, at 90 percent, whereas that of the level 9 text was much lower, at just 50 percent.

Table 4.2
**Overall Performance of Teacher Trainees on the Mathematics and English Assessments**

| Assessment | Mean | Standard Deviation |
|---|---|---|
| Mathematics | 37.77 | 10.51 |
| English/reading | 65.18 | 13.79 |
| Overall | 52.41 | 9.42 |

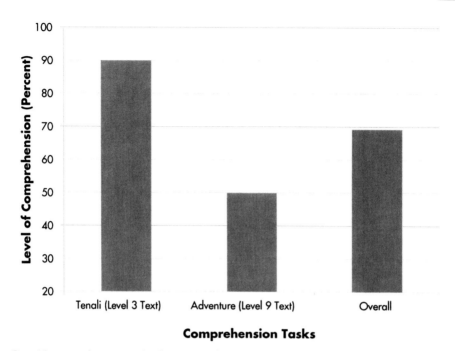

Figure 4.1 Comprehension Levels of Two Texts of Varying Difficulty by Teacher Trainees

In recent years, researchers have given substantial attention to the relationship between text comprehension and vocabulary mastery/development (e.g., Nation and Coady 1988; Graves 2009). The present study explored this relationship as well, first by testing mastery of English vocabulary in isolation and then by investigating the relationship between vocabulary knowledge and text comprehension. Figure 4.2 reports vocabulary mastery as a function of difficulty, with difficulty being operationalized in terms of the school grade by which this vocabulary is reliably mastered by schoolchildren in the United States.

Figure 4.2 reflects a significant decline in mastery by the teacher trainees in the GTTC as the difficulty level increases. The regression equation suggests a decrease in mastery of 11 percent for each jump in difficulty (which is equivalent to two grade levels or two years of age). The anomaly for level 10 was due to the choice of one vocabulary item, which is pegged as a level 10 word, though this word is commonly used in education in Cameroon.

Collectively, the data appear to imply that the level of English proficiency is functionally at approximately a grade 6 or grade 7 level (US standard) in terms of professional ability to use the language for teaching purposes. (Oral fluency is obviously another matter.)

### The Mathematics Assessment
The mathematics assessment results were of particular interest because there is a common and widespread perception in Cameroon that Cameroonians "cannot learn

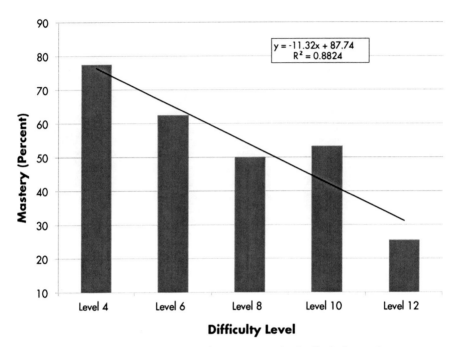

$$y = -11.32x + 87.74$$
$$R^2 = 0.8824$$

Figure 4.2 Knowledge of English Vocabulary of Increasing Levels of Difficulty by Teacher Trainees

math." It was suspected that this perception reflects an underlying reality about the learning and teaching of math at the level of basic primary education.

The math assessment drew material primarily from the curriculum for grades 5 and 6, with the addition of a small number of items designed to test acumen in analysis—that is, the ability to use mathematical, logical, and general reasoning abilities to solve mathematical or quasi-mathematical problems. The results of the math assessment appear in table 4.3.

The teacher trainees collectively scored above 50 percent in only two domains of math skills—conversions and ratios. Even in the area of basic computation, trainees scored just below 50 percent. Meanwhile, in seven domains—basic algebra, fractions, percentages, probability and statistics, symbolic representation, geometry, and graphical knowledge—trainees performed at or just slightly above the level of random guessing. (Recall, as noted above, that two of the three geometry questions were discarded due to poor photocopy quality, which made it impossible to interpret the figures referenced. Nonetheless, 119 of the teacher trainees did not answer the one remaining question correctly.) This profile of performance begins to make evident the reason why Cameroonian primary school students perform at such a low level in basic math.

Figure 4.3 compares the knowledge and skills of grade 5 students with those of teacher trainees in several domains of mathematics. Obviously, the comparisons are

Table 4.3
Performance of Teacher Trainees on the Subsections of the Mathematics Assessment

| Subsection | No. of Items | Mean Score | Standard Deviation | No. Who Answered Zero Items Correctly in This Category |
|---|---|---|---|---|
| Basic operations | 4 | 49.4 | 22.2 | 3 |
| Math facts | 4 | 46.8 | 24.6 | 11 |
| Fractions | 3 | 33.8 | 26.9 | 44 |
| Basic algebra | 6 | 25.3 | 23.1 | 47 |
| Percentages | 2 | 23.4 | 28.6 | 90 |
| Conversions | 2 | 60.4 | 34.4 | 24 |
| Probability and statistics | 2 | 32.9 | 32.3 | 69 |
| Logical analysis | 7 | 42.0 | 16.5 | 3 |
| Symbolic representation | 6 | 30.9 | 20.2 | 17 |
| Geometry (area and perimeter) | 1 | 24.7 | 43.3 | 119 |
| Graphical representation | 1 | 9.5 | 29.4 | 143 |
| Ratios | 2 | 62.7 | 35.2 | 24 |

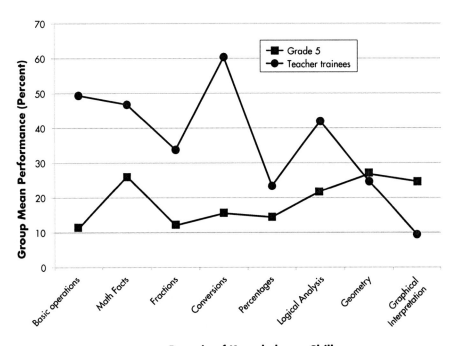

Figure 4.3 Comparison of Grade 5 Students and Teacher Trainees by Domain of Mathematics Knowledge and Skill

limited to the domains pertinent to grade 5 students. In presenting these comparisons, it must be noted that the difficulty level of the items presented to the grade 5 students within a given domain was generally below that of the teacher trainees. Therefore, the comparisons are conceptual because the difficulty level of items in each domain is calibrated to their educational level and expected knowledge/expertise.

In some domains, there is evidence that the skill level of teacher trainees (or lack thereof) is directly reflected in similar levels of skill on the part of grade 5 students. In others—basic operations, fractions, and conversions—there is a marked differential or lag. Walter and Chuo (2013) present evidence from the same area showing that for grade 6 students, there is a strong "lag" effect in the mastery of math skills. That is, when tested on grade-level material, students perform very poorly. However, when tested on material taken from earlier grade levels, their performance is much better. This may also be evidence of a more basic pedagogical issue having to do with a lack of practice or application time in the schools of the area.

## Data from the Philippines

Taylor and Coetzee (2013) used national-level data sets from South Africa to demonstrate evidence of a language-of-instruction effect; that is, the use of children's first language as a language of instruction improved educational outcomes. They did not, however, distinguish between teachers teaching in English when English was the first language of the teacher, and teachers teaching in English when English was the second language of the teacher. Almost no attention has been given to this issue in terms of its potential impact on teacher effectiveness and student learning outcomes.

Table 4.4 maps the possible scenarios on the language-of-instruction variable, identifying the most and least advantageous models for both teachers and learners. The most common of the scenarios are identified with shading. The upper left cell is widely considered the most educationally efficient model, whereas the lower right cell is very likely the least efficient model in terms of educational efficacy. Not coincidentally, the most efficient model is widely followed in the developed countries, whereas the least efficient model primarily prevails in the low-income countries.

The majority of research on the issue of the language of instruction has addressed the implications of this issue in terms of constraints on children's learning. Empirically, however, it is reasonable to inquire as to the impact on learning outcomes of instruction being delivered by teachers who are also speaking a second language. In statistical terms the question is, "How much of the variance in observed learning outcomes is due to instruction being delivered in the children's L2 (second language) versus via the teachers' L2?" In educational terms, the question can be framed as, "Is there a relationship between teacher effectiveness and mastery of the language of instruction? If so, how large is the effect size?"

Recent research carried out in an experimental MLE project in the Philippines has provided an opportunity to examine experimental data on this issue. The intent of the project was to provide instruction to children in their first language (L1)

Table 4.4
Possible Scenarios for Teaching/Learning Involving Teachers' and Students' L1 versus L2

|  | Most Advantageous for the Learner | Least Advantageous for the Learner |
|---|---|---|
| Most Advantageous for the Teacher | Learner L1; Teacher L1 (Normally the ideal; the prevailing model in developed countries; MLE programs in low-income countries) | Learner L2; Teacher L1 (Typical of the immigrant experience in developed countries) |
| Least Advantageous for the Teacher | Learner L1; Teacher L2 (Relatively rare; second-generation teachers in developed countries; seen in some immersion programs and experimental MLE programs) | Learner L2; Teacher L2 (Widespread/prevailing model in low-income countries) |

based on the general published evidence that L1 instruction improves learning outcomes. The assessment of learning outcomes was an integral part of the project designed to document the size of the L1 instructional effect.

In the implementation of the project, some of the teachers in the experimental component were L1 speakers of the L1 of the children, whereas others were L2 speakers of the L1 of the children. Project implementers assumed that the level of language proficiency exhibited by the teachers who were *not* L1 speakers of the language of instruction would have little or no negative impact on the learning of the children. The relevant data are presented in table 4.5.

The major contrast in table 4.5 is between teachers who were native speakers of the children's mother tongue and those who were L2 speakers of the children's mother tongue. Because the only obvious variable distinguishing one group from the other was whether the teacher was an L1 speaker of the language of instruction, table 4.5 allows us to estimate the effect of this variable on educational efficiency.

Table 4.5
Comparison of Results in MLE Classrooms Taught by Teachers in the Children's L1 Who Were or Were Not Native Speakers of the Children's L1

| Grade | Type of Speakers | Reading | Math | English | Overall | "Cost" (%) |
|---|---|---|---|---|---|---|
| 1 | Native | 53.8 | 46.7 | 59.9 | 52.7 | 25.4 |
|  | Nonnative | 43.9 | 32.1 | 45.3 | 39.3 |  |
| 2 | Native | 46.6 | 53.2 | 54.6 | 52.2 | 30.1 |
|  | Nonnative | 27.5 | 32.8 | 47.7 | 36.5 |  |

A scan of the table reveals that children performed at a lower level in both grades in all subjects when the teacher was not an L1 speaker of the language of instruction, even though the teacher was teaching in the children's L1. The advantage (or handicap) ranged from as little as 7 percent to as high as 20 percent. The overall size of this handicap, or penalty, is summarized in the furthest-right column of table 4.5, labeled "cost."

It is very possible that other variables explain part or all of the result, such as variation in the teaching skill and ability of the teachers or school-level variation in the entry-level ability of students. Nonetheless, the consistent pattern evident in table 4.5 certainly suggests that instructional effectiveness may be constrained by reduced language proficiency on the part of teachers.

Figure 4.4 portrays the overall pattern and scope of this effect (expressed as a discount to effectiveness) for three grades—kindergarten through grade 2. Figure 4.4 maps the year-by-year reduction in educational efficiency presumed to be due to limitations in teacher proficiency in the language of instruction. Each bar maps the "cost" or reduction in learning outcomes that appears to be associated with teaching in (the children's) L1 but not being a native speaker of that language of instruction. The cost was computed as a "discount" to the norm—that is, children speaking language X as their first language being taught in that language by trained teachers who also speak language X as their first language.

The regression equation given in figure 4.4 suggests the following: (1) the minimum loss in efficiency is approximately 18 percent (kindergarten); (2) each increase

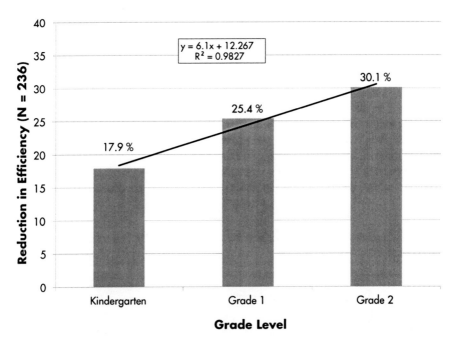

Figure 4.4 Measured Reductions in Educational Efficiency That Appear to Be Due to Reduced Proficiency in the Language of Instruction

in grade level results in an additional 6 percent loss of efficiency; and (3) language proficiency, as a vehicle of instructional efficiency, becomes more critical with each passing year. These observations are clearly reminiscent of the assertion by Thomas and Collier (1997) that the language of instruction becomes increasingly critical as the cognitive demands of instruction increase.

## Conclusion

The data from Cameroon on teaching mathematics identify what appears to be a strong relationship between teacher mastery of subject content and student performance. This finding does not appear to be an artifact of the MLE model but rather a general feature of educational policy and practice in the area. Data from the early years of the MLE experiment in Cameroon suggested that the use of the MLE model at least partially ameliorates this problem (Walter and Trammell 2010).

The data from the Philippines raise both a very specific policy issue in MLE programs and a broader policy issue having widespread implications for education in most developing countries: To what extent is educational delivery in many developing countries weakened by the delivery of instruction in a language the teachers only partially master? Clearly, if educational efficiency in developing countries is significantly compromised by the fact that most teachers teach in a language in which they lack solid proficiency, then a fundamental weakness has been identified that can only be addressed at the level of a change in educational policy.

## Notes

1. Specific identifying information is not given for reasons of security and confidentiality.
2. The analysis revealed small effects for the location and type of school that were not statistically significant. Socioeconomic status is not a relevant variable in this context.
3. This is the equivalent of a secondary school or high school in a Western context.

## References

Ball, Deborah Loewenbuerg, Mark Hoover Thames, and Geoffrey Phelps. 2008. "Content Knowledge for Teaching: What Makes It Special?" *Journal of Teacher Education* 59:389–407.

Graves, Michael F. 2009. *Teaching Individual Words: One Size Does Not Fit All*. New York: Teachers' College Press.

Mullens, John E., Richard J. Murnane, and John B. Willett. 1996. "The Contribution of Training and Subject Matter Knowledge to Teaching Effectiveness: A Multilevel Analysis of Longitudinal Evidence from Belize." *Comparative Education Review* 40:139–57.

Nation, I. S. P., and J. Coady. 1988. "Vocabuary and Reading." In *Vocabulary and Language Teaching*, edited by R. Carter and M. McCarthy. London: Longman.

Shulman, L. S. 1986. "Those Who Understand: Knowledge Growth in Teaching." *Educational Researcher* 15, no. 2: 4–14.

———. 1987. "Knowledge and Teaching: Foundations of the New Reform." *Harvard Educational Review* 57:1–22.

Taylor, Stephen, and Marisa Coetzee. 2013. *Estimating the Impact of Language of Instruction in South Africa Primary Schools: A Fixed-Effects Approach*. Stellenbosch Economic Working Papers 2113. Stellenbosch, South Africa: Department of Economics and Bureau for Economic Research at Stellenbosch University.

Thomas, Wayne, and Virginia Collier. 1997. "School Effectiveness for Language Minority Students." www.scribd.com/doc/148531990/Thomas-and-Collier-1997-School-Effectiveness-for-Language-Minority-Students.

UNESCO. 1998. *World Education Report: Teachers and Teaching in a Changing World*. Paris: UNESCO.
Walter, Stephen L., and Godfrey Kain Chuo. 2013. "The Kom Experimental Mother Tongue Education
     Project: Report for 2013." Research report presented to Ministry of Education in Cameroon.
Walter, Stephen L., and Kristine Trammell. 2010. "The Kom Experimental Mother Tongue Education
     Project: Report for 2010." Research report presented to Ministry of Education in Cameroon.

# 5

## Ghana's Complementary Education Program

KINGSLEY ARKORFUL
*University of Ghana*

ALTHOUGH THE GOVERNMENT OF GHANA has been investing significantly in formal education, not every child is able to attend a government school. In remote areas schools may not be located near enough for children to reach them safely. Some children may be precluded from attending school in the morning because families need their participation in farming or economic activities. Thus, in Ghana's Northern Region, the Complementary Education Program was introduced in 1995 to provide learning opportunities for out-of-school children between the ages of eight and fourteen years. The program, called School for Life (SfL), offers a nine-month program cycle in different communities and in nine Ghanaian languages. Using only the mother tongue as the medium of instruction, the program aims to help children attain basic literacy and numeracy skills and then to integrate the children into the formal education system (Farrell and Hartwell 2008; Casely-Hayford and Ghartey 2007). More than 150,000 children have participated in the SfL program, and some 70 percent of them have been successfully integrated into the formal school system at primary 4 or above after only nine months in the SfL program (DFID 2012). Even more arresting is that SfL learners are not introduced to the English language before enrolling in formal school, where the official language of instruction is English from primary 4 on up. The program's effectiveness has been attributed to the fact that children learn in their first language in small classes (with a maximum of twenty-five students). Each one has a book, which he or she can take home. The school hours are adjusted to the needs of the community. Literate community members who are committed to the program provide instruction using simple, effective teaching methodology. These program facilitators receive a high degree of monitoring, on-site supervision, and training by program administrators (Casely-Hayford and Ghartey 2007). Thus, though mother-tongue instruction is an essential distinguishing element of the program, it is not the only factor in the program's effectiveness.

This chapter is based on a study that examined SfL's provision of good-quality basic education and its potential to influence the quality of education in the formal education sector (Arkorful 2012). The study addressed questions of how the SfL curriculum is structured and delivered to provide opportunities for children to learn in their own language and transition to the English-based formal school, in comparison with the formal school curriculum. Highlights of the full study presented here show that whereas the use of the mother tongue is essential to SfL, other elements of children's sociocultural milieu that distinguish this program are just as important.

The study utilized documentary analysis, pupil assessment and lesson observations, and in-depth interviews with various stakeholders—all of which, when integrated, provide answers to the research questions. Documentary analysis involved scrutiny of curriculum materials for both the SfL and the formal primary school that generated information on the planned curricula. Assessing the curriculum in practice necessitated analyzing the curriculum as received by learners. This was implemented by administering English and mathematics tests to primary 4 and primary 6 pupils at ten randomly selected schools in one district of the Northern Region of Ghana. In total 387 pupils (200 in primary 4 and 187 in primary 6) participated in the assessment; 150 of which were SfL graduates in both grades. The primary 4 SfL graduates had just enrolled in the formal school, whereas the primary 6 graduates had been there for two years.

Structured observations were conducted in two each of primary 4, primary 6, and SfL classes over a two-month period. A range of interviews was also carried out with SfL learners, SfL graduates enrolled in formal school, parents, teachers, and local management committee members.

The two curricula were analyzed at three levels: planned, implemented, and attained. Analysis of the SfL curriculum focuses on whether and how it ensures that out-of-school children have the opportunity to learn within the short program cycle and transfer the skills gained to the formal school curriculum. At all levels, this curriculum was noted to prepare learners for success in formal school, in spite of barriers to integration such as a lack of English-language proficiency. The following discussion provides an overview of how the two curricula compare.

## Curriculum Focus

The SfL program does not follow the national curriculum, which relies on Ghanaian languages and English as the medium of instruction and includes seven subjects, one of which is a Ghanaian language. The SfL curriculum includes only three areas of instruction: literacy, numeracy, and life skills. Thus, in the SfL curriculum all attention is geared toward ensuring that children can read, write, and calculate—skills that are tied to the lives of the children so that learning not only is of everyday relevance to them but also can help them integrate into the formal school. The program's restrictive curriculum focus also means that both teachers and learners are not encumbered by subject areas that could distract them from their primary learning objectives. This strategy makes the most use of the learning time available to the children and motivates them to continue attending and learning. It also motivates parents to continue sending children to the program.

In the formal school, literacy and numeracy are given prime importance, but they are not woven into the overall curriculum as with the SfL program. In the formal school, English language competes with mathematics, the Ghanaian language, social science, religious and moral education, physical education, and so on. Actual formal school timetables allocate nine hours per week to the combined teaching of the

English language, mathematics, and the Ghanaian language. This compares to the fifteen hours a week devoted to literacy, numeracy, and life skills in the SfL classes.

## The Curriculum's Functional Relevance and Delivery

The topic contents of both the SfL and the formal school curricula exhibit some cultural relevance, such as a focus on family and community activities. However, the SfL curriculum's topics exhibit more immediate functional relevance for the children, as does the delivery of this curriculum. SfL lessons reflect the social, economic, and community life of the learners. The assumption is that this functionality will engender interest and will create the necessary opportunity for learners to participate in lessons. A review of the *Facilitator's Manual* suggests that the topics and vocabulary items are relevant to children living in rural environments who are using their existing knowledge of the world in beginning to learn to read (Trudell 2007; Sutherland 1992). Figure 5.1 provides the framework for a lesson in the SfL curriculum that is taught in the local language (the instructional manual is translated into each SfL language).

The coherence in the presentation given above differs from what can be seen in the formal school curriculum. For example, in accordance with the English syllabus, the first unit in *Pupil's Book 1* is "Names, Greetings and Farewell." Unit 2 is titled "Things We Know," and unit 3 is "Numbers and Shapes" (Ntumy, Bailey, and Dolphyne 2008). There does not seem to be a thematic linkage between these units. Similarly, the title of unit 27 is "Stop Thief," with a picture and reading exercise centered on catching a thief; yet the very next page shows pictures of fruit and vegetables that children are supposed to look at and name (Ntumy, Bailey, and Dolphyne 2008, 78).

Although the syllabus makes a claim that the four modalities of English (reading, writing, listening, and speaking) are integrated, they are not treated as such by means of any thematic or cognitive connections. In unit 27 described above, whereas the pictures used for illustration and reading practice are based on fruit and vegetables, the writing exercise goes under the heading "Do Not Tell Lies" (Ntumy, Bailey, and Dolphyne 2008, 78). Thus, the composition practice does not seem to have any bearing on the reading and picture discussion.

## The Language of Instruction

The study also found a discrepancy in the formal education sector between policy and practice around language and literacy instruction. Although government education guidelines state that the local language should be the medium of instruction in primary 1 through primary 3 (P1–P3), "where feasible" (Ghana Education Service 2008), subject syllabi and textbooks (apart from the Ghanaian languages textbook) do not reflect this policy because they are based on and written in English. This is therefore the language that pupils must initially learn to read and write.

Observations of formal school classes located in the communities providing SfL programs revealed an interesting scenario: A total of 42 percent of the lessons observed were conducted using a combination of the local language and English, whereas 44 percent utilized the local language. The remaining 14 percent of instruction

---

**Lesson 1: Cow**

**Objectives:** To make learners know how to care for cattle better and the need to boil milk before drinking it.

**Picture Discussion**

1. Write down the keyword.
2. What does grass give the cow? What do we do with some of the things that cattle give us? What can we do to keep our cattle neat and healthy?
3. How should we treat milk before drinking it?
4. During the discussion remember to talk about the following:
   a) Traditional and modern ways of rearing cattle.
   b) How to treat sick and/or dead cattle.
   c) The need for veterinary services.

**Keyword(s)**

This is the word through which the class is going to learn the skills of reading and writing. It has something to do with what the lesson is about (e.g., cows)

1. Write down the keyword.
   a) Say it many times.
   b) Let individual learners say it after you.
   c) Let the class say it after you.
   d) Let the class know that what you are pointing at is the keyword.
2. Introduce them to the vowels and consonants of the keyword.
   a) Let the learners know that the sounds that vibrate in the throat are called vowels:
      **i e â a ô o u**
   b) The remaining sounds are called consonants, e.g., **n h b**.
   c) Break down the keyword into syllables. A syllable has a consonant and a vowel (e.g., /na/ as in Dagbani and Ngbanyato). It can also be a consonant, vowel, and another consonant (/nam/ as in Dagbani). A syllable may also be a nasal consonant (n/m).
   d) Ask the learners to tell the number of syllables that are found in the keyword.
   e) Use the syllables to drill learners. Ask learners to combine the consonants of the keyword with the vowels of their language to form meaningful words.
   f) Treat the syllable and the syllabic family through drill.
   g) Let the learners learn to write syllables.
3. Meaningful words formation:
   a) Ask the learners to make meaningful words with the syllables.
   b) Guide the learners to use the first syllable of the keyword to form or build more words.
   c) Write each meaningful word they make on the chalkboard.
4. Sentence formation: Ask the learners to use the words they have formed in constructing simple sentences.

---

Figure 5.1 Lesson 1 of the School for Life's Instructional Manual

was conducted in English. Even though the lessons in the formal school made extensive use of the local language, in interviews the children still associated the formal school with the English language; however, SfL lessons were conducted exclusively in the local language.

## The Facilitator's Content Knowledge

Given that the study also sought to ascertain the extent to which the implemented curriculum corresponds with the planned curriculum, it was also important to address the content knowledge of the facilitators who delivered the lessons. Evidence of facilitators' content knowledge was gleaned from class observations, interviews with learners, and the facilitators themselves.

The two facilitators in the study had both been teaching SfL classes for nearly ten years and were thus well versed in the fundamentals of the SfL program. Accordingly, the evidence presented here may not be representative of all SfL facilitators. In most of the lessons observed, it was clear that the facilitators had mastery over the subject content. They were confident in their presentation and able to lead pupils in critically building on their own experiences to construct new knowledge, and get them to participate in reading, writing and numeracy exercises (table 5.1).

In all categories facilitators showed a clear grasp of the content they were expected to deliver. Learners' questions were responded to correctly 93 percent of the time, and additional information was provided 66 percent of the time. The lessons were delivered clearly, as the facilitators followed the script in the *Facilitator's Manual* and provided clear and appropriate information 90 percent of the time. Thus, the curriculum materials detailed in the SfL manual and the experiential backgrounds of the facilitators make it possible for community members who were not trained as teachers to have mastery of the learning content they deliver. Ali, one of the facilitators, indicated that "the topics I teach are all activities and functions that I as well as the children undertake daily. I have my own farm and some cattle, so all these community topics are activities I have been engaged in since a child" (April 12, 2011).

An exception in both SfL classes observed was the facilitators' difficulty in handling the topics of preventing HIV/AIDS and of information and computer technology (ICT), which had recently been added to the curriculum. ICT would seem to be a hypothetical subject, given that the schools were not equipped with computers.

Although facilitators responded to learners' questions effectively, the lesson sequence did not call for eliciting questions from the pupils. Nonetheless, there was much pupil engagement in lessons through reading sentences and writing words on the board or in their exercise books. Thus even though the lessons and the classroom interactions were always teacher initiated, the opportunity for children to answer

Table 5.1
**SfL Facilitators' Content Knowledge, Based on Classroom Observation**

| Content Indicator | % Not Evident | % Slightly Evident | % Somewhat Evident | % Evident | % Highly Evident |
|---|---|---|---|---|---|
| Shows knowledge of subject matter in lesson presentation | 3 | 0 | 0 | 11 | 86 |
| Responds to learners' questions accurately | 0 | 0 | 8 | 21 | 71 |
| Provides additional information to learners | 17 | 9 | 7 | 23 | 44 |
| Provides clear and appropriate information | 7 | 0 | 5 | 43 | 45 |

facilitators' questions and reproduce their answers either on the board or in their books was instrumental in the knowledge construction process.

Providing new information was not the responsibility of the facilitators alone. In a follow-up discussion Ali noted the following: "Where we do not have all the information, we are encouraged to bring in community members to lead or support the discussion" (May 24, 2011). Mr. Abu, who had been instrumental in developing the curriculum, also indicated that the facilitator was not intended to be a repository of all knowledge, and that the teaching and learning process was designed to encourage interaction between pupils and facilitators, with community members sometimes coming in to share their knowledge and experience. However, this was observed to take place only once during the two-month field study.

Moreover, though the involvement of others with specialized knowledge and experience is a good idea in principle and can lead to the involvement of the community, parents, and other skilled people as resource persons, it does not allow facilitators to increase their own knowledge base, especially when it comes to topics with which they are not familiar. Therefore, if suitable local resource persons were not available, classes could suffer, as observed when one facilitator was attempting to teach ICT and the prevention of HIV/AIDS.

With this exception, facilitators' competency in terms of the content of lessons was highly evident in all observations. But content knowledge is only one aspect of good teaching. It is important for the teacher not only to understand the subject in detail and be able to use the teaching manual but also to understand the importance of the subject for the pupils and be able to conduct lessons in such a way as to support the pupils' learning. Observation showed that in general facilitators provided activities that allowed pupils to practice and extend their knowledge. Lessons encouraged pupils to think independently and to link lesson content to life experiences. More than half the lessons observed took into account the range of pupils' abilities, the complexity and difficulty of lesson materials, and the place of the lesson material in the broader scope of disciplinary knowledge.

It is important to note that lesson activities were prescribed in the *Facilitator's Manual*. Little initiative was required on the part of the facilitator in devising activities aimed specifically at tackling difficult topics or subjects, and discussions with SfL facilitators revealed a certain hesitance to deviate from the guide. Thus, though the SfL is noted for its flexibility in accommodating the lifestyle of the community and its learners, there was a certain level of rigidity in the manner in which instruction was managed. O'Sullivan (2004) notes the importance of prescriptive materials that guarantee teachers stay on track and facilitate learner-centered lessons, and it appears that is the principle being utilized in the SfL. Given the fact that the facilitator is not a professionally trained teacher, scripted guides become even more crucial in ensuring that at every step of the way, the facilitator has instructions to prevent a gap between curriculum policy and practice.

By contrast, in the formal school the mismatch of curriculum policy and practice is endemic. Observations revealed that formal schoolteachers did not seem to be on top of the lessons they were delivering. In general teachers were not seen to link lessons to the lives of the children. For instance, on one occasion, I observed a reading comprehension lesson being taught through poetry in a P4 class. The poem was in English and was difficult for the children to follow. They did not seem to understand what was going on as the teacher kept on talking to them about rhyming and other literary terms without attempting to make the theme of the poem or its subject interesting to them. In general teachers were not seen attempting to change their pace or approach to ensure that learners participated in lessons. They seemed just interested in running through their lesson plans prepared for the week. There was no real attempt to ensure that the plans were delivered as intended.

## Pupil Assessment/Performance

The effectiveness of the Complementary Education Program was demonstrated in an assessment of SfL graduates' performance on standardized assessments. The SfL does not have any formal assessment process for the learners. Therefore, the study utilized the Ghana Education Service's National Education Assessment test instruments (Ministry of Education, 2012), which measure pupil competence in English and mathematics, in order to assess the Complementary Education Program's graduates and their peers in the formal school.

Of the 208 pupils assessed, 44 percent were SfL graduates (who had entered formal school in P3 or P4, with no exposure to English); 24 percent of such graduates in primary 4 managed minimum competence in the reading comprehension test, whereas 46 percent attained the target competence or proficiency level. This compares with 18 percent and 34 percent, respectively, with regard to regular formal school pupils (table 5.2).

On the grammar test (table 5.3), non-SfL pupils performed about the same as their SfL counterparts, with 29 percent of the former attaining proficiency as opposed to 28.6 percent of the latter. Discussions with teachers and pupils revealed that though the SfL focused on literacy skills, thus equipping its graduates with the ability to read and write, there was less focus on grammar in the SfL (and there was none on English). Conversely, English language lessons in the formal school seem to have focused more sharply on language usage and rules than on teaching pupils to read.

Table 5.2
**Primary 4 English Reading Comprehension Assessment (number/percent)**

| | Competency Level | | | |
|---|---|---|---|---|
| Student Type | Below Minimum Competency | Minimum Competency | Target Competency | Total |
| SfL, male | 19/29.7 | 14/21.9 | 31/49.4 | 64/100 |
| SfL, female | 8/29.6 | 8/29.6 | 11/40.7 | 27/100 |
| Total SfL | 27/29.7 | 22/24.2 | 42/46.2 | 91/100 |
| Non-SfL, male | 32/47.8 | 12/17.9 | 23/34.3 | 67/100 |
| Non-SfL, female | 24/48.0 | 9/18.0 | 17/34.0 | 50/100 |
| Total Non-SfL | 56/47.9 | 21/17.9 | 40/34.2 | 117/100 |

Table 5.3
Primary 4 English Grammar Assessment (number/percent)

|  | Competency Level | | | |
| --- | --- | --- | --- | --- |
| Student Type | Below Minimum Competency | Minimum Competency | Target Competency | Total |
| SfL, male | 27/42.2 | 18/28.1 | 19/29.7 | 64/100 |
| SfL, female | 15/55.5 | 5/18.5 | 7/26.0 | 27/100 |
| Total SfL | 42/46.1 | 23/25.3 | 26/28.6 | 91/100 |
| Non-SfL, male | 33/49.3 | 13/19.4 | 21/31.3 | 67/100 |
| Non-SfL, female | 25/50.0 | 12/24.0 | 13/26.0 | 50/100 |
| Total Non-SfL | 58/49.6 | 25/21.4 | 34/29.0 | 117/100 |

The assessment results confirm the effectiveness of the Complementary Education Program in ensuring that children acquire basic literacy and numeracy skills and transition to formal school. In P4, with no prior exposure to English, they were able to perform at essentially the same level as formal school peers who had three years of English exposure. The P6 English reading comprehension test had 38 percent of SfL graduates achieving the target competency, against 40 percent of regular formal school pupils. The results of the mathematics assessment are not presented in this chapter due to space limitations. However, they showed the SfL graduates performing at the same level as their colleagues in formal school.

## Conclusion

The key aim of this chapter has been to explain how the Complementary Education Program curriculum is implemented in order to prepare learners for entry into formal schools. Several highly practical issues have come to light concerning how facilitators manage to utilize the SfL's interactive approach and materials. It is expected that when facilitators use the SfL manual effectively, there will be an increase in effective classroom practices, particularly in such important instructional areas as pupil engagement and interaction in literacy tasks, the appropriate utilization of teaching and learning materials, pupil practice of thinking skills rather than rote learning, and enhanced facilitator feedback to pupil performance. The chapter has shown that to a large extent, facilitators have made sure that they follow the script in the manual. This was the key factor in ensuring that there was an interactive classroom environment to promote pupils' use of lesson-relevant language and the social construction of knowledge (Lave and Wenger 1991; Vygotsky 1987).

Other key factors in program success have included the functional relevance of the curriculum topics and the facilitators' mastery over the content knowledge, which was enhanced by its functionality for both facilitator and learners and ensured that classroom interaction was animated and interesting. These factors, in conjunction with the utilization of the pupils' mother tongue for all teaching and learning activities, have created a platform for dialogue that has been creative, and thus productive for knowledge construction. The functional and cultural relevance of the topics delivered via a local language has also ensured that a real community of learning has been created, with parents, facilitator, and learners coming together. Thus the Complementary Education Program's class was not separated from the community's life but situated right within the structure of the community.

However, the study does not conclude that the SfL magically creates a learner-centered environment where all teaching and learning are participatory. A review of the literature on pedagogical practices across sub-Saharan Africa showed that, by and large, most teaching and learning on the subcontinent is teacher centered and is constrained by the history and traditional social process of school (Tabulawa 1997). However, the context within which the School for Life operates breaks some traditional constraints and allows for freer interaction between the teacher and the pupil. For the SfL learner, the Complementary Education Program's class is not a real school. It is more or less a break from his or her economic chores. The environment of the class, which typically includes the presence of family members, makes the pupil feel more at home to participate.

This chapter has noted that knowledge is socially constructed in the SfL class. However, a close look at some of the processes shows that the SfL classes share similarities with the formal school in terms of teacher-initiated discourse and teacher-led elicitation of pupils' linguistic participation in the classroom. Social construction of knowledge in the SfL class is not about the individual micro-level processes or parts but is, rather, the sum of the disparate parts or processes coming together synergistically to create knowledge. The context of the class within the community, the functional relevance of the topics, the language of instruction, the locally meaningful dialogue, and the social relationship between the facilitator and learners—all coalesce to create a program and lessons within which children are able to engage energetically and produce knowledge.

In contrast, observation in the formal school showed a different situation, where there was a disconnect between the intended curriculum and the implemented curriculum with very little interaction taking place as a result of the teachers' inability or refusal to create the conditions for interactive classroom engagement. Teachers in the formal school are not obligated to ensure that learning is interactive, and though lesson plans were prepared for that purpose, it did not happen in practice. Writing instruction provides a point of contrast. At the SfL, children write almost daily about some aspect of the curricular focus for the day or week. Copying plays a minor role. In formal school, children copy what teachers write. So at the SfL, children share in generating text. It is interactive. They read, they talk, and then they write. Their writing reflects this interaction. It is a real social construction of knowledge. At formal school, they do not construct knowledge. The text that everyone copies was generated by the teacher. In formal school, pupils learn that writing belongs to the expert teacher; in SfL pupils learn that they can also be authors.

## References

Arkorful, Kingsley. 2012. "Complementary Education and the Opportunity to Learn in the Northern Region of Ghana." PhD dissertation, University of Sussex.

Casely-Hayford, Leslie, and Adom Baisie Ghartey. 2007. *The Leap to Literacy and Life Change in Northern Ghana: An Impact Assessment of School for Life*. Tamale: School for Life.

DFID (Department for International Development, Ghana). 2012. *Complementary Basic Education: Business Case*. Accra: DFID.

Farrell, Joseph P., and Ash Hartwell. 2008. *Planning for Successful Alternative Schooling: A Possible Route to Education for All*. Paris: UNESCO International Institute for Educational Planning.

Ghana Education Service. 2008. *English Syllabus for Primary Schools*. Accra: Ghana Publishing Corporation.

Government of Ghana. 1992. *The Fourth Republican Constitution of Ghana*. Accra: Ghana Publishing Corporation.

———. 2008. New Education Reform. Policy document, Accra.

Lave, Jean, and Etienne Wenger. 1991. *Situated Learning: Legitimate Peripheral Participation*. Cambridge: Cambridge University Press.

Ministry of Education. 2012. *National Education Assessment Administration Report 2011*. Accra: Government of Ghana.

Ntumy, Thomas, Donna Bailey, and Florence Dolphyne. 2008. *New Gateway to English for Primary Schools; Pupils' Book 1*. Accra: Sedco.

O'Sullivan, Margo C. 2004. "The Reconceptualisation of Learner-Centred Approaches: A Namibian Case Study." *International Journal of Educational Development* 24:585–602.

Sutherland, Peter. 1992. *Cognitive Development Today: Piaget and His Critics*. London: Paul Chapman.

Tabulawa, Richard. 1997. "Pedagogical Classroom Practice and the Social Context: The Case of Botswana." *International Journal of Educational Development* 17, no. 2: 189–204.

Trudell, Barbara. 2007. "Local Community Perspectives and Language of Education in Sub-Saharan African Communities." *International Journal of Educational Development* 27:552–63.

Vygotsky, L. S. 1987. *The Collected Works of L. S. Vygotsky*. New York: Plenum Press.

# 6

# Language Contact and Language Attitudes in Two Dagara-Speaking Border Communities in Burkina Faso and Ghana

RICHARD BEYOGLE
*University of Illinois at Urbana-Champaign*

DAGARA IS A GUR LANGUAGE spoken in the northwestern corner of Ghana, the southwestern part of Burkina Faso, and the northeastern part of Côte d'Ivoire (Bodomo 1986). An arbitrary division of the Dagara people into three neighboring West African countries is due to European colonization. From 1920 until today, this arbitrary demarcation has created an officially bilingual anglophone and francophone Dagara community, respectively, in Ghana and Burkina Faso. These political boundaries today represent a major divide and a source of mutual contact influence for the Dagara, who continue to communicate across the borders despite the differences between the official state languages adopted in the two countries.

Métuolé (1991) points out that before the division of the Dagara homelands in about 1880, the northern Dagara were living on opposite sides of the Black Volta River as one community. Subsequently, the British and French colonizers used the river as a natural boundary to partition the territory into the Gold Coast (British, now Ghana) and Upper Volta (French, now Burkina Faso).

The two countries had experienced similar contact situations as far as the adoption of their official languages is concerned; Ghana and Burkina Faso fell under British and French colonial rule in the era of the scramble for and partition of Africa. Mahama (2009) records that contact between the French colonizers and the inhabitants of Upper Volta started around the 1880s, but it was not until the 1930s that Catholic missionaries opened schools in Dissin and Dano in the Dagara homelands and started to educate the locals in French.

The first contact between the British and the Dagara in the northern territories of the Gold Coast occurred around 1900. Mahama further claims that the missionaries attempted to open a primary school in Nandom (a Dagara town, eleven miles south of the Burkina-Ghana border) in the early 1900s for the children of the new converts, but this plan had met strong opposition from the colonial authorities, who feared that the educated local Christians would undermine the authority of the native chiefs, who were being used at that time to enforce colonial rules and laws. Nevertheless, another petition was sent to the colonial authority in 1937, and that year the first boys' primary boarding school was opened in Nandom, followed in 1940 by a girls' primary boarding school in Jirapa, another Dagara town about twenty-five miles farther south of the Burkina-Ghana border (Mahama 2009, 10).

With the introduction of formal education by the colonial powers, English and French were established in the respective colonies as the only medium of instruction and communication on school compounds, and African languages were considered "inferior and less suitable for teaching" (Adegbija 1994, 104). This appears to have been a widespread attitude during colonial times, when schoolteachers were mostly Europeans, and it later became the norm in every part of Ghana.

The imposition of French in education in Burkina Faso seems to have been worse than the imposition of English in Ghana, because the French were stricter in their French-only policy in their classrooms than the British. For example, at the time of Burkina Faso's independence in 1962, although French was spoken by only about 10 to 15 percent of the total population, according to official reports, French was "the only language of instruction in all public schools from the first day of elementary school through the last day of college" (Bado 2009, 8).

## Language Attitudes

Both Ghana and Burkina Faso, like all other African countries, had multilingual societies even before they came into contact with European languages. The Dagara in Ghana were already in contact with Akan (Twi), because most of the men worked as seasonal labor migrants and returned speaking fluent Twi from southern Ghana, where Akan is widely spoken. The Burkina Dagara, conversely, were also already in contact with the two main trade languages of the region, Moré and Dioula. Native speakers of the these African languages were known traders in cola nuts, salt, and fabrics who traveled the length and breadth of Burkina and Ghana to sell and buy these products. In the postindependence years multilingualism has become a matter of special concern and an inevitable challenge for language educators and language policy planners when it comes to choosing one language as the medium of instruction, given that cultural identity signaled by language proves to be complex and delicate to handle effectively. In West Africa, for example, Fishman (1991, 354) argues that it is nearly impossible to separate language and ethnic identity as the two are intrinsically linked. Given the multilingual nature of African communities, languages perform a dual function by bringing ethnic groups together and by setting them apart from the other ethnic groups (Fishman 1991). In Burkina and Ghana, for instance, languages of wider communication like Twi and Moré presumably wielded more power, superiority, and dominance, whereas speakers of less powerful languages, including Dagara, might have felt threatened and therefore developed negative attitudes toward both the powerful vehicular languages and those who spoke them. In fact, the locals' inability to reach a compromise on the language of instruction was one of the main reasons why many African countries comfortably resorted to ex-colonial languages in order to avoid identity conflicts associated with the choice of a single language.

Adegbija (1994, 106) observes that negative attitudes toward African languages are formed because educational policymakers share the belief that the promotion and use of African languages as media of instruction might "shut the proverbial window on the world" and make it difficult for future generations to access enviable opportunities in the developed world. Adegbija also shows the general attitudinal misconception by Africans that the "implanted European languages and cultures" are more apt for education, whereas the African indigenous languages are inferior and not fit for education. As we shall see throughout this chapter these conceptions continue to be prevalent.

### Language Attitudes in Burkina Faso

Following UNESCO's reports on language policies in Africa, Chimhundu (2002, 25) records that out of the fifty-nine national languages in Burkina Faso, only about twenty have been described and are currently used for adult literacy programs. None of these languages is standardized, which means that French remains the only choice as a language of instruction and administration. What is more, some intellectuals resisted the 1979–84 major reforms that brought the use of national languages to education, arguing that the reform would "create an unfair system of two parallel schools" (Kouraogo and Dianda 2008, 34). Others have rejected outright the use of national languages as media of instruction, justifying their criticisms along the same lines argued by Adegbija. Opponents of the reforms gained decisive support when the then minister of education withdrew his child from one of the satellite schools in which the new reform was being introduced and presented the arguments that the promotion and use of local languages would limit children's opportunities in the outside world.

This example and many others could have had an adverse effect on the Burkinabe youth who were supposed to be the direct participants in and beneficiaries of the reforms. Negative attitudes toward the use of indigenous languages in the classroom and bilingual education also halted the full implementation of the new educational programs in the country, and the government has not been able to enforce the compulsory education program in the local language in public schools.

### Language Attitudes in Ghana

In Ghana, English continues to dominate in the public spheres of social and economic activity. The indigenous languages are used only in traditional contexts, such as marriage ceremonies, festivals, markets, and other forms of interpersonal interactions. This situation is reinforced by increased insistence from parents who, as Okere remarked, are eager to give their children a "head start on European languages, which they believe to be the window on the world" (Okere 1995, 182). A case in point that indicates Ghanaians' overwhelmingly positive attitude toward English is that in formal official functions, such as the president's broadcast at a national day of celebration on Independence Day and Republic Day, English remains the preferred language. Another case in point, reported by Guerini (2009), is negative attitudes among intellectuals. According to a survey conducted at the University of Ghana in Accra on the teaching of Ghanaian languages, lecturers and professors teaching indigenous languages reported feeling looked down upon by their own colleagues and other faculty members—some of whom may even refer to them overtly as "second-rate" faculty.

Guerini's research investigates language attitudes in West Africa with a focus on Ghana. Guerini reports that, according to the 2000 national census, native Akan (Twi) speakers in Ghana constitute about 43 percent of the total population, and another 40 percent speak Akan as a second language or as the lingua franca (Guerini 2009, 20). The aim of Guerini's survey was to investigate respondents' attitudes toward the use of Akan rather than English as the medium of instruction in schools in Ghana. Akan is a vehicular language, and the language of daily economic interaction, in almost all the major cities of Ghana. Other Ghanaian languages—such as Dagara, Waali, and Sissala—are not so well represented in big cities. Guerini's results were surprisingly negative toward Akan, the African language that is so widely used in Ghana: 79.5 percent of Akan native speakers and 94.9 percent of second-language speakers rejected Akan as the medium of education, even at the primary school level (Guerini 2009, 20).

In 2002 a report by the minister of education of Ghana, Ameya-Ekumfi, on Ghana's "English-only" policy in the classrooms in all schools starting with grade 1 stated the following:

1. Teachers abused the previous policy: they have used only a Ghanaian language as the medium of instruction and never spoke English in class.
2. It has been observed that students are unable to speak and write "good" English sentences even by the time they complete high school. (Ameya-Ekumfi 2002)

The report's purism and overt preference for English, I would argue, are reflections of the overall negative attitudes of Ghanaians toward the use of indigenous languages as a medium of instruction. This represents the starting point for my study.

*Theoretical Questions*
Here, I use Katz's (1960) functional approach to interpret responses to questions about language attitudes. Katz (1960, 170) proposes four basic functions for attitudes toward language: "utilitarian, value-expressive, ego-defensive and knowledge." The utilitarian function signifies that if speakers know that, by learning to speak a language, there is more gain than loss, their attitudes are more likely to be positive about that language. For the value-expressive function, Katz argues that "the individual derives satisfaction from expressing attitudes appropriate to his personal values of . . . self-expression, self-development, and self-realization." With regard to the ego-defensive function, attitudes are formed by the speakers' desire for protection from any form of current or future threat or insecurity. In other words, if a particular language does not guarantee the speaker any current or future security in any form, a negative attitude might be formed regarding the use of the language. The knowledge function refers to an organized form of social reality. If speakers, by means of a language, are able to understand the world clearly and with no ambiguous situations, this can influence positive language attitude formation.

The remainder of this chapter is divided as follows. First, I present the corpus and methodology, with special focus on the interview questions used to elicit language attitudes from participants in my fieldwork. Then I present the results of quantitative and qualitative analyses of the participants' responses and end with suggestions regarding language planning in the Dagara homelands.

## Corpus and Methodology

The data collection for my study was carried out in a fieldwork setting, using sociolinguistic interviews with a total of a hundred speakers in the border towns of Ouessa, Burkina Faso, and Hamile, Ghana, on both sides of the Ghana-Burkina border in the summers of 2011 and 2012. Participants were lifelong native Dagara residents in their respective border towns and were interviewed and recorded on a one-on-one basis by the author of this chapter, a Ghanian native-speaker of Dagara who conscientiously spoke only Dagara throughout the interviews. Each participant had obtained at least a high school diploma. Besides Dagara, all participants were fluent in their respective official languages. They answered a total of twenty-five questions during the interview, which typically lasted for thirty minutes per participant. This chapter reports on responses to two questions from the interview that are relevant to language attitudes, language status, and acquisition planning:

> Question 5.2. Do you think Dagara should be given the same official status
>      as French/English in the school curriculum? Yes/No and why?
> Question 5.3. Which language do you think should be used as medium of
>      instruction in the schools in the Dagara homelands and why?

## Results

Results are presented first for respondents in Ouessa and then for respondents in Hamile. The tables and figures display the results categorized by age group.

### *Ouessa, Burkina Faso, Respondents by Age Groups*

Responses to question 5.2, "Do you think Dagara should be given the same official status as French in the school curriculum? Yes/No and why?" by Ouessa (Burkina Faso) respondents (table 6.1 and figure 6.1) indicate that the large majority of respondents (more than 75 percent) in the four age groups are in favor of enhancing the status of Dagara. There are, however, noteworthy differences between the age groups. The youngest age group, eighteen- to thirty-year-olds, is the least favorable to such status enhancement; only 75 percent of the sixteen respondents expressed support for more official status for Dagara. The twenty-two respondents representing the educated active population (thirty-one- to forty-year-olds and forty-one to fifty years) are the most in favor (91 percent), whereas the oldest speakers (fifty-one- to sixty-year-olds) are 83 percent favorable for strengthening the language's official status. Paradoxically, however, status enhancement for Dagara in schools does not seem to extend to the use of the language as a medium of instruction for any of the age groups, including those respondents who are otherwise in favor of doing more for the local language. Regarding the preferred medium of instruction in the schools in the Dagara homelands in question 5.3, for instance, respondents in all age groups

Table 6.1
Q 5.2 and Q 5.3: Language Status and Use in Education in Ouessa, Burkina

|  |  | Q 5.2 |  |  |  | Q 5.3 |  |  |  |
| --- | --- | --- | --- | --- | --- | --- | --- | --- | --- |
| Age Limit (years) | No. of Participants | Yes | % | No | % | French | % | Dagara | % |
| 18–30 | 16 | 12 | 75 | 4 | 25 | 15 | 93 | 1 | 7 |
| 31–40 | 11 | 10 | 91 | 1 | 9 | 10 | 91 | 1 | 9 |
| 41–50 | 11 | 10 | 91 | 1 | 9 | 9 | 82 | 2 | 18 |
| 51–65 | 12 | 10 | 83 | 2 | 17 | 11 | 92 | 1 | 8 |
| Total number | 50 | 42 | 96 | 8 | 4 | 45 | 90 | 5 | 10 |

(table 6.1 and figure 6.2) expressed an overwhelming (more than 82 percent) preference for French. Eighteen percent of the forty-one- to fifty-year-old respondents
preferred Dagara as a medium of instruction in schools, but even the two older age
groups that are otherwise in strong support of Dagara do not wish to see school-
children taught exclusively in the language. As expected, based on their responses to
question 5.2, the youngest group (eighteen- to thirty-year-olds) voted as highly as 93
percent in favor of French and a very low percentage (7 percent) for Dagara in
question 5.3.

Attitudes toward language use in contact can shed light on some of these apparent contradictions. When it came to interview questions asked in the later parts of
the conversation about the reasons why respondents from Ouessa mix Dagara with
other languages, most of the answers reflected negative attitudes toward the sole
use of Dagara (or "pure Dagara") because of the prestige and power associated with
the ability to speak French or mix Dagara with French. The following comment
from a fifty-five-year-old female local farmer/trader from Ouessa is a telling example of a class-conscious approach to code-mixing and, thus, the avoidance of using
only Dagara: "Ti zɛgri ti tuɔra. Ti zuo Dagara wa won kɔkɔra omi bɔbr kɛ bɛ bangkɛ
ole no." (Translated: "We love to show too much of our social classes. Dagara
exhibit their social classes by speaking foreign languages.") This participant goes further to confirm that even the illiterate Dagara want to identify themselves with the
elites by mixing Dagara with French. She concludes: "Bɛl na saa bɛ maalia nakoli
ɛkyɛ bɛ mimi bɔbr kɛ wul bɛ minga." (Translated: "Even the illiterates want to show
that they can also speak a European language.") In light of this association between
language mixing and social mobility, it is hardly surprising that none of the age groups
in Ouessa, and especially not the youth, would be in favor of Dagara-only education.

### Hamile, Ghana, Respondents by Age Groups
The answers provided by participants in Hamile, Ghana, to questions 5.2 and 5.3
(table 6.2 and figures 6.3 and 6.4) are equally revealing. The first observation to
make is that, overall, the range of support for the enhancement of the official status
of Dagara in the school curriculum is roughly the same in Hamile (figure 6.3) as in
Ouessa (figure 6.1): 19 percent (ranging from 100 percent to 81 percent in favor ver-

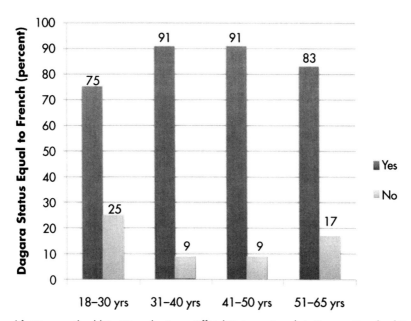

Figure 6.1 "Dagara Should Be Given the Same Official Status as French in Dagara Homelands" (Ouessa, Burkina Faso)

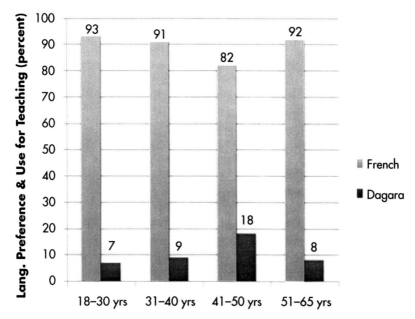

Figure 6.2 "Language Preference and Use as Medium of Instruction in Dagara Homelands" (Ouessa, Burkina Faso)

▓ Table 6.2
**Q 5.2 and Q 5.3: Language Status and Use for Education in Hamile, Ghana**

| | | Q 5.2 | | | | Q 5.3 | | | |
|---|---|---|---|---|---|---|---|---|---|
| Age Limit (years) | No. of Participants | Yes | % | No | % | English | % | Dagara | % |
| 18–30 | 23 | 19 | 83 | 4 | 17 | 23 | 100 | 0 | 0 |
| 31–40 | 6 | 5 | 83 | 1 | 17 | 5 | 83 | 1 | 17 |
| 41–50 | 5 | 5 | 100 | 0 | 0 | 5 | 100 | 0 | 0 |
| 51–65 | 16 | 13 | 81 | 3 | 19 | 15 | 94 | 1 | 6 |
| Total number | 50 | 42 | 84 | 8 | 16 | 48 | 96 | 2 | 4 |

sus 16 percent (ranging from 91 percent to 75 percent in favor). The youngest age group in Hamile is relatively unsupportive of Dagara in this respect (figure 6.3); it patterns with the group's 100 percent preference for its official ex-colonial language, English, as the medium of instruction in schools (figure 6.4). The same pattern applies, more or less clearly to all other age groups. Eighty-three percent of the thirty-one- to forty-year-olds think that Dagara should be given the same official status as English, and yet the same group objects to Dagara's use as the medium of instruction (figures 6.3 and 6.4). As for the five respondents in the forty-one- to fifty-year-old group, they are three teachers, one health worker, and one fashion designer/weaver. This group appears to show the most surprising results. All five of these respondents agreed that Dagara should be raised to the same official status as English, but when pushed further by the researcher to express their choice of language for education in the Dagara homelands, all of them rejected Dagara as a medium of instruction. Although the sample is quite small and therefore cannot be indicative of the opinion of all Dagara, these responses illustrate the high level of prestige associated with the ex-colonial official language by most Dagara literates.

Responses to later interview questions again help elucidate why the Hamile respondents appear to hold these attitudes toward their local language and English. When prompted to explain when and why they tend to mix Dagara with English, respondents associate upward social mobility with the image of a well-bred, English-Dagara bilingual. The following comment from a thirty-year-old male high school teacher confirmed the above argument: "Fo mi bɔbr kɛ nibɛ bang kɛ fo in different from them." (Translated: "The educated ones always want others to know that they are different from them.") Then the speaker argues that the only way to show one's social status is to resort to mixing Dagara with English, as in the following: "Fo mi deni a English yang a Dagara puo ka bɛ bang kɛ you are higher than them." (Translated: "As such we mix Dagara with English just to show our superiority.")

One would be tempted on the basis of the above data to argue that if at least 75 percent of respondents from Ouessa, Burkina, and 83 percent from Hamile, Ghana, agree that Dagara's status in education should be the same as French or English, then it is also expected that Dagara would be more widely sought for as a medium for education. This is clearly not the case, however, as respondents on both sides of

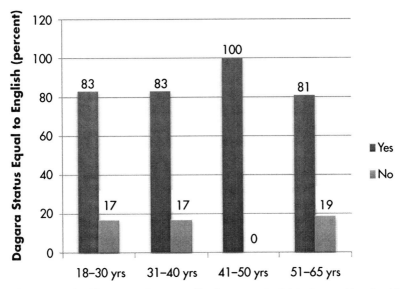

Figure 6.3 "Dagara Should Be Given the Same official Status as English in Dagara Homelands" (Hamile, Ghana)

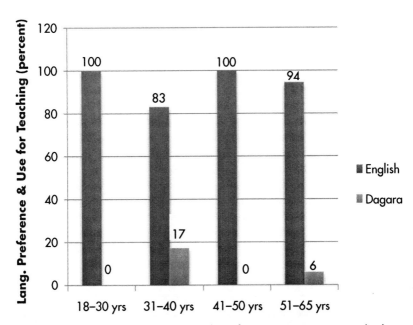

Figure 6.4 "Language Preference and Use as a Medium of Instruction in Dagara Homelands" (Hamile, Ghana)

the border appear to be in favor of widespread societal bilingualism that could be interpreted as a form of diglossia; despite obvious support for status planning for the local language, the ex-colonial languages continue to keep their exclusive "high" function in the domain of education. This presents a surprising and hitherto unreported finding that can pose a challenge to language policy planners in this region of Africa. As far as a functional approach to attitudes is concerned, it appears that most Dagara-French and Dagara-English bilingual speakers view the joint use of the two languages as more rewarding than the use of Dagara in public places. One respondent, a twenty-year-old male university student from Ouessa, Burkina, retorted for instance: "Foo kyen kpaaro zie ti piili yɛrɛ Dagara fo kon nyɛ zima zie i." (Translated: "At any Dagara social gathering, you will not be served if you start interacting with people in Dagara.") The speaker clearly points to the unconditional utility of bilingualism in the local context.

Katz's value-expressive function is another way of understanding Dagara language attitudes; as long as speakers are dissatisfied with their "individual image or self-image and personal value" (1960, 170) projected by the use of the local language, they will be ready to embrace negative attitudes toward the language. For instance, a female respondent from Ouessa asserts: "Bɛl na saa be maalia nakolia mimi yɛrɛ nia nirpɛlɛ kɛ bɛ wul bɛ minga." (Translated: "Even the illiterate Dagara try to mix Dagara with French just to show their status.")

## Conclusion and Discussion

This chapter has discussed respondents' attitudes toward the status and the use of Dagara in education in light of language contact in two Burkina-Ghana border communities in West Africa. The results teased out Dagara-French and Dagara-English bilingual speakers' overwhelmingly positive attitudes toward the status of their own language, but paradoxically showed negative attitudes toward education in the language. The pattern was particularly prevalent in responses elicited from young adults. I have argued that the likely motivations for these attitudes lie in the prestige of code-switching and code-mixing Dagara with French and English in everyday discourse. In the Dagara homelands French and English were introduced through colonization and eventually became the languages used in education and for all official programs and public forums. Because formal education is not accessible to everyone, this introduction created minority elite English- and French-speaking groups that had the means to acquire these languages. Consequently, the use of French and English words in one's discourse (Dagara) is a sign of being literate or well educated, while speaking only Dagara conveys a lower status to the speaker. From the findings reported in this chapter, it appears rather ironically that when it comes to language attitudes, status planning for the local language does not entail that Dagara is also accepted as a medium of instruction in the schools. By arguing that the joint use of English and French in bilingual discourse has a "higher value" than "pure Dagara," speakers take a strong position in favor of bilingualism. Finally, one can only agree with Adegbija that negative attitudes toward African languages seemed to have been formed and are maintained by educational policymakers who hold the belief that the promotion and use of African languages as media of instruction might "shut the proverbial window on the world" to generations of Africans (1994, 106). Some of the teachers interviewed for this chapter appear to adhere to these very beliefs. Consequently, a call for the introduction and use of African languages as media of instruction in the Dagara homeland should not ask for complete abolition of European languages in the school curricula, but rather it should advocate that the ex-colonial languages should continue to be studied together with other local languages.

## References

Adegbija, Efurosibina. 1994. *Language Attitudes in Sub-Saharan Africa: A Sociolinguistic Overview.* Bristol: Longdunn Press.

Ameya-Ekumfi, Christopher. 2002. "New Language Policy for Primary and Basic Education." *The States-man* (Accra), July 16. Available at www.thestatesmanonline.com.

Bado, Niamboue. 2009. "Bilingual Education in Burkina Faso: Where Do Parents and Teachers Stand?" Master's thesis, Ohio University. www.orthographyclearinghouse.org/images/theses/albertBado MAThesis2009.pdf.

Bodomo, Adams. 1986. "A Study of Dialectal Variation in Dagaare." Master's thesis, University of Ghana.

Chimhundu, Herbert. 2002. *Final Report, Revised: Language Policies in Africa—Intergovernmental Conference on Language Policies in Africa, Harare, Zimbabwe, 17–21 March 1997.* Paris: UNESCO. www.unesco.org/culture/ich/doc/src/00245-EN.pdf.

Fishman, Joshua A., ed. 1991. *Handbook of Language and Ethnic Identity.* Oxford: Oxford University Press.

Guerini, Frederica. 2009. "Multilingualism and Language Attitudes in Ghana: A Preliminary Study." *Ethnorêma* 4.

Katz, Daniel. 1960. "Functional Approach to the Study of Attitudes." *Public Opinion Quarterly* 24:163–204.

Kouraogo, Pierre, and Ambroise Dianda. 2008. "Education in Burkina Faso at Horizon 2025." *Journal of International Cooperation in Education* 11:23–38.

Mahama, Ibrahim. 2009. *Colonial History of Northern Ghana.* Tamale: GILLBT Printing Press.

Métuolé, Somda. 1991. *Contes Dagara du Burkina Faso.* Paris: Conseil International de Langue Française.

Okere, Theophilus, ed. 1995. *Identity and Change: Nigerian Philosophical Studies I.* Washington, DC: Council for Research in Values and Philosophy.

# 7

# Language and Education Policy in Botswana: The Case of Sebirwa

ONE TLALE BOYER AND ELIZABETH C. ZSIGA
*Georgetown University*

**THIS CHAPTER ADDRESSES** the status of the Sebirwa language in Botswana in relation to the country's language and education policy. We begin with an overview of linguistic demographics in Botswana and then turn to the specific situation of Sebirwa, presenting evidence for its marginalized, and indeed endangered, status. We then discuss how current policies on language and education in Botswana are contributing to the marginalization of all minority languages, including Sebirwa. We conclude with some success stories of language revitalization through education for other minority languages in Botswana and argue for some national-level policy changes that could aid communities in revitalizing minority languages rather than accelerating their decline. Certainly, the decline of a language cannot be reversed through government intervention and policy formulation alone, but increased government support for language documentation, as well as recognition and use of minority languages in the educational setting, can foster a sense of pride in the language and the culture of the community and can be a means for the government to affirm the acceptance and promotion of all cultures that are part of the country. Although we focus on Sebirwa, the arguments presented in this chapter are applicable to the other minority indigenous languages in Botswana that are faced with a similar plight.

## Botswana's Linguistic Demographics

Botswana is estimated to have at least twenty-nine languages (as documented at www.ethnologue.com). The most dominant indigenous language in Botswana is Setswana, a Bantu language spoken by approximately 80 percent of the population. (The term *Batswana* is used to inclusively refer to all citizens of Botswana.) English is the official national language, and Afrikaans is also spoken, especially near the South African border. The remaining twenty-six languages, about evenly divided between the Bantu and Khoisan language families, are often referred to as the minority indigenous languages. The speakers of these languages are considered to be marginalized, as their languages have no official status and their use is restricted to the home and some community cultural activities, such as religious ceremonies and *kgotla* (traditional meeting place) meetings. Many lack a standardized orthography and have limited or no written materials. Many are threatened or are critically endangered.

Some documentation and revitalization efforts are being carried out for minority languages in Botswana. Recent linguistic documentation, focused on the highly endangered Khoisan languages, is exemplified by the Research in Khoisan Studies series (most recently Witzlack-Makarevich and Ernszt 2013). Language revitalization efforts (discussed in more detail below) include Naro (Batibo 2009) and Ikalanga and Sheyeyi (Nyati-Ramahobo and Chebanne 2001). Often, the cost of carrying out the work is borne by churches, international research funders, or private donors. In some cases the work is carried out by volunteer personnel. Marginalized endangered cultures cannot rely entirely on outside resources to help remedy this situation, thus the Botswana government needs to be in the forefront of financing such efforts. Some projects have already been conducted to develop literacy in marginalized languages that can serve as models for minority languages such as Sebirwa. Revitalization for the speakers of minority indigenous languages can only come from their concerted efforts and the work of activists and language specialists, as well as support from the government on developing education materials that can not only help document the language but also be used in revitalization efforts.

We turn now to the specifics of the Sebirwa language. Sebirwa is spoken in the Bobirwa region, which includes the easternmost part of Botswana and the adjacent areas of Zimbabwe and South Africa, by the Babirwa people. It is a Sotho-Tswana language, classified in the Guthrie S30 Zone, a group of languages spoken in southern Africa. Other languages in this category include Setswana, Setswapong, Selozi, Northern Sotho, Shekgalaghari, and Sesotho. These languages have varying degrees of mutual intelligibility.

There is a great deal of variability in terms of the reported population of native speakers of Sebirwa. Chebanne (2000) estimates that there are 20,000 Sebirwa speakers in Botswana, Zimbabwe, and South Africa combined. Chebanne and Nyati-Ramahobo (2003) estimate the number of Sebirwa speakers in Botswana as 11,633 based on Botswana's 2001 census data, whereas Batibo, Mathangwane, and Tsonope (2003) put the number at 12,500. Another estimate—from Lewis, Simons, and Fennig (2013)—puts the number at 15,000 speakers in Botswana. Language data from Botswana's 2011 population census are not yet available. Census data can be hard to interpret in any case, because the language data are self-reported. As Batibo (2002) points out, for marginalized languages in Botswana ethnicity is often conflated with spoken language: People may want to identify with their ethnic group, but they do not necessarily speak the language of their ethnic group. The reverse may also occur, where speakers of a language may deny the use of their ethnic language, but claim that they speak the national language because the latter is viewed as the language of socioeconomic power.

The population of Sebirwa speakers is even harder to establish for South Africa, where Sebirwa is characterized with other languages as an "unclassified" variety of Northern Sotho. The situation is not any clearer for Sebirwa in Zimbabwe. This country is estimated to have twenty-two languages (Magwa 2010), but Sebirwa is not listed as one of them; it is listed instead as Sotho, a loose label for Sotho-Tswana speech communities in Zimbabwe. Lewis, Simons, and Fennig (2013) list Sebirwa as a dialect of Kalanga in Zimbabwe.

It is possible that one of the reasons we do not see Sebirwa listed as a threatened language by the endangered languages projects is the unclear situation with the number of speakers. An independent language census is needed to determine an accurate population of actual speakers of the language.

## Is Sebirwa an Endangered Language?

In this chapter we claim that Sebirwa is endangered. If we are to argue for the urgency of revitalizing Sebirwa, we first need to ascertain that the language's vitality is threatened. Without having conducted a survey of the language situation among the speakers of the language, we find that this becomes a difficult question to answer. For answers, we look to projects that focus on keeping records of endangered languages, the definition of an endangered language, and our research experiences among the Babirwa. We carried out fieldwork in the Bobirwa region of Botswana, conducting interviews and recording acoustic and articulatory data, in July 2012. We focused on Molalatau Village, about twenty kilometers east of the town of Bobonong and forty kilometers west of the South African border. Molalatau has a population of a few hundred people, almost all ethnic Babirwa. The results of our phonetic and phonological data collection are reported elsewhere (e.g., Zsiga and Boyer 2014); here we focus on the sociolinguistic information we gathered.

In an attempt to answer the question of whether Sebirwa is endangered, we will first look at the data from projects that keep track of endangered languages. Two major projects are often referenced as reliable sources for the vitality of the world's languages. These projects keep records of languages whose vitality is at risk, as well as the extent of the threat to these varieties. The first one, the Endangered Languages Project (www.endangeredlanguages.com), does not list Sebirwa as an endangered language. Sebirwa is also absent from the list of at-risk languages mapped out on the *UNESCO Endangered Languages Atlas* (UNESCO 2011). The absence of a language from these projects, however, does not necessarily mean that the language is thriving. It could also be an indication that no evidence has been presented to these projects to suggest that Sebirwa is a threatened language. However, *Ethnologue* (www.ethnologue.com), which also classifies languages according to the level of threat, in fact lists Sebirwa as "vigorous," which is defined as "unstandardized [but] in vigorous use among all generations."

The next step is to address the definition of what constitutes an endangered language. There is no one method for determining the vitality of a language. The UNESCO Ad Hoc Expert Group on Endangered Languages (2003) suggests six main criteria that can be used to assess the threat or lack of threat a language faces. These need to be used collectively to determine a language's vitality.

The first criterion focuses on "intergenerational language transmission," which refers to whether the language is being passed on from parents to children. From our sampling of Sebirwa in Molalatau, we noted that the language was used by the "parental generation," but not by the younger children. Among the children who did use Sebirwa, they often replaced Sebirwa words with Setswana and used a

Setswana sentence structure. One person we interviewed for the study expressed concerns that she did not speak Sebirwa and told us in code-switched Setswana and Sebirwa that

> Nna ha ke bue Sebirwa. Le ka bua le bakgekolo, ke bona ba se itseng.

> (I don't speak Sebirwa, but you can talk to the elderly, they are the ones who know it.)

This sentence is mostly Setswana, but it uses the Sebirwa form of the negative (/ha/ rather than /xa/) and the Sebirwa term for the elderly, /bakgekolo/.

Often, when we told a participant that we were looking for native speakers of Sebirwa, they would back out of the study and recommend an elderly relative. In the end, all the participants in our study were fifty years of age or older. Additionally, most speakers said that their use of the language was restricted to the home and traditional activities. In this sense, then, Sebirwa is considered definitely endangered.

The second factor involves determining the "absolute number of speakers." As mentioned above, the exact number of Sebirwa speakers cannot be clearly determined because speakers often want to associate with the language of socioeconomic power, or some say they speak the language when they are in fact referring to cultural identity. Most estimates, however, place the number of speakers at about 15,000 or less, out of a population of just over 2 million for the entire country (www.cso.gov.bw). This number, when considered in isolation from other factors, seems to suggest that the language is not endangered. The third factor outlined by UNESCO is the "proportion of speakers within the total population." For Sebirwa this is hard to determine for the same reasons stated above. However, based on what we found, it would be safe to assume that the language is not out of harm's way because we do not have 100 percent use by all the people who belong to the Babirwa community. Many of the older speakers we interviewed indicated that their grandchildren spoke very little or no Sebirwa.

The fourth factor outlined by UNESCO focuses on "shifts in domains of language use." Setswana is used in an official capacity and in education throughout Botswana, which marginalizes all other languages to varying degrees. The situation for Sebirwa is further exacerbated by the similarity with Setswana, and the extent of code-switching, especially among the younger speakers. As exemplified by the excerpt above, many speakers intermix Setswana and Sebirwa lexical items, which are usually cognate, so that even in domains where speakers would report that they are using Sebirwa, there is a strong Setswana influence.

The fifth factor is the "response to new domains and media" by the users of the language. There is some good news for Sebirwa here, as we see some Babirwa youth and cultural activists using the language on the internet in order to promote the culture. But there is no use of Sebirwa in other domains, such as television, radio, and print media. The sixth and last factor deals with the "availability of materials for language education and literacy." Sebirwa does not have an established orthography at this point, and literary materials are almost nonexistent, so on this aspect the language is highly endangered.

Based on the suggested set of criteria outlined in the UNESCO document and on our observations and comments from the Sebirwa community in Molalatau, we can conclude that the vitality of the Sebirwa language is at risk. The threat is further exacerbated by the lack of any documentation and literacy materials on the language. Other linguists have also come to the same conclusion: The language is under threat due to assimilation into Setswana (Chebanne 2000; Batibo and Seloma 2006).

## Botswana's Education Language Policy

Although English is Botswana's official language, Setswana, which is the native or second language of the majority of the population, is known as the national language, and is often used in an official capacity and as a lingua franca by speakers of the other minority languages in Botswana.

Currently, in Botswana, only English and Setswana are taught in public schools. These two languages are used as media of instruction and are also offered as subjects as part of the curriculum. From primary grades 1 to 3, all instruction for all Botswana citizen children is conducted in Setswana, irrespective of their native language, so that even children who are speakers of other languages are taught in Setswana. From primary grade 4, English takes over as the next medium of instruction, whereas Setswana is then taught as a compulsory subject for all Batswana citizens. No other languages are offered in the public school system. In some private schools other languages are offered; they are usually foreign languages such as French or Mandarin.

Much research has been done to show the importance of using the mother tongue as a medium of instruction in the early years of a child's education. In line with these well-established findings, UNESCO has made attempts to advocate for and promote early childhood mother-tongue education programs around the globe. In Botswana, however, no effort has been made to develop an early native-language education program. Currently, with the exception of Setswana, no other indigenous languages are used in the public education system in Botswana. In all cases where other languages are taught, it is through the efforts of nongovernmental organizations and community involvement, and it is also in nonformal educational settings. Although it is crucial that the community be involved in the preservation of languages, government support is also essential because the community often lacks the resources to develop materials and train the relevant personnel.

## The Predicament of Marginalized Languages

The plight of Botswana's minority languages and cultures has had a lot of attention drawn to it through studies and recommendations made by scholars and activists in Botswana (Reteng 2008; Batibo and Seloma 2006; Nyati-Ramahobo and Chebanne 2001) in past decades, but none of them have resulted in a change in language policy. The main reason put forward by those in Botswana's government who are opposed to the idea of including other languages in public schools has always been that the financial costs of such an endeavor would be prohibitive, considering the number of languages spoken in the country. All alternative ideas that are less costly have been ignored.

One suggestion for a policy change was put forward by Batibo, Mathangwane, and Tsonope (2003): offer Ikalanga in the school system. This language ranks second to Setswana in terms of the number of speakers as well as in the development of literary materials. It is a well-documented language, with an established orthography and literature, and therefore the costs associated with introducing it in the schools would not be so restrictive. An added advantage for Ikalanga is that before Botswana's independence, it was used by missionaries in the region as a medium of instruction, but its use in schools was discontinued in postindependent Botswana (Nyati-Ramahobo and Chebanne 2001). The government's response to this recommendation has been the excuse that introducing Ikalanga would result in speakers of other languages advocating that their tongues also be introduced in the school system. The government has not considered the positive aspect: By allowing the use of Ikalanga in the public school system, the government would make its willingness to recognize and promote other cultures evident, and the speakers of other languages would view this as a step in the right direction, thus enhancing Botswana's unification of its varied cultures.

Other recommendations that have been put forward have been suggestions that are as simple as teaching about "the histories, cultures, traditions, norms, and values of all ethnic groups in Botswana" (Reteng 2008, 8), so that no one culture is promoted at the expense of others.

The arguments that are put forward by the opponents of the reform in language education policy seem to be circular ("we can't do it because we can't do it") and make no attempts at any sort of compromise. Furthermore, there seems to be the ill-perceived notion that promoting other cultures and languages will jeopardize Botswana's national unity, which has been built around using Setswana as a unifying factor for all Batswana. To some extent not changing the status quo has the opposite effect, resulting in speakers of other languages feeling marginalized. UNESCO (2007, 17) promotes mother-tongue language education (MLE) because one of its many advantanges is that "government support for strong MLE programmes demonstrates to all citizens that minority languages, and those who speak the languages, are valued."

## Education Programs for Indigenous Languages

As noted above, the main reason put forward as the explanation for why other languages cannot be used as the medium of instruction in public education in Botswana is the financial burden of such an exercise. Although it is true that such a policy has financial implications, this does not mean that no action should be undertaken to preserve the other languages of Botswana. Unfortunately, for some of the languages, the situation does not allow the issue to be put on hold as they face the threat of extinction. It is these languages that are in dire need and require our immediate attention. A language policy that develops acquisition and literary programs for endangered languages should be made a priority. Botswana has several programs that have already been developed and have been carried out by nongovernmental bodies, and they can serve as models for the other languages. Some of these programs are described in this section.

The Naro Language Project in Botswana is often cited as an exemplary case of a successful language development effort. This project was initiated by the Kuru Development Trust and the Reformed Church, and it is aimed at documenting and revitalizing the Naro language. It has been conducted with efforts from missionaries, linguists, linguist-missionaries, and members of the speech community. Naro is a Khoisan language spoken in western Botswana, near the border with Namibia. Like other Khoisan languages, its vitality was greatly threatened. Today its vitality has been enhanced through the project. Work on the Naro Language Project has involved documenting the Naro language, grammar, and stories as well as developing literacy programs with educational materials for both children and adults. Preschools in the area teach the language, and many youth have joined the literacy classes. These programs have all been community efforts with very little, if any, involvement from the Botswana government. The project is credited with developing a sense of pride among the speakers of the language and also with attracting interest from other marginalized groups in the area (Batibo 2009).

Other nongovernmental efforts to develop language literacy for marginalized people in Botswana have been the development of literacy materials for Ikalanga and Sheyeyi (Nyati-Ramahobo and Chebanne 2001). These projects were possible as a result of financial support from UNESCO and collaborative work between the University of Botswana, the Kamanakao Association (which aims at preserving and promoting the culture and language of the Wayeyi people), and the Society for the Promotion of Ikalanga Language. Through these projects, literacy materials have been developed to meet the basic needs of the speakers of the languages. In the case of Ikalanga the literacy material development has focused on developing a program that would assist the speakers to gain literacy in their own language for their daily social and economic activities. Ikalanga is not considered a highly threatened language. For the Wayeyi people, conversely, the materials were more along the lines of preservation and revitalization because the speakers felt that the Shiyeyi language is highly endangered. Both of these projects have resulted in the development of curriculum resources for literacy for the language and training personnel who would be involved in the literacy programs (Nyati-Ramahobo and Chebanne 2001).

The Naro Language Project and the projects for Shiyeyi and Ikalanga have been very useful in laying the foundation for the development of literacy programs on indigenous languages. The results of these projects can be adapted to develop materials for other minority languages, so that the speakers of those languages may become literate in their own varieties and the languages will be revitalized.

## Oral Tradition as a Tool for Language Revitalization

Another strategy that can be used to revitalize at-risk languages through the school system is to use the oral tradition genre. Oral tradition has long played a role in passing on the culture and history of societies around the world. It was the traditional mode of teaching for the African family and community before the introduction of literary texts. In some instances, this is still a viable way of transmitting knowledge. However, the use of oral tradition has declined tremendously as more and more children have begun enrolling in formal schools and spending time away from home. Oral tradition is a valuable resource that can be incorporated into the school system. The absence of textbooks and orthographies therefore does not need to be a stumbling block in passing on language and culture to young children. This oral tradition can be included in the school structure, where time is set aside for students to be given a chance to practice their language variety with local native speakers through storytelling and other genres. Seeing their dialect incorporated in the school system in this manner will help foster a sense of pride for the child native speakers of the language and allow them to enhance their vocabulary and mastery of the grammatical structure of their language.

The employment of the oral mode to teach language for revitalization is not a new strategy, for it has been recommended by other linguists and educators and has been used in several other situations. Heredia and Francis (1997) point out that the oral tradition genre is an important way for learners to acquire new words and to learn the grammatical structures and the cultural aspects of the indigenous language. The importance of oral traditions for marginalized indigenous languages is affirmed by Leonard (2007, 117) in her study of Deg Xinag, a Northern Athabaskan language spoken in Alaska. Leonard points out "that speakers may use the term *xinag* (language), to refer to the vast stores of knowledge passed down to succeeding generations via the power of breath in oral traditions." Another writer, Adegoju (2008), gives examples of the elementary school he attended, where time was set aside for students to engage in storytelling, poetry, and other genres in order to enhance the status of Yorùbá. He reminisces about how "we would sing folk songs, and tell folk tales and recite lyrical poems in Yorùbá that touch on the value system of the people" (21–22). He goes on to discuss how "in order to expose one to the Yorùbá cultural belief system, we were taught some popular Yorùbá proverbs, which incorporates an African value system. We were also taught the elaborate greetings among the Yorùbá that span every time of the day, period of the year, occasion, condition, event, occupation, or vocation" (21–22).

## Conclusion

In this chapter we have outlined the Botswana language policy and shown how it alienates Batswana of other cultural and language backgrounds. We argued that Sebirwa's vitality, like that of most indigenous languages in Botswana, is endangered, as the language is being assimilated by Setswana. There are currently no literacy materials that can be used for revitalization efforts, but we suggest that oral tradition be incorporated into the education system as an initial step to help revitalize the language and culture of the Babirwa people. A second step toward the inclusion of other languages would be the development of literary materials in other indigenous languages. There are other indigenous languages in the country that already have literacy programs that serve as models.

Much has been written about the importance of preserving indigenous languages and of empowering the speakers of these languages. The reasons put forward include preserving the culture of the speakers, developing a sense of pride in their language and culture, and ensuring that these speakers do not feel marginalized by the larger society of which they are a part. To merely state that communities have the linguistic right to freely use their language in any context is not enough, however. The government needs to take steps to ensure that these linguistic rights are asserted through the inclusion of other languages in the country's language and education policies. It is only through the inclusion of other languages in education, government, the media, and other socioeconomic activities that Botswana can truly assert itself as a nation that reflects unity in diversity.

## References

Adegoju, Adeyemi. 2008. "Empowering African Languages: Rethinking the Strategies." *Journal of Pan African Studies* 2, no. 3: 14–32.

Batibo, Herman. 2002. "Integration and Ethnic Identity: A Critical Dilemma for the Minority Language Speakers of Botswana." In *Minorities in the Millennium: Perspectives from Botswana*, edited by I. N. Mazonde. Gaborone: Lightfoot.

———. 2009. "Language Documentation as a Strategy for the Empowerment of the Minority Languages of Africa." In *Selected Proceedings of the 38th Annual Conference on African Linguistics: Linguistic Theory and African Language Documentation*, edited by Masangu Matondo, Fiona McLaughlin, and Eric Potsdam. Somerville MA: Cascadilla Proceedings Project. Available at www.lingref.com.

Batibo, Herman M., Joyce T. Mathangwane, and Joseph Tsonope. 2003. *A Study of the Third Language Teaching in Botswana. (Consultancy Report.)* Gaborone: Associated Printers.

Batibo, Herman M., and Pearl Seloma. 2006. "Sebirwa and Setswapong as Distinct Linguistic and Cultural Entities." *Marang: Journal of Language and Literature* 16:3–22.

Chebanne, Anderson. 2000. "The Sebirwa Language: A Synchronic and Diachronic Account." *Pula: Botswana Journal of African Studies* 14:186–95.

Chebanne, Anderson, and Lydia Nyati-Ramahobo. 2003. "Language Knowledge and Language Use in Botswana." Proceedings of the CSO: 2001 Population and Housing Census Dissemination Seminar, Gaborone.

Heredia, Armando, and Norbert Francis. 1997. "Coyote as Reading Teacher: Oral Tradition in the Classroom." In *Teaching Indigenous Languages*, edited by Jon Reyhner. Flagstaff: Northern Arizona University.

Leonard, Beth. 2007. "Deg Xinag Oral Traditions: Reconnecting Indigenous Language and Education through Traditional Narratives." PhD thesis, University of Alaska, Fairbanks.

Lewis, M. Paul, Gary F. Simons, and Charles D. Fennig, eds. 2013. *Ethnologue: Languages of the World*, 17th ed. Dallas: SIL International. Also available at www.ethnologue.com.

Magwa, Wiseman. 2010. *Language Planning and Policy for Mass Education: A Case for Zimbabwe.* Cape Town: Centre for Advanced Studies of African Society.

Nyati-Ramahobo, Lydia, and Anderson Chebanne. 2001. "The Development of Minority Languages for Adult Literacy in Botswana: Towards Cultural Diversity." Paper presented at International Literacy Conference, Cape Town.

Reteng: The Multicultural Coalition of Botswana. 2008. "Alternative Report Submitted to the UN Human Rights Council." Gaborone.

UNESCO. 2007. *Advocacy Kit for Promoting Multilingual Education: Including the Excluded.* Bangkok: UNESCO.

———. 2011. *UNESCO Endangered Languages Atlas.* Paris: UNESCO. http://unesdoc.unesco.org /images/0019/001924/192416e.pdf.

UNESCO Ad Hoc Expert Group on Endangered Languages. 2003. *Language Vitality and Endangerment.* Paris: UNESCO. http://www.unesco.org/culture/ich/doc/src/00120-EN.pdf.

Witzlack-Makarevich, Alena, and Marina Ernszt, eds. 2013. *Khoisan Languages and Linguistics: Proceedings of the 3rd International Symposium—Research in Khoisan Studies.* Vol. 29. Series editor Ranier Voßen. Frankfurt: Rüdiger-Köppe Verlag.

Zsiga, Elizabeth C., and One Boyer. 2014. "The Sound Patterns of Sebirwa: Documentation and Some Theoretical Implications." Paper presented at 45th Annual Conference on African Linguistics, University of Kansas, Lawrence, April.

# 8

## Ethnic Language Shift among the Nao People of Ethiopia

SAMSON SEID
*Dilla University*

ETHIOPIA IS THE HOME of more than eighty-five linguistically and ethnically distinct groups, most of which have not been scientifically studied or systematically documented. As is true in every multilingual situation, some Ethiopian languages, such as Amharic and Oromiffa, are highly developed and widespread, but some minority languages, such as Nao, are confined to a specific place.

The majority of the ethnic groups are almost completely oral cultures with no written literature in their own respective languages. This means that the ethnic groups transmit their indigenous knowledge, wisdom accumulated through ages, core values, and principles underlying their cultures only orally or ritually.

The few studies of Ethiopian minority languages have almost exclusively focused on the description of the languages' grammar. The one linguistic work on the Nao language published in recent decades is a "phonological sketch" (Yilma 1994). Although describing the structural properties of a language is not a problem in itself and has been one of the central concerns of linguistic research, the scope of contemporary linguistics is not only confined to descriptions of languages' grammar but also includes sociolinguistics, which studies language in relation to society. Sociolinguistic studies, and in particular language contact investigations, are scarcely available on Ethiopian languages, and Nao is no exception. Hence, this chapter intends to fill this gap.

Nao is one of the minority languages spoken in Ethiopia, and minority languages in general are assumed to be threatened by extinction. However, being a minority language does not invariably mean that the language is endangered, or that its speakers are faced with a language shift (Fasold 1984, 217; Brenzinger 1997, 276). It is thus not appropriate to say that Nao is either an endangered or a safe language simply by virtue of its being spoken next to the dominant language in the region, Kefinoono, or based on its lack of official status, or based on the demographic conditions (geographical location, numerical strength) of the group, or so on. Some factors may favor language maintenance, and others may favor a language shift in a given speech community. These types of factors are investigated in the present chapter, which focuses on the Nao ethnic people settled in the Keficho community.

## The Language and the People

Nao (also known as "Nayi") is an Omotic language of the Afro-Asiatic language family spoken in western Ethiopia. The 2007 census listed 7,188 speakers, with 1,137 identified as monolinguals.

Most of the speakers of the language live in two separate areas. The largest group lives in the Decha district of the Kaffa Zone. The nearest city to their region is Bonga. A few live in Dulkuma village in the Shoa Bench district, and some in the Sheko district, having moved there in the period 1976–77 as a result of conflicts between local feudal lords and the military government (Yilma 2002, 4). The language is notable for its retroflex consonants (Yilma 1994), a striking feature shared with closely related Dizi, Sheko, and nearby (but not closely related) Bench. Nao, together with the Dizi and Sheko languages, is part of a cluster of languages variously called Maji or Dizoid.

## Language Use among the Nao

One way of discussing the state of language maintenance and shifts is to investigate whether there is a movement from the habitual use of one language to another in certain domains. In other words, when a domain hitherto reserved for an indigenous language begins to be "invaded" by another tongue, a language shift can be said to be in progress, whereas separating using the language in different contexts represents a case of stable bilingualism or language maintenance (Fasold 1984, 211). The intrusion of a dominant language into the domains of an old one, leading to its total replacement, does not take place overnight. The gradual replacement of a minority language can take place over several generations. The data and analysis presented below were taken from different age groups: the older generation, fifty years of age and older; the middle generation, thirty to fifty years; young adults, twenty to thirty years; adolescents, ten to twenty years; and children, up to ten years. This is an indispensable diagnostic tool for forecasting the stability of the language. If there are speakers from every age group, then the language will not die out for at least another forty to fifty years.

### Language Use at Home

Because the home setting is believed to be the last stronghold where a minority language can be maintained and thus not become a total loss, the intrusion of the new (dominant) language in this sphere portends the worst situation for the survival of the old one (Downes 1998). The data, which were obtained from interviews and personal observation, demonstrate that Nao and Kefinoono are both used at home, with the former being the dominant language at home among elder groups. Conversely, where the interaction is between children and parents, the medium of interaction is solely Kefinoono. Children are frequently socially exposed to predominant speakers of Kefinoono, both in and out of school. Parents have said that the main reason why they use Kefinoono at home with their children is that it is the medium of instruction in school. The most important factor influencing language use at home is the age of the participants in the interaction. If the speakers are among the older age groups, they tend to use Nao rather than Kefinoono. When the participants are middle aged and young people, they tend to choose Kefinoono instead of Nao. Thus, the older generations present a more traditional pattern of social interaction than the younger ones. Older persons use Nao more often than younger ones, who often use Kefinoono as their first language. Consequently, one can argue from this that Nao is in actual jeopardy in the home setting among the younger generations.

### Language Use in Neighborhoods

The neighborhood is one of the informal or intimate domains deemed crucial for minority-language maintenance (Baker 1996; Fishman 2001). In fact, in the context of the Nao-speaking community in the Decha district, the neighborhood is predominantly occupied by Kaficho people. Regardless of their age differences, most Nao community members argue that Kefinoono rather than Nao is used to a remarkable degree. In the neighborhood, Nao seems to give way to the dominant tongue, Kefinoono.

Some speakers of Nao explain the decline of the mother tongue and the increasing influence of Kefinoono in terms of neighborhood interactions. A considerable number of Kefinoono speakers are not capable of speaking Nao. Conversely, the Nao people are proficient in speaking Kefinoono. So to accommodate the Kaficho people, the Nao people are being expected to acquire Kefinoono. Therefore, most of the traditional meetings that would once have required the use of Nao are now totally replacing it with Kefinoono. From these two settings (domains), we can understand that there is a shift occurring from relatively stable bilingualism in the home setting toward a less stable bilingualism in the neighborhood setting.

### Language Use in Places of Worship

It is generally assumed that a language will have a better chance of maintenance when it is used in the religious activities of its respective speakers (Fishman 1990; Baker 1996). But my findings indicate that the Nao language has no use in the religious activities of the Nao community. As I was told by my informants, the introduction of modern religious institutions (i.e., those of Christianity), along with the construction of churches in the area, engulfed traditional religious institutions, which were mainly using the Nao language. In addition, the majority of the Christian priests and deacons speak Kefinoono and Amharic. Hence, every religious service would be held in either Kefinoono or Amharic.

### Language Use in the Marketplace

The market setting is known as a place where heterogeneous peoples from diverse linguistic groups gather to exchange commodities. When these people of diverse linguistic backgrounds meet, the question is which language is used in their interactions. The data obtained from my interviews and observations reveal that the Kefinoono language is dominant for communication in the marketplace. It is possible to say that Kefinoono is the lingua franca of the market setting, where people from diverse linguistic backgrounds communicate. The main reason for the use of Kefinoono is that most of the people who speak a minority language also speak at least one dominant language, in this case Kefinoono. Conversely, speakers of the dominant language are less likely to acquire minority languages.

### Language Use in Schools

Schools are believed to be one of the main agents for spreading languages (Fishman 1985). The data obtained from my interview and research observations with school-children show that there is no room for the use of the Nao language at all in school. The school is largely filled by speakers of Kefinoono.

All the schoolchildren interviewed were monolingual speakers of Kefinoono, even though they had Nao family backgrounds. None responded with any level of skill in the Nao language. Similarly, Yilma (1994, 4) also showed that in Decha, young people no longer speak the language. In the classroom situation, children were being taught in Kefinoono. Kefinoono is used in such locales for two basic reasons. First, Kefinoono is the official language of the school offices and is the medium of instruction, at the primary level, as well as a school subject, up to grade 4. Second, most teachers as well as staff members are native speakers of Kefinoono. The observed speech behaviors in the classrooms and on the playgrounds are thus the result of these factors.

### Language Use in the Workplace

As regards the administrative/workplace sphere, based on observations in different offices in the Decha district, I found exclusive use of Kefinoono and Amharic, whereas Nao was not used. The former but not the latter have been given official status in the administrative sphere. Some elders explained that Nao had been used in some traditional institutions, such as those dealing with arbitrations, and at local meetings. However, these traditional institutions are not used often in the present situation due to the expansion of the modern court system, health institutions, and various governmental offices, which require the use of Kefinoono. In general, then, Kefinoono is used in both formal and informal settings.

### Language Use in the Media

New areas for language use emerge as community living conditions change. The Nao language enjoys widespread use by the broadcast media. A community-based FM radio station broadcasts three times a week but only for an hour.

### Language Use for Various Functions

The only functions in which speakers reported relatively dominant use of Nao is when dreaming and getting angry. And even there, the interference of Kefinoono is still noteworthy. Conversely, Nao and Kefinoono are used equally when people count, sing, and pray. It needs to be remembered that these domains apply only to the older generations, whereas the use of Nao is not observed among the younger generations at all.

## Language Shifts in Nao

The Nao people in the Decha district of the Kaffa Zone have maintained their own culture, tradition, and language for several centuries. They have maintained their own cultural values in spite of the strong influence of the surrounding Omotic people and some Cushitic-speaking peoples. However, at the present time the Nao people are suffering and losing their cultural values and ethnic identity due to the influence of the surrounding community.

My findings indicate that most Nao people are monolingual. They speak only Kefinoono as a means of communication. Because the Decha district is currently governed predominantly by the Keficho people, the Nao people have found it necessary to learn to speak languages other than their mother tongue. Due to the excessive influence of the surrounding Omotic, particularly from Kefinoono speakers, many Nao people have become monolingual Kefinoono speakers. As in the typical language contact situation, language socialization causes the language with the greater role or position to dominate the weaker minority language. Nao has no writing system and no level of standardization, and it is clearly endangered.

## Factors Accelerating Language Shift

Language shift is very difficult to impose from without. Direct attempts by external forces to suppress a language may not be successful for the simple reason that people resist such pressure. Displacing a community's indigenous language is equivalent to displacing its deep system of belief. And even when individuals consent to assimilation, it is enormously difficult to give up one's native language. Languages can die, however, in a more complex and gradual way, through the assimilation of their speakers into other cultures.

The lion's share of responsibility for a language shift is within the language communities of the Nao themselves. No doubt these changes frequently take place in reaction to the external pressures that weaken the bond that holds communities together. Ultimately, however, the speakers themselves are responsible, through their attitudes and choices, for what happens to their native language. Families choose to speak the language only in certain limited domains such as the home. Many community elders decline to promote Nao and accommodate using Kefinoono in formal and informal domains. Such decisions are not made in a vacuum, however, and they may not be deliberate. The data gathered for this chapter, based on observations in the community, illustrate some of the key factors involved in this language shift.

### Economic Factors

Economics has been stated to be the most prominent factor affecting language shifts in Nao communities. One of the most common factors that lead a community to shift from one language to another is that the acquired language is thought to be economically beneficial by its adoptive community of speakers (Holmes 1992, 65–66). In line with such arguments, the Nao people acquired Kefinoono so as to accommodate the Keficho in order to obtain jobs and education. And because Kefinoono is being used for educational and administrative purposes, the Nao are becoming more and more inclined to use Kefinoono. The linguistic group in a lower economic condition may thus tend to abandon its linguistic tradition in favor of another dominant language.

### Demographic Factors and the Settlement Pattern of the Nao

For the members of an ethnic group, living in their native homeland is important for preserving their language. The prevalence of this factor, in combination with several others, has preserved many indigenous Ethiopian languages. Conversely, resettlement, especially when it is forced, is a negative factor; for some languages, it has had devastating consequences, and it has been unfavorable for the Nao people.

Currently, the Nao live in two separated areas. The largest group live in the Decha district of the Kaffa Zone. The nearest city in their region is Bonga, which is the capital of Kaffa. A few Nao people live in Dulkauma village in the Shoa Bench district, and some live in the Sheko district of the Bench-Maji Zone.

As regards the historical origin of the Nao people, not many written documents have been transmitted to the present generations. However, using oral history information and books by travelers and ethnographers, it is possible to reconstruct the origin of the Nao people. On the basis of these records, it is possible to say that the Nao people came to the present area as a result of movement from an earlier homeland in the Bench-Maji area. The Nao were forced to move to the Decha district in the period 1976–77 as a result of conflict between the government and local feudal lords (Yilma 2002, 4). In addition, a large proportion of the population of the country generally migrates from one locality to another and to the different corners of the country in search of work and a better life.

Once the Nao settled permanently in the Keficho area, where Kefinoono is the predominant language, both ethnic groups chose integration rather than segregation. This has clearly been manifested in their marriage custom and traditions, so the Nao are being integrated with the Keficho community over the course of time. One of the consequences of the Nao's in-migration has been the emergence of language contact, and thus the members of the Nao community are almost unavoidably shifting toward the use of Kefinoono.

## Language and Cultural Contacts of the Nao with Keficho Communities

Language contact, or contact between different linguistic groups, of course is not a recent phenomenon; it dates back to the earliest times of human history. In ancient times contact between languages required some degree of physical contact between two or more linguistic groups—for instance, via migration, state formation, trade, or pilgrimage. Such contact is assumed to be as old as human history for the fundamental reason that nature does not provide or satisfy all human needs or desires in a language group's immediate surroundings. People have been in continuous contact with each other as they have addressed their various material needs and nonmaterial desires. Such contacts can be either peaceful or violent, but in the process people have always brought their various sociocultural identities, deliberately or accidentally, into contact, and language contact has been an inevitable part of this comprehensive process. And the more contact there is with other cultures and other languages, the more vulnerable a given ethnically based language may become.

Although language contact does not directly lead to language endangerment, it may severely affect the attitude of a given community or its population toward its own language. The Keficho have a written language that is the bearer of a powerful traditional belief system, a large population, a complex civilization with a long recorded history, and a technologically more complex culture. In comparison, the Nao live in a smaller area and have fewer speakers, and their history is unwritten. In this situation the Nao are more influenced by the more "developed" Kefinoono language, which has led to the partial or complete adoption of much of the culture and language of the Keficho people by the Nao, who in the process have lost much, if not all, of their native language.

The cultural proximity between the Nao and Keficho peoples is another factor that favors the language shift from Nao to Kefinoono. With this regard, Baker (1996, 45) suggests that cultural dissimilarity between groups that are in contact favors language maintenance, whereas cultural similarity may facilitate a language shift. The Nao and Keficho communities have very similar marriage customs, funeral ceremonies, traditional rituals, and religious beliefs, among other similarities. In such a situation where there is a close cultural affinity between minority and dominant groups, a language shift is more likely to happen from the minority (Nao) to the dominant (Keficho). Thus, over a long history of contact between the Nao and the Keficho, the Nao have adopted many customs and traditions from the Keficho people. Nao informants explained that the traditional cultural system of the Nao has shifted to that of the Keficho people. And this shift in culture has been accompanied by a shift in language.

### Education
From the time of their establishment up until 1991, Ethiopian schools used Amharic as the medium of instruction. But after the fall of the Derge regime in 1991, different languages were introduced. Today, in the Kaffa Zone, the medium of instruction for grades 1–4 is Kefinoono. Moreover, Kefinoono is taught as a subject in grades 5 through 8. In the Decha district, Nao children attend schools where they are taught in Kefinoono. After they complete their elementary school grades, these children move to the neighboring town of Bonga to continue their education. In most of the secondary schools, English is used as the medium of instruction, and both Kefinoono and Amharic are taught as subjects.

The effect of this educational situation on the Nao children, and thus the future of the language, is clear: Children speak Kefinoono and adopt it as their first language. At the present time, the use of Nao is limited to the elders of the community, and they hardly communicate with their children using Nao. Among the Nao, most children do not understand even words in Nao. Therefore, this means that the language shift has created a generation gap; the younger generations do not connect with their historical heritage, but adapt themselves to the new language and culture.

### The Medium of Social Services
Throughout the region, social services are provided using the regional language of the government. If the Nao people want to access social services—such as the judiciary system, health services, or government offices—they need to use either Kefinoono or Amharic. Again, this situation influences the Nao people to abandon their language.

## Conclusion

The Nao people have experienced a language shift. Due to the excessive influence of the surrounding Cushitic- and Semitic-speaking peoples, the Nao are now becoming monolingual Kefinoono speakers, with the Nao language continuing to exist only as a substratum. The intense and extended form of the Nao people's migration has played a significant role in this language shift. Because the Nao people are currently governed under the government of the Kaffa Zone, they have found it necessary to learn to speak the dominant languages rather than their mother tongue in order to benefit from the opportunities that these majority languages afford. Therefore, the Nao have already adopted Kefinoono as their language and are abandoning the use of Nao. Among those who send their children to school, there is strong pressure to use Kefinoono (and to some extent Amharic), which serves as the medium of instruction for Nao children. It is also the language of all social service offices. Most children from Nao families speak Kefinoono as their first language. This continuous language shift among the Nao has again resulted in a generation gap. Members of the younger generation have abandoned using their own language and maintaining their culture. As a result, the Nao people, who are already intermixed with the groups of Kefinoono speakers through intermarriage and other social practices, feel only a loose or insignificant attachment to their ethnic identity. Nao as a language and as a culture is no longer being transmitted to and no longer being absorbed by the next generations.

## References

Baker, Colin. 1996. *Foundation of Bilingual Education and Bilingualism*, 2nd ed. Clevedon, UK: Multiligual Matters.

Brenzinger, Matthias. 1997. *Language Contact and Displacement*. In *The Handbook of Sociolinguistics*, edited by Florian Columns. Oxford: Blackwell.

Central Statistical Authority. 2008. *Summary and Statistical Report of the 2007 Population and Housing Census*. Addis Ababa: Central Statistical Authority.

Downes, John. 1998. *Language and Society*, 2nd ed. Cambridge: Cambridge University Press.

Fasold, Ralph. 1984. *The Sociolinguistics of Society*. Oxford: Basil Blackwell.

Fishman, Joshua. 1985. "Language Maintenance and Ethnicity." In *The Rise and Fall of the Ethnic Revival: Perspective on Language and Ethnicity*, edited by Joshua Fishman. Berlin: Mouton.

———. 1989. *Language and Ethnicity in Minority Sociolinguistic Perspective*. Philadelphia: Multilingual Matters.

———. 1990. "What Is Reversing Language Shift (RLS) and How Can It Succeed?" *Journal of Multilingual and Multicultural Development* 11, nos. 1–2: 5–36.

———. 2001. *Can Threatened Languages Be Saved?* Philadelphia: Multilingual Matters.

Holmes, Janet. 1992. *An Introduction to Sociolinguistics*. London: Longman.

Paulston, Christina Bratt. 1994a. "Multilingualism and Language Policies." In *Linguistic Minorities in Multilingual Settings*, edited by Christina Bratt Paulston. Amsterdam: John Benjamins.

———. 1994b. "Social Factors in Language Maintenance and Shift." In *Linguistic Minorities in Multilingual Settings*, edited by Christina Bratt Paulston. Amsterdam: John Benjamins.

Yilma, Aklilu. 1994. "A Sketch of the Nayi Grammar." *SLLE Linguistic Reports* 16:1–20.

———. 2002. *Sociolinguistic Survey Report of the Nayi Language of Ethiopia*. Dallas: SIL International.

# 9

## The Role of Language and Culture in Ethnic Identity Maintenance: The Case of the Gujarati Community in South Africa

SHEENA SHAH
*University of Cape Town*

THIS CHAPTER FOCUSES on the importance of the Gujarati language and culture for the ethnic identity development and maintenance of young people living in the Diaspora context of South Africa. Thirty-seven current and former students of a heritage-language school in South Africa completed surveys, semistructured interviews, and language tests. Using the participants' own words, this chapter reports on the views they hold on aspects of their Gujarati identity in a multiethnic and multiracial South Africa. Findings show that they generally identified strongly as Indian. Although proficiency in Gujarati is for the most part low among the participants and they increasingly view the Gujarati language as unimportant in defining their ethnic identity, ethnic culture and religion are viewed as integral aspects of their Gujarati identity.

### The Gujarati Community in South Africa

The Gujarati community has its origins in the state of Gujarat in India, and Gujaratis began settling in South Africa starting in the 1870s. Although the first Indians in South Africa came as indentured laborers to Natal between 1860 and 1911 to work on sugar plantations, Gujaratis came at their own expense as traders and were known as "passenger Indians." They settled first in Natal; many later migrated to the Transvaal. Unlike the indentured laborers, who worked under fixed contracts, the "passenger Indians" had the status of free rather than bonded people. Ninety-five percent of the passenger Indians were Gujaratis, of whom two-thirds were Muslims and one-third were Hindus (Klein 1986, 2–3). The passenger Indians traded in goods, such as Indian spices and clothing, mostly with their fellow Indians.

The number of people of Indian origin in South Africa approximates 1.2 million (Lal, Reeves, and Rai 2006) and constitutes about 3 percent of the total South African population (Desai 1997, 1; Klein 1986, 2). The majority are of Tamil origin. The Gujarati population constitutes about 3 percent of the minority Indian population and is thus "a minority within a minority" (Desai 1997, 1). Klein refers to the Gujaratis in South Africa as "a middleman minority" (Klein 1986). Klein explains that middleman minorities are minority groups in the country that they currently inhabit, a country to which they themselves migrated or to which their descendants migrated. They hold middle-ranked roles, concentrate on entrepreneurial businesses, and maintain strong ties with their ethnic groups and ancestral countries.

## Language Maintenance for Gujaratis in the Diaspora

Despite the seemingly unavoidable shift to the dominant language(s) of society for Diaspora communities in general, Gujarati tends to be one of the better-maintained languages among Indian languages today (see, e.g., Mugler and Mamtora [2004], on Fiji; Roberts [1999], on New Zealand; and Sridhar [1993], on the United States). Various factors have enabled Gujarati communities located outside their homeland to maintain their language and culture and thereby their ethnic identity in a Diaspora setting. One important factor is that many Gujarati households are composed of three generations and today often still include monolingual Gujarati grandparents, which thus facilitates language maintenance. Another factor is that Gujaratis generally marry within their community and sometimes even within their subcaste (Oonk 2007; Shah 2007), which is another way in which "ethnic boundaries" (Oonk 2007, 157) are maintained.

However, the newer generations of Gujaratis in the Diaspora seem to be gradually shifting away from their heritage language and sometimes even their heritage culture. Oonk's (2007) study investigated the shift from Gujarati to English among three generations of the Hindu Lohana community in East Africa. Although the first generation of East African Hindu Lohana participants in his study were still able to speak, write, and read Gujarati fluently, the second generation already displayed signs of difficulty in writing Gujarati, and the third generation may have spoken Gujarati at home with their (grand)parents but were mostly unable to read or write it. One of the factors cited in his study to explain this shift was that the Gujaratis in the third generation had "a more international outlook" (Oonk 2007, 82), which encompassed a need to become fully proficient in English. An earlier study by Oonk (2004) illustrated how the cultural practices among the same community in East Africa were shifting. The changing cultural practices included altering food habits and marriage policies. The men in his study went from marrying Hindu women from the same subcaste (i.e., Lohana) who were raised in India to marrying Hindu women outside the Lohana subcaste who were raised in East Africa. In addition, they went from being strict vegetarians and nondrinkers to eating meat and drinking alcohol.

In the South African context, Desai (1992, 1997) reports on how the Gujarati community is actively trying to maintain its ethnic identity and language by setting up linguistic (i.e., heritage-language schools), cultural, and religious organizations. Through such community efforts, Gujarati is cited as proportionally being the most-spoken Indian language in South Africa (Desai 1992, 4). Mesthrie (2007) agrees with Desai (1992, 11) and claims that Gujarati is "the best-maintained Indian language [in South Africa] in the twentieth century," but he highlights the fact that caution is needed when making such statements, because passenger Indians arrived after the first indentured Indians, and as a result Gujaratis in South Africa had fewer years of contact with English than other Indians. According to Mesthrie (2007), class plays a key role. Gujaratis in South Africa belong to the middle class, whereas other Indian languages in South Africa (e.g., Hindi, Tamil, and Telugu) often historically became associated with indenture. As such, a language shift to English was a means to escape the world of indenture and poverty for speakers of these other Indian languages.

## Methodology

This study uses mixed methods that combine both qualitative and quantitative approaches and incorporate both sociolinguistic and applied linguistic techniques. The mixed-methods design used in this study is the *triangulation design* (Creswell et al. 2003), whereby qualitative and quantitative data are collected and analyzed separately but concomitantly, with each approach being given equal weight. The mixing of the data takes place when the qualitative and quantitative data are merged, or when the results of two or more approaches are integrated or compared side by side in a discussion.

Thirteen males and twenty-four females of between fifteen and twenty-eight years of age participated in this study. All these participants were born and grew up in Lenasia, a predominantly Indian suburb of Johannesburg, and were second-, third-, or fourth-generation South African Gujaratis, with the majority being in the third generation.

All the participants were either current students or recent graduates of the Shree Bharat Sharda Mandir (SBSM) School located in Lenasia, and all had studied or were currently in their final years of studying Gujarati at the school. The goal of the SBSM School is to provide a good-quality, affordable education based on the Hindu ethos in a multicultural society. It was first established as a Gujarati vernacular school in 1936 as a means to maintain Indian culture and educate children in Indian languages such as Gujarati, Hindi, and Sanskrit. Today it is a private educational institution that runs a main school in English in the mornings and an optional Gujarati school in the afternoons. At both the main school and the optional afternoon school, heritage learners of Gujarati are taught their ancestral language, culture, and religion.

For this study, the participants completed three tasks. First, they filled out a survey consisting of fifty questions. The survey was divided up into four sections: (1) demographic information, (2) language information, (3) questions related to issues of identity, and (4) Gujarati school experience. Second, they took part in a semistructured interview, which lasted approximately an hour. This interview was a follow-up from the questionnaire and contained questions related to the role of language and culture for ethnic identity maintenance in the Diaspora. Third, they completed a short oral language proficiency test with a native speaker of Gujarati, in which they answered seven questions in Gujarati.

## Findings: Oral Proficiency Scores

Using a holistic proficiency scale ranging from 0 to 25, two native speakers of Gujarati individually evaluated the language proficiency of the participants on the basis of the short oral proficiency test and later met to discuss their individual ratings in an attempt to reach a consensus on any disagreements in their individual ratings. This process, sometimes referred to as coding socialization (Philp, Oliver, and Mackey 2006), was performed for the entire data set. The two raters evaluated the language proficiency of the participants both before and after coding socialization with a high correlation (respectively, $r = 0.686$, $p < 0.01$; and $r = 0.920$, $p < 0.01$).

The participants' oral proficiency scores range from low (6.5 units out of 25) to very high (23 units out of 25), with an average score of 13 units out of 25. With the exception of a few participants, many struggle with the oral language proficiency test, as indicated by the self-evaluations of their language proficiency: "I can hardly speak Gujarati" (Anita), "I don't know much Gujarati" (Rekha), and "I can't speak Gujarati perfectly" (Suraj).

## Findings: Maintaining Language at Home

Gujarati is generally not maintained in the home environment, and English is cited as the home language for most of the participants. These findings, which were obtained from the semistructured interview, are also confirmed by the quantitative results from survey data. Gujarati, if used, is limited to certain domains (e.g., common Indian grocery items) or specific people (e.g., monolingual grandparents). Parents and grandparents are often described as speaking to their children in English, even for India-born parents and grandparents residing in South Africa. Some participants even describe their level in Gujarati as being higher than that of their parents.

Several participants make comparisons between black Africans and themselves in terms of language maintenance and patterns of language use. The parents of black Africans are described as enforcing the use of the ancestral language at home and English at school. Gujaratis (and other Indians in South Africa), conversely, are described as speaking English both at home and at school: "What happens is that we are speaking English all the time and then when we really have to speak Gujarati, then we do, you know? . . . If we had to carry on speaking the language at home, then we would have been fluent at it. Like let me give you an example: The Africans in this country, their African language is native to them, you know, Zulu or whatever, then they will speak their language at home, but when they come to school, then they will be forced to speak in English" (Shilpa). The home environment therefore does not allow for the maintenance of the mother tongue, because Gujarati is generally not employed by parents and/or grandparents when conversing with their children and vice versa.

## Findings: Maintaining Language at Gujarati School

Although Gujarati is generally not used in the home environment, some participants describe their use of slang or "kitchen Gujarati" in the home, whereas the Gujarati school is defined as a place where the participants learn "pure Gujarati." However, their acquisition of "pure Gujarati" is often through memorization. The Gujarati teachers at the SBSM School are described as employing a more "old-fashioned Indian way of teaching" (Neelam) by giving their students essays to learn by heart, which they then regurgitate verbatim for tests and examinations. As a result, many participants in South Africa have difficulties answering questions for which they have not already memorized set answers, such as those in the oral proficiency test.

Samir, who scored the highest in the proficiency test, does not believe that a school is where languages can be acquired: "To speak you need something external. A school can't teach you to speak Gujarati. Well, that's my personal opinion. You can't learn to speak Gujarati at school. You need something from home. It's a nice place to refresh it, and to improve here and there, but you need something from home." So though the school provides the opportunity for the participants to be exposed to Gujarati, the methods of teaching employed by the teachers at the school seem to not be apt for gaining high proficiency in the language.

## Findings: Maintaining Culture and Religion

All the participants have been heavily involved in Indian cultural activities during their childhood (e.g., performing Indian dances, playing Indian musical instruments, etc.), and the Gujarati culture is generally viewed as an integral aspect of their Gujarati identity, which is successfully maintained by all at home, at school, and through various community organizations. For example, at home, through ethnically endogamous marriage patterns (i.e., marriages that are not only within the Gujarati community, but also often within the same caste and subcaste), other aspects of culture are maintained (e.g., dietary habits). At school, several hours every week are dedicated to cultural activities (e.g., organizing Indian dance performances) and to teaching students about aspects of Gujarati culture.

Religion is viewed as an integral aspect of their Gujarati identity and is successfully maintained by all at home, school, and the temple. The participants attend religious ceremonies, follow religious customs and practices, and perform religious rituals. Religious knowledge is often acquired at the school (e.g., during assemblies and through religious activities that the school organizes, like the celebration of religious days). The school is integral in transmitting religious knowledge to the students, more so than the home at times, because the India-born teachers often have more knowledge about religion than the locally born parents: "That's one thing I'm very thankful to the school for is that they taught us a lot about our religion. . . . We would do the *Ramayana* (an ancient Indian religious epic), we would do the *Mahabharata* (another ancient Indian epic), we would do the *Bhagvat Gita* (the 700-verse Hindu scripture that is part of the *Mahabharata*), they used to teach us Hindi, so the *bens* (a term used to refer to their Gujarati teachers) were more like mothers that taught me those small things that my parents being South African couldn't do" (Kinari).

Knowing Gujarati enables the participants to access religious songs, prayers, and scripts in the original language, rather than having to rely on translations in English, and thus enables them to fully participate in religious activities and functions. As illustrated by Kalpa below, knowing how to read Gujarati enables her to access religious writings and scriptures in the original language:

> With me, the biggest plus point for Gujarati is that our *guru* [spiritual teacher] gives *ashirwad* [blessing] only in Gujarati. Our *sadguru santos* [true teachers],

they give—they use a bit of English here and there, but if you don't understand the main points which are in Gujarati, you're lost. Our main scriptures, *Vachanamrut* [the Lord's spoken word], *Shikshapatri* [the Lord's written word], *Swamini Vato* [the Guru's word], there's English translations, but if you read the Gujarati, it makes more sense. Our *bhajans* [devotional songs], like you know with the ā, they put the like the *matra* [symbol] on top in the English text and you get confused, so you mess up, but if you like use Gujarati, it's fluent, you can understand it, you can sing it well. So for me, Gujarati is a plus point. (Kalpa)

## Findings: Attitudes toward the Heritage Language

The participants in South Africa increasingly view the Gujarati language as unimportant in defining their ethnic identity, whereas ethnic culture and religion are viewed as integral aspects of their Gujarati identity: "As a Gujarati person, it's important to know your culture, it's important to know your religion, it's nice to know your language, it's not key. . . . The key language is English; it's spoken throughout the world" (Rakesh). Many do not make a connection between language and culture, but instead view the two as separate concepts: "Language is not that important for your identity, as long as you know your culture, that's all that matters for Gujarati" (Asha). "You should know about your religion and culture. All those values. But not knowing Gujarati is not going to make you less of an Indian" (Keval). So even though the South African participants generally identify strongly as Indian, knowing Gujarati is for the most part not considered to be an important ethnic identity marker.

Second, English is considered the key language to know and use in South Africa, and Gujarati is regarded as rather useless in South Africa except in a limited number of domains (e.g., the religious domain, as noted in Kalpa's point above): "If you go anywhere around the world, you're not gonna use it [Gujarati] unless you go to India." Furthermore, Gujarati is not considered useful on a professional level. One participant explains why he chose not to continue with Gujarati for Matrik, the qualification received on graduating from high school at the age of eighteen and the minimum university entrance requirement for South African students: "It's not about getting an A, it's about what's going to help me afterwards" (Suraj). Such views may partly be due to the Department of Education's failure to promote community languages in South Africa. Although the SBSM School is the only school in the country to offer Gujarati as a Matrik subject, there are no real incentives for the participants to study the language up to the Matrik level. Scores in Gujarati are generally not taken into account by university officials who are evaluating university applications except in cases of low scores in other subjects.

## Findings: The Future of Gujarati in South Africa

In the past Gujarati was cited as being the best-maintained and most-spoken Indian language in South Africa, and the participants confirm that this is still the case in present-day South Africa through the comparisons they make with other Indian languages. The participants describe how their other Indian friends (e.g., Tamil and Hindi) do not know or understand their ancestral languages, but Gujaratis at least seem to know the basics of Gujarati. Despite this, an overwhelmingly large majority of the participants feel that Gujarati does not have a promising future in South Africa.

First, Gujaratis in the diaspora are described by the participants as becoming increasingly Western and modern in their outlook on life. This has led to diminishing numbers of students at the SBSM School, partly because of a lack of interest on the part of the children, who might not see the value of learning Gujarati, but also because the new generation of parents are not native speakers of Gujarati for the most part and are increasingly becoming interested in sending their children to other extracurricular activities (e.g., swimming, karate, violin) rather than to Gujarati school. It has also led to changes in lifestyle and living patterns, with increasing numbers choosing to move away from Indian areas to other areas and increasingly choosing to live in two-generation households. For example, those participants who have moved to other suburbs of Johannesburg and have attended school there are often unable to attend Gujarati school in the afternoons because they live too far away.

Second, the survey results indicate that the new generation of parents is increasingly speaking English to their children. One of the main ways in which Gujarati can be maintained is through intergenerational language transmission. A lack of intergenerational language transmission increases the likelihood of a language shift. This trend is likely to continue in future generations. Although some parents and other older people have the desire to pass Gujarati down to the younger generations, there is a realization among the participants that this may be unrealistic: "If they have to learn from me, they would be learning the wrong stuff" (Mayuri).

## Conclusion

This chapter has highlighted how young South African Gujaratis increasingly view Gujarati as unimportant in defining their ethnic identity. Conversely, ethnic culture and religion are viewed as integral aspects of their Gujarati identity and are successfully maintained at home, at school, and through various community organizations. Although most South Africans are already displaying extremely low levels of proficiency in Gujarati, and though this pattern is likely to continue among future generations, this chapter has shown that the loss of proficiency in the heritage language does not necessarily entail the loss of ethnic identity. Language shift tends to precede cultural shift, so in some cases, although ethnic minority communities may no longer be able to express their ethnic identity through linguistic means, they may instead resort to expressing their ethnic identity predominantly or solely through cultural means (e.g., see Canagarajah 2008; Khemlani-David 1998). In terms of Giles's (1979) ethnic boundary model, these speakers are moving from a "hard linguistic/soft non-linguistic" quadrant to a "soft linguistic/hard non-linguistic" quadrant. As illustrated by the participants in this study, when people feel strongly that maintaining their identity is important, they will find ways to do so, whether through language or through nonlinguistic means (e.g., cultural practices, religious beliefs, attitudes) or both.

## References

Canagarajah, A. Suresh. 2008. "Language Shift and the Family: Questions from the Sri Lankan Tamil Diaspora." *Journal of Sociolinguistics* 12:143–76.

Creswell, John W., Vicki L. Plano Clark, Michelle L. Gutmann, and William E. Hanson. 2003. "Advanced Mixed Methods Research Designs." In *Handbook of Mixed Methods in Social and Behavioral Research*, edited by Abbas Tashakkori and Charles Teddlie. Thousand Oaks CA: Sage.

Desai, U. K. 1992. "The Gujarati Language amongst Gujarati Speaking Hindus in Natal." Master's thesis, University of Durban-Westville.

———. 1997. "An Investigation of Factors Influencing Maintenance and Shift of the Gujarati Language in South Africa." PhD dissertation, University of Durban-Westville.

Giles, Howard. 1979. "Ethnicity Markers in Speech." In *Social Markers in Speech*, edited by Klaus Rainer Scherer and Howard Giles. Cambridge: Cambridge University Press.

Khemlani-David, Maya. 1998. "Language Shift, Cultural Maintenance, and Ethnic Identity: A Study of a Minority Community—the Sindhis of Malaysia." *International Journal of the Sociology of Language* 130:67–76.

Klein, Gary D. 1986. *South Africans of Gujarati-Indian Descent: Cultural, Structural and Ideological Dynamics*. PhD dissertation, Temple University.

Lal, Brij V., Peter Reeves, and Rajesh Rai, eds. 2006. *The Encyclopedia of the Indian Diaspora*. Singapore: Editions Didier Millet.

Mesthrie, Rajend. 2007. "Language Shift, Cultural Change and Identity Retention: Indian South Africans in the 1960s and Beyond." *South African Historical Journal* 57:134–52.

Mugler, France, and Mamtora, Jayshree. 2004. "The Gujarati Language in Fiji." *Te Reo* 47:29–61.

Oonk, Gijsbert. 2004. "The Changing Culture of the Hindu Lohana Community in East Africa." *Contemporary South Asia* 13:7–23.

———. 2007. "'We Lost Our Gift of Expression': Loss of the Mother Tongue among Indians in East Africa, 1880–2000." In *Global Indian Diasporas: Exploring Trajectories of Migration and Theory*, edited by Gijsbert Oonk. Amsterdam: Amsterdam University Press.

Philp, Jenefer, Rhonda Oliver, and Alison Mackey. 2006. "The Impact of Planning Time on Children's Task-Based Interactions." *System* 34:547–65.

Roberts, Mary Lucy. 1999. "Immigrant Language Maintenance and Shift in the Gujarati, Dutch, and Samoan Communities of Wellington." PhD dissertation, Victoria University of Wellington.

Shah, K. 2007. "Passing on the Culture in the Diaspora: Inter-Generational Communication of Cultural Identity amongst Gujaratis in the USA." PhD dissertation, Wayne State University.

Sridhar, Kamal K. 1993. "Meaning, Means, Maintenance." In *Language, Communication, and Social Meaning: Georgetown University Round Table on Languages and Linguistics*, edited by James E. Alatis. Washington DC: Georgetown University Press.

# 10

# "The Palm Oil with Which Words Are Eaten": Proverbs from Cameroon's Endangered Indigenous Languages

EYOVI NJWE
*University of Bamenda*

CHINUA ACHEBE, a renowned novelist of African descent, figuratively made reference to the undisputed fact of the relevance of proverbs in language when he said that they were "the palm oil with which words are eaten" (Achebe 1958, 14). The importance of proverbs, especially in spoken language as well as written texts, cannot be overemphasized for the color and flavor they introduce and sustain in language. In our study of some endangered Cameroonian languages, we saw the need to investigate and preserve these forms because they tell the stories, experiences, and cultural heritage more vividly than other forms of language use. In this chapter I present proverbs from a number of endangered Cameroonian languages, organized according to theme. Although the figurative expressions are unique to each language, the common themes illustrate experiences shared across the language groups. For example, each of the following proverbs expresses in a different way the idea that two heads are better than one:

Kom:
ŋgen ŋgen ni ngoyn ni ɲim ta ʒi wo - wʊl taw u bassi i fiaŋ
River Ngen Ngen meanders at the Ijim Forest because it had nobody to straighten its course.

Ngwo:
Ndimi kpe mbe ə ɲimi ndʒi mboʔoŋga mbe ə ni ʒi?
The river said it lost its course because it was alone.

Mbili:
iŋstɛ gwa kuɲu nga jɫ ləgə jɫ ŋtwigə laɑdi
A stream that flows alone has so many bends.

Mankon:
ŋki Itɔkə be ke tsi zig zig
A river meanders because it is alone.

As can be observed, the proverb expression is more interesting and compelling.

Proverbs are "wise sayings." They express a deeper meaning than the observable external meaning. The examples of proverbs given above are not actually about any river or flowing water. In the above examples, the users of those languages, through the proverbs, wish to express the fact that people are community beings and must relate to each other and cooperate in order to function well. The same theme is expressed differently in the following proverbs:

Ngwo:
    ndzob nwa? Kema ga bo
    A single bangle makes no noise.
    *or*
    Abwo nwa? Kema kodo bo' bo
    A single hand cannot tie a bundle.

Mbili:
    abugu ji mo'o lege nka nibu nkwiri ni
    A single hand cannot tie a bundle
    *or*
    atə ji mɔʔɔ lema áka kɔ gəyə
    A single tree cannot make a forest.

Kom:
    ncha mo' ni kum wi
    One bangle cannot make a noise.
    *or*
    awu a mo' kaa'a ki be' la kul ibu'
    One hand cannot tie a bundle.
    *or*
    aban no mi gha a ghesi iimsi
    Nothing is above us to undo when we work as a group.

Bamoum:
    Ndi pwo me turei ŋgab tide?
    One finger cannot take or steal meat from the pot.

To continue with our discussion on proverbs in Cameroonian languages, I begin with a definition and categorization of proverbs. Then I explain the sources of the proverbs presented. The next section presents proverbs from Cameroon in the light of themes connected with cooperation, hard work and industry, stubbornness, disobedience, love, promiscuity, and decency. I also look at themes of greed, selfishness, and wickedness, as well as virtues of humility and gratitude, patience, and endurance. I conclude with a discussion of the importance of proverbs in Cameroon's multilingual society and of the role they may play in language revitalization.

## What Is a Proverb?

The genre of "proverb" has no generally accepted definition. According to Madumulla (1995, 1998), the renowned scholar Archer Taylor, fondly referred to as "the

Father of Paraemiology," preferred to identify and describe proverbs by the use of characteristic features rather than by definition. Madumulla also recounts the efforts of Ruth Finnegan, an anthropologist who carried out in-depth research on African oral literature in the 1970s, admitting the difficulty or the impossibility of arriving at an exact definition of the term "proverb." In an attempt to provide a definition for a proverb, Finnegan borrowed from James Howell (1659) and said that "a proverb is a saying in more or less a fixed form marked by 'shortness, sense, and salt' and distinguished by the popular acceptance of the truth tersely expressed in it" (Finnegan 1970, 427).

The proverb is not the only form that lacks a widely accepted definition. There are many forms and concepts in the field of humanities and other areas with the same problem. Therefore, different definitions are provided, adjusted, and accepted according to various needs. In this chapter, where I examine the thematic distribution or implication of proverbs in Cameroonian languages, Fergusson's (1983) definition is most appropriate: "A proverb is a succinct and memorable statement that contains advice, a warning or prediction, or analytical observation. Its form is usually terse, figurative and rich in metaphor and most often poetic." In addition, I would add that a proverb is an expression that contains a general or universal truth.

## Types of Proverbs

Arriving at the categorization of proverbs is as challenging as providing a definition for proverbs. This is so because a proverb is easily confused with other formulaic genres, such as riddles and puns. This is the situation for English proverbs, for which there are many synonyms, and among which making distinctions is difficult. Such synonyms include the adage, maxim, aphorism, saw, gnome saying, apothegm, and many others. In the case of Africa, paraemiologists have found that in certain ethnic groups, the proverb genre shares names with the folktale, parable, riddle, and saying; it is not seen as an independent entity. Madumulla (1998) observes that this tendency of oral literary genres to share a name is due to their syncretic nature; that is, they simply merge into each other.

Despite these constraints, scholars have attempted to classify the proverb corpus. Schipper (1991) proposes that African proverbs can be divided into two main groups:

- Clear, direct statements—that is, moral sayings and mottos.
- Proverbs in metaphorical form, such as in Kom, when it is said that "you have fetched water in a basket," meaning you have made futile attempts.

However, Schipper immediately notes that in their application, the direct proverbs may also become metaphorical.

Proverbs may also be categorized by authorship, as either known (eponymous) or unknown (anonymous). Proverbs in the anonymous category fall within the realm of the collective voice of the past. However, this does not imply that the proverbs in this category came about spontaneously. Each proverb text has an author behind it. However, the proverbs in this category have been made part of a collection.

The eponymous category of proverbs are associated with personalities who are known in history for their inventiveness in creating wise sayings. There is the example of King Solomon in the Bible, to whom is attributed the authorship of the Book of Proverbs. The Sumerian king Shuruppak (2600 BC) is claimed to have composed wise sayings for his son Ziusudra. Yet another is Akkadiom (1550 BC), who wrote the "Counsels of Wisdom." Another anthology of proverbs in this category is the instruction of Pta-Hotep, said to have been composed by Pharaoh Isesi for his son. Although these names are associated with collections of proverbs, it cannot be established without doubt that the attributed eponymous proverbs were indeed the work of these people.

The sources of the proverbs presented here are varied. The proverbs of Kom origin come from a collection titled *Itaŋikom: Timlini-i-Kom Proverbs*, produced by SIL Cameroon (1997). Proverbs in Lamso' are from *Ŋgàn se Nso, Nso Proverbs*, from the Center for Applied Linguistics (2001). Proverbs from Ngwo were collected from my parents and the Ngwo Cultural Association's Bamenda Chapter. The others were obtained from students at the University of Bamenda, who in turn collected them from their parents and grandparents. They were assembled, organized, and presented in this work by the author.

## Proverbs of Cameroon
The proverbs that follow are grouped by theme. Each proverb is presented in the original language, in the orthography of that language, followed by an English translation.

### Unity and Cooperation
The theme of unity and cooperation, which was introduced at the beginning of this chapter, is also found in the following:

Lamso':
> Lav mbì-iì shìíy e rə́
> A debating house stayed open; or, where there is disunity there is bound to be some obstacles.
> *or*
> Kiwó kimò' ón ki y ò' yii kúr kifá
> One hand cannot tie a bundle.

Oku:
> kenchiten lu etəm, kenkiabsən iuu ifəi
> United we stand, divided we fall.

Oroko:
> Itongi basusu isa didaka
> Many hands make light work.

Libum:
> Bongabi you ngerr
> There is strength/power in unity.

Bamessing (Ndop):
>     Kədʒie mo? Je? Dzen ŋgeibe?
>     A straw of a broom does not sweep the house.
>     or
>     beto? bja bou tʃja ke mo?
>     Two heads are better than one.

### Forgiveness

There are proverbs on the theme of forgiveness:

Ngwo:
>     fúʔúrú bit bwɛ girì
>     Cover faeces and catch termites.

It is good to forget someone's wrongdoings so as to benefit from him. In Lamso' it is expressed with the same meaning:

Lamso':
>     Á té' já. e koò' ..ò'
>     Cover faeces catch termites.

Still on the theme of forgiveness, in Kom we have:

Kom:
>     ɨchfɨ ndo nɨ bòwàyn lum gô' kɨ àzì—azɨ
>     The door of a father's house is ever open.

The child can decide to be stubborn, but the father is ever ready to forgive him or her when the child comes back to plead with the father for forgiveness. This proverb would be used by a father promising always to forgive his obstinate child.

### Industry and Hard Work

There are proverbs on the theme of industry and hard work:

Pinyin:
>     kà miʒe? mbo ndoŋgkfu
>     No food for a lazy man.

Lamso':
>     shinən shé shuù shi yò' yii bá rì lá
>     A noisy bird builds no nest.

Oroko:
>     Ndʒoku esa teneke ekote
>     An elephant is not tired of carrying its tusk.

Limbum:
>     mu nkeh ki sohsi mboh yinger a blibi
>     When a child washes his hand clean, he can dine with elders.

Bafaw:
> nlu emeu è baŋi karti e peum daso muna a paki mutu
> The head that refuses to study will end up carrying loads in the motor park.

### Stubbornness
On stubbornness, we have the following examples:

Ngwe:
> Ntesah eʒe te lih jup tʃela? Moye? a tee le pe?
> A stubborn fly follows its mother to the grave.

Ejagham:
> nzezeŋ ŋi tʃa jog ni ejig ojɛm
> A stubborn fly follows the corpse to the grave.

Mbili:
> Muo de ju? meeg, ko? jug ʃoʃe
> A child who does not listen to the mother's advice throws away her treasure.

Kom:
> wain ve wu ntala wu nvuwi a tÓ
> A stubborn child does not listen to warnings.

Lamso':
> Ma mgbitu wɔŋɔ ŋku ba wu tseatfɛt
> A stubborn child dies prematurely.

### Greed
On the theme of greed, the same proverb runs across many languages, stating that "those who eat alone fight (or die) alone."

Oroko:
> Wa rake moiti, akondo wa moit
> Those who eat alone die alone.

Limbum:
> je momndʒin kwei momndʒi?
> He who eats alone fights alone.

Oku:
> wei we əbjien wen nyiŋ ni kuo nyiŋ
> He who eats alone fights alone.
> *or*
> nwa si yinger mim ŋgi kui mim ŋgi
> He who eats alone dies alone.

Mungaka, Ngwe, Bafut, Ejagham, Mbili, Bafaw, and many others use the same expression on the theme of greed.

### Respect for Elders, Humility, Patience, and Endurance
There are proverbs on the themes of respect for elders, humility, patience, and endurance. We have the following examples:

Mbili:
>Mbilig le kɑ to'o ʃa tʃege
>Your shoulder cannot grow above your head.

Oku:
>ɑ ŋɑm kewo ke kə ɲese we
>Don't bite the finger that fed you.
>*or*
>buo je əb fofən wiy ɲyam əb wakən
>A patient dog eats the fattest bone.

Mungaka:
>WΛnti mjun beʊ ŋkɑbi
>Respect people to gain wealth.
>*or*
>ŋgwe bé ŋgriu ta ntieu ntoʔ ɑtuʔ
>Your shoulders cannot grow above your head.

Babanki:
>ɲiŋtə ɲiŋtə túʔ ndʒìwù:
>When you run all day, darkness falls.

>ndʒeʔtə dʒeʔtə túʔ ndʒìwù
>When you walk all day, darkness falls. In other words, those who run and those who walk will still meet darkness. (The race is not to the swift.)

### Love

Kom:
>Kcŋ wɑin na va ta wa kcŋ genzhia
>Love your neighbor as you love yourself.

Bafut:
>akɔŋnə tʃa ŋkabə
>Love is more than money.

## Proverbs and Language Revitalization
From the above, we can see that proverbs are very important in the languages of Cameroon. Todd (1971, 85) had earlier remarked on this when describing pidgin speakers of West Cameroon: "Among pidgin speakers in West Cameroon, too, the ability to sum a problem to recognizable proportion by a humorous comment is indeed highly prized and very few conversations take place in which proverbs do not occur."

This was in her description of proverbs in Cameroon Pidgin English "Kamtok." She went further to provide a link between Krio and Cameroon pidgin, observing that the two have much in common. She further suggested that an analysis of the proverbs of Cameroon vernacular languages, like the examples provided in this work, can shed light on the sources, the structure, and the potentials of West African proverbs.

Cameroon has been classified by Grimes (2000) as one of the world's most linguistically diversified countries. According to the 2008 census, Cameroon has a population of 18.5 million, approximately 0.02 percent of the world's population. Yet with 286 languages, it accounts for almost 5 percent of the world's languages. The mean number of speakers for each language is about 60,000. The extreme multilingual situation of the country has provided many opportunities for contact between languages.

The languages of Cameroon are of both unequal prestige and unequal vitality. There are two official languages, French and English, from the colonial background of Cameroon. These two official languages enjoy high prestige and high vitality. They are superposed on a lingua franca of pidgin English in the country's Northwest and Southwest regions, that have spread to the big cities of the rest of the eight regions. There is another pidgin tongue called Camfranglais. In addition, there are the 284 indigenous languages spoken in the nation. My worry is that this multilingual situation, which favors the foreign colonial languages and the pidgins, has endangered many of the country's indigenous languages and has brought some to the brink of extinction.

Various attempts have been made and methods have been proposed to revive the languages. Here I propose the use of proverbs from the various languages in language revitalization. Proverbs could be included in radio, television, and educational programs. I suggest that different programs, especially entertainment and those that feature conversations, could help the situation. In the collection of some of the corpus used in this chapter, I discovered that the students were very excited and enthusiastic to participate in providing the proverbs from their indigenous languages. Many of them had to get their parents, grandparents, and elders from their respective villages to assist them.

Again, the collection of proverbs presented in this chapter goes a long way toward expressing the belief of the people in the themes handled here. This collection will also be preserved and referred to by present and future readers, some of them of a later generation. In the view of Ashu (2010), proverb collection and usage promote cultural awareness and create situations where learners share with one another their personal experiences and traditions.

## References

Achebe, Chinua. 1958. *Things Fall Apart*. New York: Anchor Books.
Ashu, Comfort Eneke. 2010. *Riddles, Folktales, and Proverbs from Cameroon*. Bamenda: Langaa Research.
Center for Applied Linguistics. 2001. *Ɖgàn se Nso, Nso Proverbs*, vol. 1. CAL Edition Series 8. Washington DC: Center for Applied Linguistics.
Fergusson, Rosalind. 1983. *The Penguin Dictionary of Proverbs*. New York: Penguin Books.

Finnegan, Ruth H. 1970. *Oral Literature in Africa*. Oxford: Clarendon Press.
Grimes, Barbara F. 2000. *Ethnologue: The Languages of the World*, 14th ed. Dallas: Summer Institute of
 Linguistics.
Howell, James. 1659. *Proverbs*. London.
Madumulla, J. S. 1995. *Proverbs and Sayings: Theory and Practice*. Dar es Salaam: Institute of Kiswhali
 Research.
———. 1998. "Proverbs: 'A Pack of Lies?'" *UTAFITI Special Issue* 4:257–74.
Schipper, M. 1991. *Source of All Evil: African Proverbs and Sayings on Women*. Chicago: Ivan R. Dee.
SIL Cameroon. 1997. *Itaŋikom: Timlini-i-Kom Proverbs*. Yaoundé: SIL Cameroon.
Todd, Loreto. 1971. "West Cameroon Pidgin Proverbs." *Journal of West African Languages* 7, no. 2.

# 11

# The Linguistic "Glocal" in Nigeria's Urban Popular Music

TOLULOPE ODEBUNMI
*University of Ibadan*

THE PHENOMENON OF "WORLD BEAT" has been aptly described as the "Africanization of world pop music and the Americanization of African pop" (Feld 1994, 245). Among other things, it signposts one aspect of the larger flows and interminglings among cultures that are increasingly aware of themselves and of others. Transcultural influences in the realm of World Music are, for the most part, understood as manifested in style, mode, and identity-performance. In this chapter I look at the centrality of language for this hybrid musical culture by considering the linguistic features of pop music of Nigeria, especially the hip-hop music produced and consumed by urban youth. The dynamics have changed since the 1970s, when the success of such an artiste as the juju music bandleader King Sunny Ade helped implant African popular music in the imagination of the world. Ade's musical oeuvre is in the Yorùbá language; yet, even though the late rap artiste Dagrin (1987–2010) did his songs in Yorùbá as well, the distance in approach to social reality between these two musicians is evident in their linguistic performance. If genre accounts for differences in linguistic performance in this case, then we can say that Dagrin aspires to be true to the nature of his genre by foregrounding in his language the transgressive linguistic usage of hip-hop, established first by black Americans and transplanted to the rest of the world. The concept of "glocalization" explicates the process whereby the interpenetration and cross-fertilization of linguistic elements and forms from both local and foreign languages occur in the popular music of Nigeria. The emphasis here is on Yorùbá hip-hop.

## Background

During the past two decades, there have been many innovations in the Nigerian music industry, and they are very much in evidence in the influence of hip-hop on popular music in the country. The result is a transgressive genre, which evolves by the day, and Nigerian popular music has now become a global phenomenon that attracts fans all over the world, especially in the Diaspora.

Hip-hop started in the Bronx Borough of New York City in the early to middle 1970s. It has since spread to the rest of the world. As Alridge and Stewart (2005, 190) observe, "Hip-hop has developed as a cultural and artistic phenomenon affecting youth culture around the world"; they also enumerate its "four fundamental elements: disc jockeying (DJing), break dancing, graffiti art, and rapping (emceeing)." Of these elements, rap music seems to be the most widespread. Hip-hop was first introduced to Nigeria in 1981 with a track titled "The Way I Feel" by Ronnie. From that small beginning, hip-hop has come to find a ready home in the country, suited as it is for projecting and interrogating certain social tendencies in urban youth culture, thus speaking to a broader participation in the development of a black aesthetic: "Hip-hop aesthetics, steeped in polyrhythm, antiphony, an orality of social commentary, and a vital embodiment of all of the above, is repositioned by Sub-Saharan black African, Afro-Caribbean, and Brazilian youths because of their connection to the transiting black aesthetic itself" (Osumare 2005, 266).

The steady growth of hip-hop in Nigeria became noticeable in the late 1990s. Seyi Sodimu, the Remedies, Plantation Boyz, Rugged&Raw, Trybesmen, and Ruff, among others, made up the mainstream. The underground included Swat Roots, Tuck Tyte, and Coal City Finest. The release of "Ehen" (Nigerian Pidgin for "Is That It?") in 2003 by Ruggedman totally redefined Nigerian hip-hop, and there was a reawakening of this genre in the music industry. This period marked a turnaround in the industry and fellow musicians knew they had to be "on top of their game," as they say in hip-hop parlance. There was a much more conscious effort to appeal to the needs and tastes of younger people in Nigeria, and to stage hip-hop as both a subculture and countercultural movement, albeit with a heavy dose of "Nigerianness" as opposed to just imitating the concerns and practices of American hip-hop musicians. One marker of this new concern was an influx of linguistic elements from urban youth practice into Ruggedman's songs, including the use of Nigerian Pidgin slang terms and the mixing of these with expressions from other Nigerian languages. Other hip-hop musicians followed suit in this practice of doing rap music in Nigerian languages.

Language has always played a huge role in the development of hip-hop in Nigeria. Indeed, the language of popular Nigerian music has been greatly transformed by hip-hop culture, as this chapter seeks to show. The place of language in this global youth cultural movement cannot be overemphasized, for, as Alim (2009, 5) notes, the Global Hip-Hop Nation is characterized by, among other things, its commitment to "subversive language ideologies." The Nigerian version of hip-hop's linguistic subversion has already begun to catch the attention of scholars of language; Omoniyi (2009) has attempted to map out the matrix and strategies of a "Naija Style" in this regard.

This chapter examines the continuities and changes (ruptures) in the use of Yorùbá in musical performance acts and for staging identity among urban youth. Ultimately, this means that I am concerned about the debate over the future of the Yorùbá language, particularly in relation to the position taken by purists who are worried about decay and decadence in linguistic practice. Indeed, as Barber (2000, 155) points out, some scholars see the Anglicization of African languages as something negative, a "sad by-product of cultural and mental colonisation." In the case of Yorùbá, she observes that it is feared that the intrusion of English vocabulary, syntax, and structure signposts "language dilution and eventual language loss" or death. Barber (2000, 155–56) reaches the conclusion that there is no doubt that the purist had a point. The younger generation of school-educated children did suffer a kind of linguistic deprivation compared with their elders, and lacked the extraordinarily versatile and productive command of linguistic registers which was typical of the older and less "educated" Yorùbá people. There are many university students and members of the educated elite who ruefully admit that they are unable to complete a sentence in Yorùbá without lapsing into English. However, not all uses of loan words and borrowed syntax are signs of a helpless acquiescence in language loss. Many genres of Yorùbá popular culture import elements of English into a thriving Yorùbá linguistic medium to make specific points or create specific effects. In this way they turn the linguistic interface into a critical frontier.

It is this frontier interface of language use in Nigerian popular music, best exemplified by hip-hop artistes in the country, with which this chapter is largely concerned. There is a whole world of difference between the linguistic practice of, say, King Sunny Ade, the juju bandleader, and that of the rapper Dagrin, even though they are both Yorùbá musical performers. This whole world of difference is called into being by the intensification of "glocal" factors in the sense that whereas hip-hop has come to us in Nigeria from outside, there has been a very conscious effort to create a Nigerian version of it, and linguistic strategies have played a vital role in this enterprise. Language is central to hip-hop, and the interaction between rap and language from society to society is one way of showing "how globally circulating musical styles are received and used outside their points of origin in the so-called 'centre' or 'core' countries of production" (Solomon 2005, 1).

## The Concept and Process of the "Glocal"

"Glocalization" is a concept that captures the phenomenon of "global cultural flows" (see Appadurai 1996) and the commingling of goods, ideas, styles, genres, practices, and languages, in this contemporary period hitherto thought of as being marked by the mere globalization of Western cultural products. It is a heuristic concept, whereby "investigating the international diffusion of a culture, one is essentially inquiring into an interactive dialogic process that links discrete sites and real people" (Osumare 2005, 266). "'Glocal' is the term used to describe a hybrid space, in which the global is adapted to the local (and perhaps vice versa)" (Mesthrie and Bhatt 2008, 153). The issue is to raise "a more general awareness of the importance of 'glocalization' or the interaction and merger between local cultures and global processes" (Turner 2010, 6). The concept relates to two key issues in the transformation of societies in a world where people are being made more aware of the self and the other on account of the flows enabled by media technology:

1. What are the outcomes of such flows: homogeneity or heterogeneity?
2. What informs these flows: imposition (by the global powers, especially the United States) or inventiveness (at the local peripheries)?

As explicated by Robertson (1992, 35), glocalization involves the "linking of localities" and the "invention of locality." And it has "led to the emergence of . . .

world music, gourmet cooking, and ethnic body adornment" (He 2007, 8). Of course, in time past, similar processes took place in the way societies shared cultural things. Diffusion and syncretism were concepts used by anthropologists to explain these processes. This is not to say that what is happening now has always happened before. As Trouillot (2001, 129) argues, there are "changes in the spatialization of the world economy and changes in the volume and, especially, the kinds of movements that occur across political boundaries." As one anthropologist puts it, "Historians and sociologists, especially those concerned with translocal processes . . . and the world systems associated with capitalism . . . have long been aware that the world has been a congeries of large-scale interactions for many centuries. Yet today's world involves interactions of a new order and intensity, [facilitated and] accelerated by [technologies of] transfers and innovations" (Appadurai 1996, 27–28).

Linguistic practices are implicated in every one of these glocal processes of exchange in the world's cultural economy. Goods, ideas, and artistic forms may be taken as semiological systems with their own "linguistic admixtures" (Barthes 1968, 10), so that when a commodity or idea comes from the outside into another society, it brings along with it a linguistic repertoire that may well run into a new fate in its new locale. Language itself is often the main, and not just a secondary, item in these glocal flows. In relation to language use, the development of world Englishes, for instance, is a glocal phenomenon, with English "being appropriated by local speakers, and in that process . . . diversifying and developing new dialects" (Schneider 2003, 233). The spread of musical forms is one way in which languages and linguistic practices travel from place to place, and in the process these languages and linguistic practices are appropriated and, probably, transformed in usage.

## World Beat: A Glocal Process

In the light of the glocal heuristic, it can be seen that there is much more to World Beat than its being merely "the Africanization of world pop music and the Americanization of African pop" (Feld 1994, 245). Mainly what is stressed in considerations of World Beat is the conflation of the technologies and styles of genre fusion (e.g., Sunny Ade's infusion of the electric guitar and synthesizers into his sound ensemble, which includes traditional instruments like the talking drum) and the new creations that emerge from such fusion (e.g., Fela's sonic arrangements, which blend elements of jazz, funk, and soul with the hypnotic effects of traditional trance sequences to create the distinctive style of Afrobeat). If we situate Nigerian hip-hop in the larger frame of World Beat, then Nigerian hip-hop also becomes the product of a glocal process. This means that we can accept as new things the musical products emerging from the practice of Nigerian hip-hop artistes who devise ways of making the genre their own. These products are not just imitations of American rap but also a marriage of the elements of rap with elements from more indigenous styles fostered through the element of individual creativity. This idea of a commitment to fusion is evident in Dagrin's statement in the song "Pon pon pon": "A ma fi rap wrap yín pọ̀" (We will wrap you all up with hip-hop). The wordplay in this line is a common feature of Yorùbá orature. Even though Dagrin's beat and feel are definitely hip-hop, his linguistic deployment, whereby words (in this case, "rap" and "wrap") are brought into the same semantic field on the basis of their sonic resonance, is a very common Yorùbá practice. Osundare asserts of this practice in Yorùbá orature that "common sounds can be invested with new meanings (and vice versa?) even beyond the institutionalized matrix of onomatopoeia" (2000, 27). This practice of conjuring a semantic field by placing words that sound similar side by side is, perhaps, what has been described elsewhere as "declarative palindromes" (Hess 2007, 146). Nigerian artists do not only sample linguistic practices in hip-hop in the United States; they also look into traditions of local oral performance, and these are fused in ingenious ways to create something unique.

## The Languages of Nigerian Hip-Hop Music

Sunny Ade largely harnesses the features of Yorùbá oral-musical-poetic performance. This has made it easy for his genre of music to be incorporated into the category of the traditional. Thus what may have been seen as novel and foreign in Sunny Ade and juju music as a whole is now taken as very traditional. However, Fela is still considered unique, and he stands out of that category. Linguistic practice is important in making this distinction. Fela and Ade both use the traditional poetic form of call-and-response. But Fela is not considered to have done Yorùbá music because, in his linguistic practice, he privileged Nigerian Pidgin for casting his songs of defiance against the political order in Nigeria. Ade, conversely, privileged Yorùbá, and he depended a lot on the features of Yorùbá praise poetry. His linguistic practice remained within the ambit of the standard form of the language. The influences on urban music in Nigerian society today go beyond the technology of sound production and fusion. The hip-hop tradition caught on fast in Nigeria and led to the prominent, but no less nuanced, appearance of the "linguistic glocal" in urban youth music in Nigeria. By the linguistic glocal is meant realizations of the genre expectations that underlie the transgressive linguistic practice of American hip-hop acts as well as hip-hop acts anywhere else in the world. The use of objectionable language is an overt strategy of transgression (Solomon 2005). However, linguistic transgression in hip-hop language does not always resort to this strategy. Rather, the rule is to "keep it real." This is achieved by modifying the language along the parameters of authentic street practice. Apart from the use of Nigerian Pidgin in many of these hip-hop songs, rapping is done in a mixed language that combines linguistic and prosodic elements from both English and, say, Yorùbá. The first hip-hop songs were done in English and Nigerian Pidgin. But the artistes became more daring, doing hip-hop in Yorùbá especially in the late 1990s—for example, Maintain ("I Catch Cold"), Seyi Sodimu ("Love Me Jeje"), and Remedies ("Sade"). Rhythm was not a problem, but rhyme was. Tonal languages are known for being highly rhythmical, and it is possible to see elements of rap in even Sunny Ade, just as some researchers go as far as the performance of the griot in West African societies in tracing the origin of rap music (Omoniyi 2009). At first the rappers overlooked the problem of rhyme and simply forced Yorùbá into the hip-hop "beat." Dagrin solved the problem by means of a "mixilingual" (pace Brann 1989) practice in his song lyrics. He made Yorùbá rhyme by introducing words from other languages and slang terms (for an account of how the problem of rhyme was resolved by Japanese hip-hop artistes, see Manabe

2006). This strategy has made it possible, for example, for Dagrin to do both internal rhymes and end-rhymes, sometimes with the rhymed words alternating between Yorùbá and English. In "Ghetto Dreams," we get these examples from Dagrin:

Aìmóye ìgbà tí mo dìde tí mo tí subú (Nobody knows the number of times I've risen and fallen)

Aìmóye èébú tí wón ti pè mí ló lórí ibú (Nobody knows the number of insults in which I've been called the accursed one)

Aìmóye àjẹ́, aìmóye osó (Nobody knows the number of witches, nobody knows the number of wizards)

Aìmóye many times tí mò ń play free show (Nobody knows the number of times I've performed without pay)

Mo ní dream láti mòwé bíi Wole Soyinka (I had a dream to be as educated as Wole Soyinka)

But problem mi ni pé àwon sisi yimika (But my problem is that I am surrounded by ladies)

Mo ni dream lati lọ school kí n di Professor (I had a dream to become a Professor)

Owó ló dámi dúró bíi bus tí àwon èrò fẹ́ sò (But lack of money stopped me like a bus from which commuters are alighting).

The emergence of Yorùbá rap may speak to the fact often reiterated in relation to the Yorùbá that their society is "highly cosmopolitan and dynamic. The Yorùbá have lived in large cities for centuries and have complex markets, sophisticated philosophical systems, and a general openness to the incorporation of foreign styles and technologies" (Campbell and Waterman 1995, 38). But beyond this openness to the foreign, transgression is not such a novel practice among the Yorùbá given their robust tradition of ribald festivals and masquerades, where language is utilized for an overall parodic effect. But recently, there has been a certain parody in hip-hop of Yorùbá linguistic practice itself, as can be seen in the phenomenon of postproverbials, where "a radical overturning of the form of the traditional proverb" is fast becoming standard practice (see Raji-Oyelade 1999). However, whereas the postproverbial is a subversion of the proverbial, with the latter serving ultimately as the originary template, there is also the phenomenon of the "autoproverbial" in Yorùbá hip-hop, that is, a proverb that does not emanate as a reaction from some earlier wise saying but is rather the artiste's own contribution to the traditional repertoire that was hitherto thought of as being fixed and finite (Raji-Oyelade 1999). In "Impossible" by Jabless featuring Ajasa, we have the following:

Mí ò le f'ata rodo se roll-on (I cannot use chili pepper as roll-on)

Mí ò le f'eja kíka se bangle (I cannot use dried fish as a bangle)

Mi ò le f'éjò se belt (I cannot use a snake as belt)

Mi ò le s'aluwala l'express (I cannot do [Muslim] ablutions on the expressway)

Òrónro eran wón ní fé lo jé (Nobody eats goat's bile)

O wà nínú plane o ní fé lo bé (You're on an airplane, you won't want to jump out).

Thus has hip-hop's attitude of transgressive linguistic practice, a necessary aspect of the genre anywhere it finds expression, been localized in the Nigerian milieu. The features of Yorùbá oral poetry are nevertheless still present in Yorùbá rap, such as repetition (in "Mercies of the Lord" by Jungalist featuring Dagrin), noncasual language, and figurative language. Showing an awareness of this glocal mix, Dagrin made the promise that the time would come when "O ma fi hip-hop jó bàtá" (i.e., Hip-hop will be used to do the bàtá dance). And indeed, bàtá is very similar to break dancing. In recognition of Dagrin's contribution to the linguistic practice of urban youth music in Nigeria, the tribute song done to memorialize his premature death ("My Pain") is one of the most polyvocal, polyrhythmic, and hetero-glossic performances ever created in the country. This tribute to Dagrin displays staggering linguistic innovativeness. Multiple voices are heard in the song because it was done by various artistes. Part of the transgression includes the placement of the tune of a Yorùbá Christian hymn, "A ó pàdé lésè Jésù" in a hip-hop context. And even traditional Yorùbá poetry (ewì) is incorporated into the ensemble of this same track overlaid with a hip-hop beat. The languages of this particular song, with the very words taken from different cultures and styles, reflect the ethnomusicological expanse of Nigerian music. In "Mercies of the Lord," the languages used in the rampant code-switching and code-mixing that characterize the song include:

Igbo: Chineke nna ekelem o (God, I give you thanks)
Yorùbá: Nigeria, ojojúmó là ń jí ríyà (Nigeria, every day we wake up into suffering)

Ragga Patois (a form of the language of reggae): Me look around the place and what me see . . . (I look around and what do I see . . .)

Nigerian Pidgin: While some dey do juju because their magga no dey pay (Some people ["yahoo boys" (i.e., internet scammers)] do black magic because their dupes do not fall for their tricks)

Code-mixing of Itsekiri and Yorùbá: Oritse mi mo bé ọ o (My God, I beg you)

Ijọ: Tamara sésé iyé (God, come to my rescue).

## "Glocal" Factors in Nigerian Hip-Hop
Indeed, the linguistic usages of these musicians indicate their responses to "glocal" factors. First, they know that hip-hop culture includes the deployment of language to self-identify in particular ways. For example, Dagrin uses Yorùbá slang to show that he is coming from urban street culture but is also situated within a Yorùbá/Nigerian milieu. As Omoniyi argues, these artistes use local languages to mark out

their own space within the hip-hop world. They do so against "wholesale assimilation by global hip-hop culture and to carve out an independent glocal identity" (Omoniyi 2006, 198).

Second, they are also aware of the need for astute marketing strategy because hip-hop is serious business. They have to display their unique selling points. If they rap in the language of American artistes, then what are they really offering? As has been noted of hip-hop elsewhere—for example, Turkish hip-hop (Solomon 2005)—Nigerian hip-hop has become a "transnational movement." Nigerians in the Diaspora now listen to hip-hop done by Nigerian artistes based back home. They need to feel the authentic thing, and language plays a role here. It makes a lot of sense to foreground this linguistic unique selling point. Akon, for instance, has done songs with some Nigerian musicians in which he sings in pidgin ("Chop My Money," by Psquare) and in Yorùbá ("Damiduro," by Davido).

Third, the hip-hop artistes demonstrate clearly how dialogue can be sustained among the diversity of languages spoken in Nigeria. Their approach and attitude are a refreshing departure from the rancor that usually arises when the issue is raised over the need for an official language in Nigerian political circles. As Iwara (2008, 20) has observed, "Nigeria is typical of those countries of Sub-Saharan Africa that are not only saddled with an official colonial language to which only a minority of population have adequate access, but which also possess many rival ethnic languages from which it is generally considered to be politically inexpedient to choose one as a national language for use throughout the country." But in the linguistic practice of hip-hop artistes in the country, this typical tendency is done away with. They do not search for one language to elevate above all others, but rather throw all into the same mixilingual pool, including the English language. These artistes show active awareness of the multilingual Nigerian society, and thus pitch their appeal in awareness of the need for unity in diversity.

## Conclusion

The languages and linguistic strategies employed in the different spheres of popular culture more or less indicate how people relate to issues in the wider social landscape. Nigerian hip-hop displays linguistic features that locate it at the juncture of a "glocal" confluence. It goes without saying that the transgressive linguistic attitude found in these songs is a genre marker of hip-hop anywhere in the world. But having admitted this, we can also say that the linguistic gestures in Nigerian hip-hop deeply reflect urban youth culture in the country; otherwise, the music would not be abiding by the dictum of "keeping it real." Its linguistic realness, as has been pointed out (Omoniyi 2009), is such that it has become a staple of the Nigerian Diaspora and other peoples of the world. But there is even more to the linguistic practice of Nigerian hip-hop musicians when we consider that they use language to pitch their appeal in order to capture the local and global markets, and that they are able to transcend the bickering that erupts when the language issue is raised in the political circles. These artistes therefore transgress the politics of the language question by demonstrating how the different languages can together be put to use to achieve very potent effects. In relation to the fortunes of one of the three major languages in the country, Yorùbá in this case, the purists may not be happy with the dilution or even decay that they observe in the linguistic practice of Yorùbá hip-hop artistes. But this practice, much as it is substandard, is a reflection of urban street usage, and perhaps is a pointer to how the language will survive within its glocal milieu.

## References

Alim, H. Samy. 2009. "Straight Outta Compton, Straight *aus München*: Global Linguistic Flows, Identities, and the Politics of Language." In *Global Linguistic Flows: Hip-Hop Cultures, Youth Identities, and the Politics of Language*, edited by H. Samy Alim, Awad Ibrahim, and Alastair Pennycook. New York: Routledge.

Alridge, Derrick P., and James B. Stewart. 2005. "Introduction: Hip-Hop in History: Past, Present, and Future." *Journal of African American History* 90:190–95.

Appadurai, Arjun. 1996. *Modernity at Large: Cultural Dimensions of Globalization*. Minneapolis: University of Minnesota Press.

Barber, Karin. 2000. "The Use of English in Yorùbá Popular Plays." In *Kiss and Quarrel: Yorùbá/English Strategies of Mediation*, edited by Stewart Brown. Edgbaston: University of Birmingham.

Barthes, Roland. 1968. *Elements of Semiology*. New York: Hill and Wang.

Brann, Conrad. 1989. "The Terminology of Babel: A Suggestion." *Journal of West African Languages* 19, no. 2: 125–27.

Campbell, Patricia Shehan, and Christopher Waterman. 1995. "Christopher Waterman on Yorùbá Music of Africa." *Music Educators Journal* 81, no. 6: 35–43.

Feld, Steven. 1994. "Notes on 'World Beat.'" In *Music Grooves*, edited by Charles Kell and Steven Feld. Chicago: University of Chicago Press.

He, Shaoyi. 2007. "Internet Multilinguality: Challenges, Dimensions, and Recommendations." In *Linguistic and Cultural Online Communication Issues in the Global Age*, edited by Kirk St. Amant. Hershey PA: Information Science Reference.

Hess, Mickey. 2007. *Is Hip-Hop Dead? The Past, Present, and Future of America's Most Wanted Music*. Westport CT: Praeger.

Iwara, Alexander U. 2008. *The Linguistic Situation in Nigeria and Its Implications for Sustainable Development: Da mihi locum stare et terram movebo*. Inaugural Lecture. Ibadan: Ibadan University Press.

Manabe, Noriko. 2006. "Globalization and Japanese Creativity: Adaptations of Language to Rap." *Ethnomusicology* 50, no. 1: 1–36.

Mesthrie, Rajend, and Rakesh M. Bhatt. 2008. *World Englishes: The Study of New Linguistic Varieties*. Cambridge: Cambridge University Press.

Omoniyi, Tope. 2006. "Hip-Hop through the World Englishes Lens: A Response to Globalization." *World Englishes* 25, no. 2: 195–208.

———. 2009. "'So I Choose to Do Am Naija Style': Hip-Hop, Language, and Postcolonial Identities." In *Global Linguistic Flows: Hip-Hop Cultures, Youth Identities, and the Politics of Language*, edited by H. Samy Alim, Awad Ibrahim, and Alastair Pennycook. New York: Routledge.

Osumare, Halifu. 2005. "Global Hip-Hop and the African Diaspora." In *Black Cultural Traffic: Crossroads in Global Performance and Popular Culture*, edited by Harry J. Elam Jr. and Kennell Jackson. Ann Arbor: University of Michigan Press.

Osundare, Niyi. 2000. "Yorùbá Thought, English Words: A Poet's Journey through the Tunnel of Two Tongues." In *Kiss and Quarrel: Yorùbá/English Strategies of Mediation*, edited by Stewart Brown. Edgbaston: University of Birmingham.

Raji-Oyelade, Aderemi. 1999. "Postproverbials in Yoruba Culture: A Playful Blasphemy." *Research in African Literatures* 30, no. 1: 74–82.

Robertson, Roland. 1992. *Globalization: Social Theory and Global Culture*. London: Sage.

Schneider, Edgar W. 2003. "The Dynamics of New Englishes: From Identity Construction to Dialect Birth." *Language* 79:233–81.

Solomon, Thomas. 2005. "'Living Underground Is Tough': Authenticity and Locality in the Hip-Hop
    Community in Istanbul, Turkey." *Popular Music* 24, no. 1: 1–20.
Trouillot, Michel-Rolph. 2001. "The Anthropology of the State in the Age of Globalization." *Current
    Anthropology* 42, no. 1: 125–38.
Turner, Bryan S. 2010. "Theories of Globalization: Issues and Origins." In *The Routledge International
    Handbook of Globalization Studies*, edited by Bryan S. Turner. Oxford: Routledge.

# 12

## Language Use in Advertisements as a Reflection of Speakers' Language Habits

LEONARD MUAKA
*Winston-Salem University*

**ADVERTISING AS A FIELD** transcends several disciplines. This chapter contributes to this interdisciplinary field from a sociolinguistic perspective by focusing on billboards that form the linguistic landscape of Kenyan and Tanzanian urban centers. Although the field of linguistic landscapes has made major progress in other parts of the world, the East African region and Africa in general are only beginning to see studies on linguistic landscapes emerge. Examples from the region include Higgins (2009), who deals with Tanzania and Kenya; Stroud and Mpendukana (2009) on South Africa; Bwenge (2009) on Tanzania; and Legère (2012) on Tanzania as well. The purpose of this chapter is therefore to take a closer look at the linguistic landscapes of Kenya and Tanzania using an eclectic sociolinguistic framework that will contribute to the field by discussing advertising in light of the underpinning political, ideological, and economic realities that play out in language policies and language practices in the two countries. Although the chapter looks at the two East African countries linguistically, the focal points are the linguistic landscapes of three cities. In Kenya the chapter focuses on the capital city of Nairobi and the coastal city of Mombasa. In Tanzania the focus is on the city of Dar es Salaam, the country's commercial capital. Given the strategic locations of these three cities, their advertising audiences are diverse. Mombasa is a coastal town largely dominated by Swahili speakers. However, it is also a major port that serves not only Kenya but also other Eastern African countries that are landlocked, such as Uganda, Congo, Burundi, and Southern Sudan. This is also true of Dar es Salaam, which in addition to being the commercial capital of Tanzania is also the country's major port. Nairobi is a major business hub for the entire Eastern African region, which makes it difficult to focus on the local residents alone. In examining the signage in the three cities, I bore these factors in mind. Previous studies have often divided linguistic landscapes as either private or public (Landry and Bourhis 1997). In Kenya and Tanzania this division is evident; however, a category that combines the two forms is warranted. To incorporate this new category, I have created the semipublic/semiprivate category to account for signage that does not fall squarely in one category as outlined in previous research projects. These billboards involve partnerships between the government and nongovernmental entities, and they provide different possibilities for how language is used. Other groups in this category include parastatal organizations.

## Background Information about Kenya and Tanzania

Kenya and Tanzania are neighboring countries with a singular feature that makes this study both interesting and important. The two countries share a linguistic characteristic in that they both embrace Swahili as a national as well as an official language, yet they also proclaim English to be their language for official and international communication. Where they differ is how, through language policies and language ideologies, each country has embraced these two languages. This section discusses these differences.

### *Tanzania's Language Policy and Situation*

Although Tanzania has more than 120 languages (Mutembei 2013), a quick review of its language policies shows how much the language policy under colonialism played a major role in the past and has been maintained with modifications in the current sociopolitical climate. Blommaert (1999) examines Tanzania's language ideology, which was based on Ujamaa (African socialism), and notes that, before the country gained its independence, Swahili was the language of political mobilization and the medium of instruction at the primary school level. When the ruling party, the Tanzania African National Union, came into existence, there was a ready instrument to use in the mobilization of the Tanzanian people. As in other societies where local languages existed alongside colonial languages, Swahili was used in lower spheres of education, but English was used in the higher spheres of social and political life (Blommaert 1999). One assumption that has been made about Tanzania is that everyone speaks Swahili, but this is only somewhat true. Although some people are born into families that speak Swahili and therefore acquire it from childhood, others learn it as a second language or acquire it along with their parents' first language. After independence the ease with which politicians expressed themselves in Swahili made the promotion of Swahili an easy sale and an added asset for them and the people. The influence of Julius Nyerere, the first president of Tanzania, made this even easier. Nyerere embraced the language in his speeches to promote African socialism, the core of the Arusha Declaration of 1967. As a consequence, the entire society viewed Swahili as a marker of African socialism and as an identity marker for the people of Tanzania and their culture. To the proponents of the Ujamaa ideology, Swahili symbolized independence, Africanhood, Tanzanian citizenship, and freedom, whereas, according to Blommaert (1999), English became more a symbol of neocolonialism, oppression, and imperialism. For instance, these divergent views are captured in a play by Ebrahim Hussein (1971), who reexamines these phenomena after the Zanzibar revolution of 1964. Although Nyerere later began to urge his country to embrace multilingualism by learning English, Swahili had already been engrained in people's lives as the language of the common people and the language through which the country perpetuated its manifestos and policies. Times have obviously changed, and the efforts to promote Swahili seem to have been abandoned with the collapse of the Ujamaa hegemony and the current political alliances that

Tanzania as a country has established. However, Swahili remains the language of the majority, and, in fact, it has essentially marginalized all the other Tanzanian languages. Tanzania still embraces Swahili, but the reemergence in Africa of the influence of the Western powers, especially the United States, through globalization and the free market, has seen Tanzania gravitating more and more toward a capitalist mentality. This mentality seeks to be aggressive economically by hosting foreign investors who do not necessarily speak Swahili. Although the proposed new Constitution identifies Swahili as the national and official language, some Tanzanians question the place of Swahili in a globalized society where English dominates the world's markets.

### Kenya's Language Policy and Situation

Kenya, which gained its independence in 1963, boasts at least forty-two ethnolinguistic groups. Within these many groups, the dominant ones numerically include the Gikuyu, Luo, Kalenjin, and Luhya. Unlike Tanzania, Kenya was colonized solely by the British during the colonial period. Kenya's coast, however, came into contact with other national groups, such as the Arab world, before colonialism, and thus its linguistic landscape is painted with some Arabism, which raises the question of the purity and status of Swahili. The approach of the British to language was to promote local languages when they deemed it beneficial to their course of action, and to promote English when they deemed the status of English to be in jeopardy. Nabea (2009) argues that though English was promoted, local languages were discouraged due to their potential unifying force. For the British, Kenya was viewed as similar to South Africa (Mazrui 1986; Mazrui and Mazrui 1998). The British liked Kenya, and they wanted to settle there—the white highlands in Kenya are a testimony to their liking of the country. Therefore, based on both political and other interests, language policies in Kenya have not been consistent; they have changed based on the political regimes.

Language policy in Kenya is conspicuous in its schools but almost absent in its public life outside educational institutions. Unlike in Tanzania, however, English has been used as the medium of instruction from fourth grade to college. In cosmopolitan communities ethnic languages are not used in schools; instead, Swahili is used in conjunction with English as the languages of instruction starting in first grade. Kenya's Parliament uses both English and Swahili, and members of Parliament must pass a proficiency examination in both languages before they are allowed to vie for public seats.

On paper and in its most recent Constitution of 2010, Kenya recognizes all ethnic groups and their languages. Kenya's major challenge, however, is the attitudes of the population toward the language of education. Because English is introduced at the very beginning of a child's educational career, local-language or Swahili-mediated instruction has not been supported by the population, as Swahili has in Tanzania (Muaka 2009). It is also important to note here that, as opposed to Tanzania's Ujamaa/ socialistic political and economic ideology after the Arusha Declaration of 1967, Kenya went in a liberal direction, taking a capitalistic approach to economic matters. This has also led to less ingenuity in language use among speakers in public, except in public institutions, where the use of local languages is discouraged. As already observed above, this is the route currently being adopted by Tanzania, a nation that for a long time was viewed as an exemplary model of Swahilization and Africanhood identity.

Institutionally, therefore, Kenya has established English as the medium of instruction and Swahili as the national language. Although Swahili is also an official language and can be used in any official domain, English seems to dominate the business of the government. Therefore, whereas most Kenyans speak these two official languages, they also may speak several other indigenous languages due to intermarriages or necessity as members of communities that interact with each other. Given the history of Kenya and its interaction with foreign cultures of English hegemony, it has been noted by scholars (e.g., Mazrui 2004) that the use of English is more visible in government offices than in marketplaces. They acknowledge, however, as Muaka (2009) also notes, that outside the public domain, English has begun to compete for space with indigenous languages in unofficial domains.

## The Study

The study described in this chapter is situated in the context of language policies of these two countries. The chapter utilizes visual data collected over a period of three and a half years from 2010 to 2013 in Nairobi, Mombasa, and Dar es Salaam. More than three hundred digital photographs of billboards were taken in these three cities in an effort to understand how advertising language choices in asymmetrical multilingual settings are made and used to express the linguistic habits of the inhabitants of these speech communities. Questions guiding this study include:

- What are the language choices in public signage?
- How does language choice in these settings reflect and represent the language policies of each country?
- What language dynamics do the billboards represent?
- Given their sociopolitical ecologies, do the countries in question represent similar or different language choices?
- Finally, what relationship exists between language displays and language policies in the two East African countries?

### *Conceptual Framework*

Signage and advertising in general are multidisciplinary, and therefore they call for a multifaceted approach to adequately address the issues they convey. The eclectic sociolinguistic framework (Landry and Bourhis 1997; Shohamy, Ben Rafael, and Barni 2010; Spolsky 2004; Shohamy and Gorter 2009; Bakhtin 1981, 1986) sheds more light on how public signage on billboards perpetuates language ideologies and how these ideologies are contested through current language trends in urban settings. Consequently, this study combines several approaches—discourse analysis, Bakhtinian concepts of multivocality and heteroglossia, language policy, and ideology—in an attempt to understand signage in the three major multilingual urban settings identified.

Because this chapter is concerned with language policy matters, I first consider the work of Spolsky (2004), in which he talks of three elements within language policy: language management, practice, and beliefs. His model helps to delineate whether language management strategies transfer into actual language use, both in signage and speakers' daily practices. His argument is that effective language policies can have a positive impact on language use. Elsewhere, Spolsky (2009) observes that when language policies marginalize some languages, they lead to the dominant ideology, which in effect can result in a monolingual situation. He further notes that when people are marginalized, they develop strong resistance to the dominant language hegemony and enable the creation of bilingual advertising. By drawing on his model, I seek to explain how advertisers are influenced by the policies that are in place. I also seek to identify the creators of those advertisements to discern the connection between language practice and language management.

For Spolsky (2004), depending on how language policy is executed, certain language ideologies and attitudes will influence language practices. These concepts are intertwined, so a discussion of one of them automatically leads to a consideration of the other one. In a way, Spolsky's views are similar to Bakhtin's (1981, 1986) concept of multivocality. In his examination of language, Bakhtin argues that there are different voices in any given act. In East African advertisements, and in particular Kenyan advertisements, different languages are used. These languages represent different voices—voices of young people, adults, and those of ordinary Kenyans.

Language policies in both Kenya and Tanzania identify Swahili and English as both national and official languages to be used in public domains. In Bakhtin's words, this is an attempt to create order; it is an ideal situation that societies strive to achieve. However, as Bakhtin (1986, 141) further points out, "language is always languages." It has already been noted that both Kenya and Tanzania are multilingual, with both autochthonous and former colonial languages interacting in people's repertoires. This resonates with what Bakhtin notes above when he states that there are always many different ways of speaking, variations that reflect the diversity of social experiences, conceptualizations, and values. In the East African situation, language use reflects the effects of historical and social forces that these speech communities have undergone. In this chapter I argue that language choice and practice reflect the attitudes and the realities of East Africans in their day-to-day lives. And as Bakhtin notes, there is always creativity in language use. Language is a social product that is affected by society just as much as language affects the society within which it is used. Language practice, which is itself affected by language ideologies, cannot be detached from its sociopolitical and historical contexts. House and Rehbein (2004) attest to this position when they note that the media reveal much about social realities. However, though this is true, they equally posit that the media can also be creators of reality. In other words, the frameworks used in this chapter help the reader to see how discourse on billboards is a representation of how language and discourse interact with the sociopolitical realities of speakers in their respective speech communities.

Within this broad understanding of society, linguistic diversity emerges as language changes over time in response to societal dynamics. For Bakhtin language change is not systematic but rather messy, as it responds to real people's actions in their daily lives. Although purists view language as a systematic system, Bakhtin's views seem to suggest that language change does not begin systematically. Perhaps after it has been adopted by speakers, then it can become a norm. However, what has been observed in this school of thought is that as a consequence of diversity, people speak differently on different occasions and due to a variety of factors, such as profession, age, social class, and region. Consequently, Bakhtin's concept of creativity becomes very important as we examine hybridity, which is manifested in people's speech as well as the billboards that this study examines in both Kenya and Tanzania. Thus, though there are language policies or language management (Spolky 2009), globalization, evolving political and economic mentalities and ideologies, and marketing strategies are in the hands of a generation that embraces multilingual communication, which includes both legitimate and unofficial linguistic varieties. These changes reflect linguistic landscapes as much as these linguistic landscapes reflect the linguistic realities of the people in the cities investigated. With reference to Bakhtin's notion of heteroglossia, languages do not exclude each other; rather, they intersect with each other in many different ways, resulting in different language varieties. This concept supports the idea of creativity, which manifests itself in hybrid constructions, a focal point of this chapter.

### Research Methodology

In this study more than three hundred digital photographs of city billboards were taken in Nairobi, Dar es Salaam, and Mombasa and were subsequently analyzed. The photographs were taken along the main city center streets and roads and also on the route from the airport toward the city center and in adjacent neighborhoods. Photographs of billboards that displayed the same items were taken to determine whether language use changed based on the location or country. Because these cities are strategically positioned economically, their businesses are vibrant and there is so much that passersby get to see. In order to fully understand the linguistic landscape that these cities display, one must also consider the creation and design of the signage. A distinction between private and public signs (see Landry and Bourhis 1997) enables us to determine how language policy intersects with language practice on the ground. Besides taking pictures and documenting them as a method of data collection, I utilized unstructured interviews. It is only possible to gain an understanding of the cultural nuances and contexts that lead to certain choices of words by consulting those who speak the languages involved, spend their lives in the culture, and understand the dynamics of their speech community.

## Findings

Language choice in advertisements depends on a variety of factors: the product, location, and audience. Language choice is likely to illustrate the cultural, social, political, and economic circumstances of the targeted population and its region. However, not every single sign will capture all the circumstances that define the people of a given region. In this section different categories of language choice on billboards are analyzed qualitatively to capture the linguistic habits of the groups

Table 12.1
Languages Used on Billboards in Three East African Cities

| City | English Only | Swahili Only | Swahili and English | Total per City |
|---|---|---|---|---|
| Nairobi | 62, or 62.6% | 9, or 9.1% | 28, or 28.3% | 99, or 100% |
| Dar es Salaam | 40, or 31.3% | 60, or 46.9% | 28, or 21.9% | 128, or 100% |
| Mombasa | 50, or 61.7% | 11, or 13.6% | 20, or 24.7% | 81, or 100% |
| Total per category | 152, or 49.4% | 80, or 25.9% | 76, or 24.7% | 308, or 100% |

under discussion. The following are the categories by which different billboards are analyzed: English only, Swahili only, and a mix of Swahili and English. Table 12.1 shows the proportions of each category of billboard observed in each city. In the following sections I report on language asymmetry, language symmetry, and language hybridity; language in Kenya and Tanzania in the eyes of the advertisers; and semi-private advertisements in both countries. Finally, the chapter ends with a commentary on the whole research project.

### English and Swahili Billboards

In figure 12.1 the advertisement depicts a scene that one is likely to encounter in a Kenyan urban neighborhood between a landlord or landlady and his or her tenant or between roommates. The billboard combines urban Swahili (asking "Will you move this round/time?") in bold capital letters with use of a smaller font for the English text. This is an advertisement by the Nation Group Ltd. to advertise a contest that could potentially increase newspaper sales. The Nation Group publishes the most

Figure 12.1 An Advertisement for an English-Language Newspaper in Nairobi, Using Both Swahili and English

popular English daily in Kenya, *The Daily Nation*, which is also now sold all over East Africa. The company also publishes a Swahili version, *Taifa Leo*. It is therefore unusual that this English paper can place an advertisement with Swahili words in bold. What is the motivation? As already outlined, signage can depict how language is used and it can also be influenced by speakers' habits. Figure 12.1 shows how the impact of society on the media forces the newspaper to build on people's habits (Bourdieu 1991). The advertisement also depicts how language is practiced by the paper's readers, even though its main medium is English. Although they use English as their main language of publishing, advertisers prefer to use Swahili to connect with their larger audience, as has been observed by Bell (1984). Therefore, though the majority of advertisements are still only in English, a mix of English and Swahili continues to gain currency in all the cities studied.

Billboards that use Swahili can be found in all three cities, as shown in table 12.1. However, most of these billboards are found in Dar es Salaam. Generally, these billboards convey the regular linguistic habits of the local audience. The data from Kenya reported here are a little surprising because, given that Mombasa is the cradle of Swahili, one would have expected it to have as many billboards in Swahili as Dar es Salaam, but this is not the case. Only 13.6 percent of the billboards in Mombasa are displayed in Swahili compared with 46.9 percent of the billboards in Dar es Salaam.

### Language Asymmetry

Under the category of language asymmetry, billboards that show both languages in unequal proportions are analyzed. In figure 12.1 the choice of language remains English, even though Swahili is foregrounded in the form of a question: UTA-HAMA ROUNDI HII (Will you move this round/time)? The rest of the ad is in English, with the byline and the extra text being displayed in English. This is a Kenyan advertisement in Nairobi, and it clearly shows the dominance of English. Swahili is used to initially connect to the audience, but the rest of the information is conveyed in English. One can also tell that ROUNDI is "round" in English but has been Swahilized. Most speakers would write it as RAUNDI rather than ROUNDI, as spelled in figure 12.1.

In figure 12.2 a similar disproportionate use of language is observed. A politician vying for a seat uses English everywhere else except in the word ALILETA (he or she brought). The politician was vying for the governor's seat in Nairobi. What seems to be represented here is the liberty that the politician accords his designer to include both English and Swahili in the advertisement. In his campaigns, however, the politician uses mostly Swahili, because the majority of the people who come to listen to his speeches are more comfortable speaking Swahili and their local languages. This shows the underlying power of Swahili, a power that is not always expressed in language policy. However, the use of both English and Swahili also demonstrates the multilingual nature of the society, a situation that has been aided by an educational language policy that valorizes English.

The billboards in Tanzania do not, however, show many examples of this type of code-switched discourse. Most of them are in Swahili, with a few English lexical

Figure 12.2 A Political Advertisement in Nairobi

items. In the next sections we see examples that illustrate the most noticeable code-switching in the Tanzanian market scene.

### Swahili-Only Billboards

In both Kenyan and Tanzanian cities, billboards using only Swahili were observed. In Kenya, most of these billboards were observed in Mombasa. In figure 12.3 the image shows a billboard advertising flour with the display text using Swahili only.

Figure 12.3 An Advertisement for Flour in Mombasa

Figure 12.4  A Billboard in Dar es Salaam, Using Swahili

The ad's text, "Unga wa Jamii kwa matokeo bora" (Societal Flour for better results), clearly shows that the target of the advertisement is homemakers, who are typically women in Kenyan culture. However, the message on the flour packet itself is expressed in English. Conversely, figure 12.4 is a representation of many billboards in Dar es Salaam where "pure" Swahili is used. In figure 12.4 the advertisers

Figure 12.5  An Advertisement for a Kenyan English-Language Newspaper

use older people to convey their message, even though the intended reader could be a younger person. The ad says, "Tuma pesa kuongeza tabasamu lao" (send money [to them] to increase their smile). The Kenyan market would probably have used an advertisement (e.g., the one shown in figure 12.12) that employs urban or informal Swahili, that is, Sheng.

### English-Only Advertisements

English-only billboards were more noticeable in Kenyan cities than in Tanzania. The choice of English is a reflection of language ideology that is current in Kenya. Figures 12.5 and 12.6 are typical. Figure 12.5, an advertisement for a newspaper, further exemplifies the dominant language ideology, which views English as a marker of knowledge. This means that knowledge can only be gained through the English language. It would be rare to see a billboard that says smart people read the *Taifa Leo* or *Mwananchi* Swahili newspapers. The text in the Coca-Cola advertisement (figure 12.6) in Nairobi is all in English. It is a further illustration of the dominant language ideology.

### Language Symmetry

In her study of advertisements in Lira town, Uganda, Reh (2004) found some advertisements that displayed the same message in more than one language. The data sets investigated in this chapter show this same occurrence, especially in Dar es Salaam. Most government and semigovernment organizations have begun to display their writing in both English and Swahili.

Figure 12.6 A Coca-Cola Advertisement in Nairobi

Similar to Reh's study, this study found several billboards that displayed the use of Swahili and English symmetrically. On the same billboard the identical message was displayed in two or more languages. The prominence given to both languages did not, however, symbolize the same status or perceptions by the audience. What these types of advertisements show is advertisers' desire to connect with their audience (Bell 1984). Putting Swahili side by side with English is meant to facilitate communication on either side. The sign in figure 12.7 is an insurance advertisement that promises its clients that it does not matter what language they speak. All their insurance needs can be met in their language. This billboard is in four different languages—English, Swahili, Afrikaans, and Hindi. In a linguistically diverse city such as Dar es Salaam, the signage is meant for both local people and those from other societies where those languages are spoken.

The billboard shown in figure 12.8, posted by the University of Dar es Salaam for its fiftieth anniversary, provides its message in two languages. Legère (2012) observed that in Tanzania, most Swahili signage was being replaced with signs in English, especially on university premises. Clearly the billboard in figure 12.8 attests to this trend, with the English version of the text being at the top and the Swahili one at the bottom. Tanzania's gradual acceptance of English seems to appear not only in this advertisement but also in the Institute of Kiswahili's billboard shown in figure 12.9. Unlike the main university billboard, which prioritizes English, Swahili is prioritized in the one that addresses Swahili studies. Although table 12.1 shows that the majority of signs in Dar es Salaam are in Swahili, the use of bilingual signs in English and Swahili is increasing.

### Language Duplication

The foregoing language alternation that is so common in Dar es Salaam was not common in the two Kenyan cities studied. However, what was observed in Kenya

Figure 12.7 A Billboard in Dar es Salaam Advertising Insurance in English, Swahili, Afrikaans, and Hindi

Figure 12.8  A Sign Promoting the University of Dar es Salaam

was the same message displayed on separate billboards in English and then in Swahili. A good example are the OMO detergent billboards (figures 12.10 and 12.11), which demonstrate this kind of language choice by advertisers. What is also interesting is that there does not seem to be any clear motive for doing this, except perhaps to acknowledge that both Swahili and English are used and therefore speakers have access to both.

Figure 12.9  A Sign Promoting the Institute of Kiswahili

Figure 12.10 An Advertisement for OMO Detergent, Using Swahili

Figure 12.11 An Advertisement for OMO Detergent, Using English

### Language Hybridity: Swahinglish and Sheng

Higgins (2009) examines how English is localized in East Africa and shows different forms of hybridity, including in advertisements. In Tanzania hybridity appears in advertisements that use Swahinglish (Swahili and English), and in Kenya Sheng or Engsh are very common. These advertisements are mostly private, but semiprivate billboards seem to portray this type of language choice as well. Bakhtin (1981) notes that the notion of heteroglossia underscores the importance of hybridity through language creativity in showing the consequences of multilingualism. This type of multilingual communication (House and Rehbein 2004) was very much evident in billboards observed in Kenya. Figure 12.12 shows a political billboard ad placed by a young presidential candidate during the 2013 elections. These advertisements started running in 2012, when the presidential campaigns started in Kenya. Peter Kenneth was one of the presidential candidates, and his main target was youths. His style of presentation was therefore influenced by the audience he sought to reach (Bell 1984). In his main slogan, "TUNAWESMAKE," Peter Kenneth sought to appeal to youths by letting them know that they could make it.

### Analyzing TUNAWESMAKE

The targeted audience in the billboard shown in figure 12.12 is the young voter who speaks not the standard form of Swahili but a hybrid variety that incorporates different varieties. This variety is commonly referred to as Sheng in Kenya, and a

Figure 12.12 A Presidential Campaign Advertisement in Kenya, Using Sheng

somewhat similar version occurs in Tanzania in the form of Swahinglish. The advertisement illustrates both syntactic and phonological creativity:

TU, We

NA, Tense

WES, Can (standard Swahili would be *weza*)

MAKE, make

The intended meaning is "We can make it."

Language hybridity is not just restricted to political slogans, for other advertisers also take advantage of this form of communication by mixing Swahili and English. In some cases mixing could be viewed as borrowing, as with the word "paypoint" in figure 12.13, but it is a very consistent practice in other advertisements, as can be observed in figure 12.14, which is for Family Bank and highlights how mobile banking has eased money transactions. In both Kenyan and Tanzanian cities, the emerging markets have largely contributed to hybridity and creativity. Mobile telephones, an important part of life for East Africans, have made informal interactions that mix different languages in a single interaction an important element of language practice, so it is not surprising that an advertisement for a mobile phone would mix languages. This is the interaction that Bakhtin's (1981, 1986) approach introduces, and it shows multilinguals' creativity: Changing language reflects a changing society. Similar examples of hybridity can be observed in

Figure 12.13 Code-Switching from Swahili to English in a Kenyan Advertisement

Figure 12.14 An Advertisement for Mobile Banking

figure 12.15, in which Kenya Power encourages people to connect power to avoid cold showers ("shower freezer").

### Language Practice and Language Policy?
The dominance of English in Kenyan advertisements reflects the impact that language policies have had on speakers in public domains. However, creativity as witnessed in advertisements shows the forces from below that do not necessarily adhere

Figure 12.15 An Advertisement for Kenya Power

to the written policies. These language users draw from these policies by mastering English and then creatively blending it with local languages. The majority of Kenyans do not follow a monologic approach in their daily speech. Billboards in Kenya have begun to reflect this dialogism, which also reflects how different people construct their identities.

The data from Tanzania show similar trends. There are more and more hybrid billboards, especially in Dar es Salaam. Consider, for instance, figure 12.13 which, though largely loaded with Swahili, does include a single English word—"paypoint." These multilingual billboards illustrate an attempt by the advertising world to connect with its audience in a linguistic form that is current and unrestricted. The dominance of Swahili in Dar es Salaam reflects the language ideology that has been held by Tanzanians for many years.

### Language Use in Private and Semiprivate Advertisements

Language choice on billboards in both Kenya and Tanzania depends mostly on the sponsors of the advertisements. In this chapter attention has also been paid to those billboards that demonstrate collaborations between government agencies and private partners. In these types of advertisements, government policies seem to dictate the language used. In the Kenyan scenarios, the language is either Swahili or English, whereas in Tanzania it is mostly Swahili. In figure 12.16 the Kenyan government, in partnership with the US Agency for International Development and the UK Department for International Development, mounts a billboard that aims to eradicate malaria by urging residents to sleep in mosquito nets. As can be seen in the picture, both English and Swahili are used. Although Swahili fronts the main text area, the text at the bottom that identifies the sponsors and region is in English:

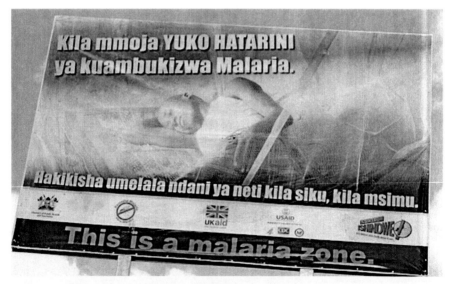

Figure 12.16 A Billboard Promoting the Use of Mosquito Nets, Sponsored by the Government of Kenya in Collaboration with Foreign Aid Groups

Figure 12.17 A Billboard in Dar es Salaam, Sponsored by the Government of Tanzania and the African Development Bank

"This is a malaria zone." The ad is a product of a partnership between the Kenyan government and foreign government agencies that shows a symbiotic relationship between the two languages. This ad is meant for areas where Swahili is the main language used, even though other languages are spoken. As can be seen in figure 12.17, in Dar es Salaam most of the text is in Swahili but, in the billboard sponsored by both the government of Tanzania and the African Development Bank, both English and Swahili are used. It shows a concerted effort by the government to reach its audience in Dar es Salaam in a language they understand better.

### Kenya and Tanzania in the Eyes of Advertisers

The East African region boasts of trade collaborations among the countries involved. Some Kenyan products are found in grocery stores in other countries to the extent that if you are inside one store, you might think you are in Kenya. In Tanzania, for instance, most stores sell Kenyan products, and Kenyan television channels are broadcast. Likewise, Coca-Cola is obviously an American product, but it is also sold in Kenya and Tanzania, and very few people would think of it as a foreign product because of how it has been localized.

Spolsky (2009) makes a similar observation when he discusses the impact of globalization in the media and advertisements. It can be argued that although Coca-Cola is originally from the United States, the marketing of the product has been localized to suit consumers in particular countries. Figure 12.18 was taken in Dar es Salaam and it is the same Coca-Cola billboard displayed in figure 12.6 above for the

Figure 12.18 A Coca-Cola Advertisement in Dar es Salaam

Kenyan market. The only difference is the language used. In Tanzania Swahili is used, but in Kenya English is the language chosen to convey the message. The actors are Kenyan, even though no one would notice whether they were Kenyans or Tanzanians. What this further demonstrates is the language ideologies that have guided these two countries for a long period of time. In figure 12.10 the display of OMO detergent in Kenya is in both English and Swahili. In Tanzania the advertisement is only displayed in Swahili.

## Conclusion

Language choice on billboards reflects the language policies adopted in both countries examined here. On one hand, private linguistic landscapes recognize the actual language practices of the people by embracing hybridity with ingenuity. On the other hand, where the sponsors of an advertisement are government units, either both languages are used interchangeably or only one language is used. When both languages are used, there is no hybridity observed. The decisions seem to be dictated by the audience, a factor that shows government units are more conscious of the people's habits than in the past. Hybridity, however, shows both creativity and some form of contestation from below in reaction to the dominant ideology of either English or Swahili. Although Tanzania has always been viewed as the custodian of standard Swahili, elements of street Swahili, hybridity, and code-switching are becoming common trends in people's lives.

In spite of different sociopolitical standpoints, both Kenya and Tanzania recognize the importance of Swahili and either use it in their public spaces or devise creative ways to use it alongside English that no longer symbolize elitism. The informal sector, private media houses, information technology, and aggressive marketing by different entities such as telephone companies make word play an interesting phenomenon of language practice in the two countries.

## References

Bakhtin, M. Mikhail. 1981. *The Dialogic Imagination*, edited by Michael Holquist. Translated by Caryl Emerson and Michael Holquist. Austin: University of Texas Press.

———. 1986. *Speech Genres and Other Late Essays*. Translated by Vern W. McGee. Austin: University of Texas Press.

Bell, Allan. 1984. "Language Style as Audience Design." *Language in Society* 13, no. 2: 145–204.

Blommaert, Jan. 1999. *State Ideology and Language in Tanzania*. Cologne: Köppe.

Bourdieu, Pierre. 1991. *Language and Symbolic Power*. Cambridge MA: Harvard University Press.

Bwenge, Charles. 2009. "Language Choice in Dar es Salaam's Billboards." In *The Languages of Urban Africa*, edited by Fiona McLaughlin. New York: Continuum.

Higgins, Christina. 2009. *English as a Local Language: Post-Colonial Identities and Multilingual Practices*. Buffalo: Multilingual Matters.

House, Juliane, and Jochen Rehbein, eds. 2004. *Multilingual Communication*. Philadelphia: John Benjamins.

Hussein, Ebrahim. 1971. *Mashetani*. Dar es Salaam: Oxford University Press.

Landry, Rodrigue, and Richard Y. Bourhis. 1997. "Linguistic Landscape and Ethnolinguistic Vitality: An Empirical Study." *Journal of Language and Social Psychology* 16:23–49.

Legère, Karsten. 2012. "Swahili and English in Dar es Salaam: Billboards, Shop Signs, and Homepages." Paper presented at 43rd Annual Conference on African Linguistics, New Orleans, March.

Mazrui, Ali Al'Amin. 1986. *The Africans: A Triple Heritage: A Commentary*. Santa Barbara CA: Annenberg/CPB Project.

———. 2004. *English in Africa after the Cold War*. Clevedon, UK: Multilingual Matters.

Mazrui, Ali Al'Amin, and Alamin Mazrui. 1998. *The Power of Babel: Language & Governance in the African Experience*. Oxford: J. Currey.

Muaka, Leonard. 2009. "The Dynamics of Language Use among Rural and Urban Kenyan Youths." PhD dissertation, University of Illinois at Urbana-Champaign.

Mutembei, Kai Aldin. 2013. "Swahili Language and Culture." Lecture presented at Makongo, Dar es Salaam.

Nabea, Wendo. 2009. "Language Policy in Kenya: Negotiation with Hegemony." *Journal of Pan African Studies* 3, no. 1: 121–38.

Reh, Mechthild. 2004. "Multilingual Writing: A Reader's Oriented Typology—with Examples from Lira Municipality (Uganda)." *International Journal of the Sociology of Language* 170:1–41.

Shohamy, Elana Goldberg, and Durk Gorter, eds. 2009. *Linguistic Landscape: Expanding the Scenery*. New York: Routledge.

Shohamy, Elana Goldberg, Eliezer Ben Rafael, and Monica Barni, eds. 2010. *Linguistic Landscape in the City*. Buffalo: Multilingual Matters.

Spolsky, Bernard. 2004. *Language Policy*. New York: Cambridge University Press.

———. 2009. *Language Management*. New York: Cambridge University Press.

Stroud, Christopher, and Sibonile Mpendukana. 2009. "Towards a Material Ethnography of Linguistic Landscape: Multilingualism, Mobility and Space in a South African Township." *Journal of Sociolinguistics* 13, no. 3: 363–86.

# 13

## The Persuasive Nature of Metaphors in Kenya's Political Discourse

**LEONARD MUAKA**
*Winston-Salem University*

**THE AIM OF THIS CHAPTER** is to analyze Kenya's political discourse with an emphasis on the metaphors politicians use. The chapter uses Raila Arnollo Odinga, a controversial and influential figure in Kenyan politics, as the main focal point in a discussion of Kenya's political discourse. By focusing on Odinga's political parables in his campaigns leading to the 2007 and 2013 presidential elections, the chapter identifies the stylistic strategies utilized by politicians to engage and identify with their audiences from different ethnic groups. Quite often, the (mis)interpretations of these metaphors lead to further debates.

To examine these debates I invoke a number of approaches that deal with both political discourse and metaphor. These approaches include critical discourse analysis (Van Dijk 1993, 1997), critical metaphor analysis (Charteris-Black 2004, 2011), ideology (Fairclough 1992; Jones 2012), and cognitive theory of metaphors (Lakoff and Johnson 1980; Ungerer and Schmid 2006). The foregoing frameworks complement each other in showing how politicians seek and win their participants' involvement in their political agendas by evoking cultural nuances and experiences known to both politicians and potential voters.

More than sixty different metaphorical linguistic instances were examined to establish patterns of how politicians strategically use language to win votes and to present their opponents negatively. The data used in this chapter were drawn from Kenyan online media, including radio shows, mainstream live and recorded television programs, newspapers, and other privately run internet media sites. The period under consideration here covers the 2007 to 2013 Kenyan general election campaigns.

### Metaphor in Political Discourse
Politicians hope to influence and persuade voters by using different rhetorical strategies in their political campaigns. Whatever strategies politicians use, including metaphors, each politician exploits the strategies that are understood within his or her social and cultural world. As Mooney and colleagues (2011) note, politicians need to speak to their audiences persuasively and inclusively if they hope to win elections. When language is used metaphorically, listeners and readers are able to

create images in their own minds and associate them with certain contexts. Lakoff and Johnson (1980, 3) argue persuasively that when people speak metaphorically, they are likely to influence the way other people think and behave. For them, "metaphor is pervasive in everyday life, not just in language but in thought and action. Our ordinary conceptual system, in terms of which we both think and act, is fundamentally metaphorical in nature."

The persuasive nature of political discourse is realized in the context of ideology, an important construct that manifests itself through language. Ideology can be defined as a set of beliefs that are held by a group of people and through which they view their world (Jones 2012). The scope of the group can vary greatly. For example, the group can be defined at the gender level, community level, ethnic level, or national level. This mutual worldview can be dominant and in such situations it is held as hegemonic. However, Mooney and colleagues (2011) warn that ideological power struggles can ensue if other groups contest the hegemonic ideology in their society. In the case of societies that are divided along ethnic lines, ethnic conflict can easily occur.

In Kenya political discourse is manifested at the national level in a manner that mirrors not only the political ideologies of the different political figures but also the various ethnic communities that make up the Kenyan nation. Kenya has roughly forty-two ethnolinguistic groups that also represent how the country is divided regionally. Politicians from each one of these ethnic groups form political parties that draw heavily from their ethnic bases. However, no victory at the national level can be garnered without alliances that involve multiple political parties, especially since the one-party system was abandoned in the early 1990s, following many years of the Kenya African National Union's dominance of Kenyan politics.

## Language and Politics

Political discourse has attracted much attention from different scholars around the globe, including Orwenjo (2010), Charteris-Black (2011), Obeng (2003), and Nabea (2010), among others. The main focus of such works has been to examine how politicians use language as a political tool to win elections and to defend their positions and policies. Politicians rely on the spoken word to contrast their track record with that of their opponents.

Although many voters would like to make their voting decisions based on a politician's honesty, morality, and integrity, in a pool of so many choices, each politician needs to have some style and form of self-presentation that can ultimately influence the voter's decision (Charteris-Black 2011). Politicians capitalize on their strengths and, in an attempt to be persuasive, resort to metaphors that can help convey their arguments effectively. For the majority of the audience that follows politics, the spoken language is the primary mode politicians use to communicate in persuading them. Charteris-Black further notes that politicians employ humor, metaphor, and myth telling to make their speeches more appealing and effective.

## Theoretical Framework

To capture these essential rhetorical strategies discussed above, I introduce several approaches in this chapter. First, the chapter utilizes Lakoff and Johnson's (1980) cognitive theory of metaphor analysis to show how politicians seek participants' involvement in their political agendas by evoking the cultural nuances embedded in metaphors known to both politicians and voters. The new thoughts that metaphors offer to the listeners broaden their understanding of the situation at hand.

Another important theoretical framework that is utilized in this chapter is critical discourse analysis (CDA), as proposed by Van Dijk (1993) and by other scholars, such as Paltridge (2013). CDA shows how political discourse can be a medium for producing, maintaining, and reproducing power inequality through established sociopolitical structures. The addition of CDA helps paint a vivid picture of power struggles among politicians through metaphor. Additionally, CDA takes note of how dialogues are manipulated and dominated in turn-taking to sustain and reproduce inequality. It is, however, important to acknowledge that there are obviously other strategies that speakers use to maintain an edge over their interlocutors.

Charteris-Black's (2004, 2011) critical metaphor framework, and its treatment of how metaphorical language is used to persuade audiences, adds another dimension to the current analysis. He describes this as an approach that analyzes metaphors with the aim of identifying the intentions and ideologies inherent in language use. For Charteris-Black and other scholars, metaphor involves meaning transfer that the audience has to interpret. At the same time each metaphor is guided by an ideology that mirrors people's specific sets of beliefs and assumptions (Jones 2012). In this chapter ideology is examined because of its crucial role in discourse analysis.

In the Kenyan case tact, strategies, and energies were all invested in the 2013 contest between two powerful politicians, Raila Odinga and Uhuru Kenyatta, and, by extension, between their running mates. This was despite the fact that there were eight presidential aspirants in the March 2013 general elections. Charteris-Black (2004) observes that metaphors are very important tools for persuading voters to align with candidates' ideological standpoints. Through their political ideologies, such candidates are able to exert their worldview and maintain a hegemonic power base that some people take to be the norm. Politicians in this study always attempted to create this disposition within their political bases.

## The Kenyan Political Scene

Kenya is a young nation that just celebrated fifty years of independence from British colonial rule in 2013. This fifty-year period has seen the country go through different highs and lows in politics. Always seen as a haven of peace in a volatile region, Kenya prided itself on being a promising democratic nation for a long time. For the most part until 1992, Kenya was a one-party state. However, with the repeal of a section of the Kenyan Constitution, Kenya officially became a multiparty state. The opposition was weak, however, and with the same political and judicial structures in place, no real change occurred. In 2002 the first opposition leader, Mwai Kibaki, was elected the president through an alliance of several parties. Kibaki defeated the Kenya African National Union's ruling party candidate, Uhuru Kenyatta, and ascended to the presidency. Since then, political freedom has continued to be experienced in the country amid problems that young democracies encounter.

In 2007 former political allies parted ways and contested for the same presidential seat. Odinga and Kibaki were the front-runners. However, in an election that was expected to see Odinga emerge as the winner, the country was thrown into a pandemonium after Kibaki was declared the winner. The 2007 postelection violence left the country wounded. Many people, especially in the Rift Valley region, were killed. In the last election, of March 2013, Uhuru Kenyatta, who contested for the presidency with his running mate, William Ruto, defeated Odinga. However, at the time of writing this chapter, the two leaders face charges at the International Criminal Court for their alleged involvement in the 2007 postelection violence and killings.

Kenyan politicians depend upon their ethnic backing, with very few addressing issues that face the country as a whole. Because of the country's ethnic-based politics, any politician who seeks leadership at the national level must, by necessity, form alliances with leaders from other ethnic communities to guarantee votes from those communities.

Odinga is a politician who is described by Babafemi Badejo as an enigma in Kenyan politics (cited by Mueller 2009). He is the immediate former prime minister, and he has unsuccessfully contested for the Kenyan presidency three times since 1997. In 2007 Odinga claimed that former president Kibaki had robbed victory from him. In the 2013 elections Odinga claimed that the Jubilee coalition had colluded with the Kenyan Independent Electoral and Boundaries Commission to deny him a clear presidential victory at the ballot box. Although there were no riots in 2013, Odinga and his supporters stated that they did not agree with the Supreme Court's judgment after their unsuccessful petition, but they had accepted the verdict for the sake of peace in the country.

Odinga, who likes to entertain his followers, attributes his skills with proverbial language to his childhood socialization. In an interview with the *Sauti Zetu Show* on July 28, 2013, he noted that his use of metaphorical language is grounded in his childhood, when he observed and listened to his uncles speak in parables in their conversations. He noted that sayings help make the point clear to his audience when they compare concepts with familiar things in their lives.

Although politicians can skillfully entertain and pull in crowds, the question that needs to be asked is whether Kenyan politicians engage in issue-based politics or personal attacks. A snapshot of the data collected seems to suggest that verbal attacks at the personal level dominate rallies and that little room is left for real issues. This lack of a discussion of real issues may lead to unqualified candidates being elected to represent the people.

## Metaphor Analysis

To analyze the strategies used by Kenyan politicians, this chapter identifies several metaphors that were consistently used by Odinga during his political campaigns from 2007 to 2013:

1. the soccer commentary/soccer metaphor,
2. the half-bread metaphor,
3. the analog-versus-digital metaphor,

4. the featherweight/heavyweight metaphor,

5. the madman metaphor, and

6. the cat-versus-rat metaphor.

### The Soccer Metaphor

Several of Odinga's well-known metaphors revolve around soccer. One great advantage he has is that he knows his base very well, and one thing upon which most critics agree is that he knows how to connect with his audience. For more than twenty years, Odinga represented the Kibera constituency in Nairobi, an area that is regarded as the largest slum in Africa. He uses the soccer analogy whenever he is addressing large crowds. He resonates and connects with his audience using this metaphor because soccer is the game of the people. A cultural connection is therefore established (Zinken 2003). In Odinga's game metaphor, there are a referee, linesmen, and players, and Odinga plays the role of commentator and successfully employs the soccer register, as it is known by his audience. His skillful use of the game metaphor also allows his audience to see how he brings political victory to his supporters. Just as players change clubs and get traded, Odinga's soccer metaphors change as he incorporates new and different players in his team. His teams always have an edge, and he is usually the one who gets the final pass to score.

The CDA framework indicates that power is never equal and is produced and reproduced by the structures in place (Fairclough 1992). Odinga's metaphors, while engaging the voter, also demonstrate how the political structures that are in place help in sustaining the status quo (Van Dijk 1993). In one of these soccer metaphors Odinga notes that when he remained with the goalkeeper alone and scored, he was ruled offside. In another instance the goalposts were moved (Orwenjo 2010). In reality no goal post can be moved when the game is on; however, Odinga's metaphors demonstrate how he is able to appeal to his base emotionally using soccer, a cultural game they understand well, to appreciate the political realities of their country.

Musalia Mudavadi, a politician who quit Odinga's party to run for the presidency, uses Odinga's own rhetorical strategy and Kenya's pastime, soccer, to redefine Odinga's metaphor. Mudavadi notes that one of the world's greatest soccer players was Pelé. However, he tells the audience that Pelé is no longer the best player. He was the best player at some point, but he is no longer the best player because other younger and better players have emerged. In particular he singles out Lionel Messi, the Argentinian player who plays professional soccer in the European soccer league. Mudavadi's ability to retain the same soccer metaphor but to respecify the theme by introducing two players who are not even Kenyans is also an indication that as a Kenyan politician, he is aware of the cultural experience of the majority of Kenyan soccer fans. Mudavadi's strategy illustrates how speakers can either retain a metaphor with or without modification, or contest it altogether (Chilton and Ilyin 1993). Retaining the soccer metaphor while employing different players from the ones Odinga uses shows an evolving political representation in Kenya.

The examples presented here connect both politicians to their followers by creating vivid images while at the same time equating politicians to players in a game. In each case followers understand that ultimately what they want their politicians to do is win elections. But to enable them to win, the politicians must play a game of positioning and repositioning.

### The Half-Bread Metaphor

Odinga engaged his audiences after the 2007 postelection violence by telling the story of the half-bread that was shared. Kenya's 2007 political violence led to a shared government between Odinga and Kibaki. In the days that followed, this would be viewed as similar to how a loaf of bread is shared. In Kenyan culture it is not unusual for someone to go to a kiosk and buy a half loaf of bread. When reflecting on the compromise after the 2007 elections, Odinga stated the following: "Si Tukasema basi, ilikuwa ni yetu lakini mmetunyanganya sasa pasua katikakati chukua nusu mwachie sisi nusu. Sio? Basi chukua nusu na sisi tuchukue nusu [We said, OK, it was ours, but you have stolen it from us and so now break it into two halves and leave us with a half, right? OK then, take half and we take the other half]" (*The Standard*, December 18, 2012).

As a rejoinder to this metaphor that Odinga often shared with his supporters, his political opponents in the ruling party of Mwai Kibaki reused the metaphor to claim that Odinga's party did not share its portion among its members equitably. They presented Odinga's party as wanting to keep power among a few people, while bribing those who would have otherwise exposed power abuse in the party. Here is the text that was reported in *The Standard* newspaper:

> Tulishika tukagawana. Nusu ikawa yetu nusu ikawa ya ODM na yote ikawa sawa sawa. Yetu tulishika sisi tuligawana sawawasa bila shida yo yote. Lakini ODM wakati walipopatiwa yao badala ya kugawa vizuri wapatie watu wao, wao walianza kuweka kwenye mifuko na halafu wanatolea wengine kamoja; shika kidogo shika kidogo. [We took and split it into two equal halves; one to us and the other half to ODM (Orange Democratic Movement). On our part we shared equally without any problem. But when ODM was given their half, instead of sharing it equally with their people, they started putting some of it in their pockets while giving small portions to some of their members.] (*Citizen TV*, December 14, 2012)

During his campaigns, Odinga also used a different metaphor that parallels the half-bread metaphor. In this analogy, reported in *The Standard* (March 1, 2009), Odinga talked of a hunter who had to share his kill with a bystander: "You assisted with a weapon that I used to spear the animal. But when I dashed to the bush I found another man pulling the carcass, claiming it belongs to him. In the process of staking my rightful claim, people started fighting over the animal and I agreed to share it to avoid more bloodshed."

In the foregoing metaphor, the use of hunters represents political rivals who were both fighting for the presidency (the animal). The metaphor captures the quest for power between the main political coalitions after the election results were disputed. It also shows how many people lost their lives as a compromise was sought. The import of this parable is how Odinga presented himself as a patriot who, for the love of the country, agreed to share executive power with Kibaki after the 2007 elections even though he believed he had won the elections. Yet those from other parties who capitalized on the metaphor showed the mistrust that Odinga's party demonstrated.

Charteris-Black (2011) observes that politics is concerned with acquiring, maintaining, and sustaining power by legitimizing one's actions while delegitimizing opponents (see also Chilton 2004). In the foregoing scenarios, the metaphor of sharing clearly shows the desire of one group wanting to maintain power and the other group challenging the status quo. Each opponent claims that he has been fair and generous but that his opponent has acted unfairly and selfishly. In the end, after noting that each party would have a share of the much-coveted power, a settlement is reached. However, one point that must be observed here is that when a politician uses rhetorical strategies, he banks on the assumption that, culturally, the audience will connect with him and infer the meaning of the metaphor (Lakoff and Johnson 1980).

### The Analog-versus-Digital Metaphor

Raila Odinga and his former running mate and ally, William Ruto, parted ways following a dispute over land issues related to the internally displaced people after the postelection violence of 2007. However, in his attack on old politicians, Ruto and the current president, Uhuru Kenyatta, always referred to such politicians as "analog politicians." What this metaphor attempts to convey politically is that the electorate should phase out the old crop of leaders and politicians who have outlived their usefulness due to their age. In the world of technology, most systems are changing from analog to digital formats and, in the case of Kenya, politicians such as Kenyatta and Ruto view themselves as the leaders of the digital generation. The transfer and creation of new meanings are what make this metaphor interesting.

However, Odinga counters this argument and provides his own perceptions of how he thinks the analog metaphor should be interpreted. As a trained mechanical engineer, Odinga tells his followers that he understands the digital world better than his political opponents. Although this may be construed as a literal interpretation of the metaphor, it can also acquire an extended meaning that portrays Odinga as a seasoned politician who understands the political history of Kenya and the fight for democracy in modern Kenya better than his opponents.

In the analog/digital metaphor, abstract concepts are easily conceptualized when the audience is pushed to think about a change that comes with new ideas and political plans (Lakoff and Johnson 1980). Thus the younger politicians promised the electorate changes, whereas the old politicians were presented and viewed as nonreformists and empty talkers. What is also critical in this metaphor is how Odinga becomes defensive when someone else uses a metaphoric strategy to describe him politically.

### The Cat-versus-Rats Metaphor

Although Odinga would sometimes begin or end his campaigns with the style used in telling a riddle, he would always end up telling a tale. It is safe to argue that

Odinga's metaphoric style benefits from Africa's oral traditions, where stories are told in parables and it is up to the audience to figure out how this metaphor applies to the current political climate. Politicians tailor their speeches and campaigns for a given audience (Jowett and O'Donnell 1992), but at the same time, they are always aware that other listeners or readers who are not present will nonetheless later have access to this message. This is what Chilton and Ilyin (1993) refer to as interaction between actors that is distantiated in time and space and in which there are ongoing conversations between stakeholders. Odinga's stories are always told in Swahili, the language of the masses. Here is Odinga's tale on rats versus cats: "Rats once had a plan of putting a bell around the cat's neck to alert them whenever danger loomed. However, no one volunteered to take up the task of tying up the bell around the cat's neck" (*The Standard*, August 11, 2011).

This metaphor targets the so-called Group of Seven alliance members (Uhuru, Wamalwa, Ruto, Balala, Ngilu, among others), who at that time were eager to remove Odinga but had not decided on who would face him at the ballot box for the presidential seat. In this metaphor, Odinga skillfully portrays himself as the cat and the Group of Seven members, who are afraid of him, as the rats. For Kenyan audiences, it is easy to recognize this connection because of their shared cultural experiences of the roles cats play in homes. Kenyans keep cats not just as pets but also as partners who can scare away snakes, rats, and other enemies. Therefore, a metaphor like this fits very well within the cultural significance of metaphors. And, borrowing from cognitive linguistics (Ungerer and Schmid 2006; Zinken 2003), I argue that the understanding of this metaphorical language depends on appreciating the cultural knowledge needed to interpret metaphors.

### The Nile Perch and Sardine Metaphor

Odinga's ancestral land is in western Kenya near Lake Victoria. The proximity to the lake makes fish a staple food among his ethnic group. The linguistic repertoire of these people clearly reflects both their cultural and environmental experiences. On December 18, 2009, when talking about politicians who had taken land from the people, Odinga referred to powerful politicians metaphorically, using a fish analogy. As already stated, most of Odinga's metaphors are in Swahili, the national language. Therefore, on this particular occasion, Odinga referred to those politicians as *mbuta* (Nile perch) and then went further to call the people who had been displaced *omena* (sardines). However, the fish terminology has been borrowed from Luo, Odinga's first language: "Kwa wale ambao wametoka ni ile samaki ndogo ambayo inaitwa omena. Lakini kuna mbuta. Bado iko. Na hiyo ndiyo mbuta inapiga kelele ambayo mnasikia. [For those who have left, they are the small fish, which are called sardines. But there are still the big fish, called Nile perch, and they are the ones still making the noise you hear]" (*The Standard*, December 18, 2009).

Politicians who were implicated in this scandal were not members of Odinga's party, and they were not happy that their names had been tarnished by Odinga's claims. When one of them, Zakayo Cheruiyot, a local politician at the time, reacted, he used the same metaphor to counter Odinga's accusations. He noted: "I am not *mbuta* and there are no *omenas* in my place. We have not called them *ng'ombes* [cows], the Luos, and we do not expect them to call us fish" (2009, translation mine).

This politician went further to describe Odinga as someone who was crazy and jealous. The kind of verbal exchange that ensued between Odinga and the implicated politicians reflects what Fairclough (1992) refers to as "intertextuality" (one text referring to another), a term attributed to Bakhtin's (1981) work. This further supports the view that when a metaphor is uttered, its interpretations are triggered for both the intended local audience and bystanders. The rhetoric that emerged appealed to the audience's emotions, just as the counterattack appealed to Odinga as an audience. In both cases reactions came from people who were not in the immediate audience.

What is significant in this verbal exchange is the use of personal pronouns "we, them, and us" that appeal to a larger audience. *I want to say I am not mbuta and there are no omenas in my constituency. We have not called them ng'ombes, the Luos, and we do not expect them to call us fish.* Clearly in this text, the verbal war goes beyond individual attacks to involve the community. It is no longer just the political rivalry and differences between the politicians involved; the rivalry escalates to the level of ethnicity. When Cheruiyot says, "we have not called them *ng'ombes* [cows], the Luos," this involves all the people who identify themselves as Luo,and the defense is for all who identify with Cheruiyot—namely, the Kalenjin community. It is no wonder that ethnic tensions are triggered by politicians' choice of words and how they frame their utterances. Again, this is a confirmation of the power of words and how they can work for the good of the politician or the destruction of the community involved.

### The Madman Metaphor

Although for the most part politicians target their political opponents, it is also possible for those who consider themselves to be insiders to part ways with their bosses. In the case of Odinga, one of his influential advisers, Miguna Miguna, differed with him and decided to accuse him of political and legal violations (*The Standard*, August 18, 2012). In his defense, when addressing his audience Odinga used a metaphor to question Miguna's credibility by making reference to a madman. He told his audience that there was once a man who had gone to the river to bathe and then noticed a madman come along and steal his clothes while he was in the river. He told the crowd that his response was to jump out of the water and chase after the madman naked. He then posed the question: "Who between the two appeared to be mad?" Amid applause and laughter from his audience, Odinga told the crowd that "a madman has taken my clothes but I will not run after him. I will buy new ones" (*The Standard*, August 18, 2012). Odinga did not address the issue directly, but he still gave a satisfactory response to critics and to his supporters who wanted him to comment on the fallout with his senior aide.

### The Chicken Metaphor

Odinga's ultimate goal is to woo voters into his party and to retain the ones he already has. Although a politician can have great ideas, he or she must also have a way to connect with the audience by discrediting other opponents (Chateris-Black 2004, 2011).

In one of his campaign rallies in western Kenya, where he has a large following, Odinga warned his voters of the actions of the other parties by likening his former running mate, Musalia Mudavadi, to a chicken being lured by corn only to be captured for slaughter. Mudavadi, who served under different governments and rose to the position of vice president under President Moi, had differed with Odinga and quit Odinga's Orange Democratic Movement Party to join the United Democratic Front. Odinga wanted his allies and supporters to know the tricks his political opponents were using to delegitimize his credibility (*The Standard*, September 1, 2012). Mudavadi later unsuccessfully contested for the presidency, falling behind both Odinga and Kenyatta, who had also dumped him after making a promise that he would be the ticket bearer of the Jubilee coalition, currently headed by Kenyatta.

Politicians can be persuasive because they know their audience. Although most of what has been discussed has been what Odinga does to woo voters and to persuade them through metaphors and parables that discredit his opponents, his political allies find ways to lobby for him. Leading up to the 2013 general elections, Odinga allied with many politicians across the nation whose task was to pitch for his presidential bid. A metaphor that they adopted to silence one of his potential opponents, Eugene Wamalwa, was in an analogy to a boxing match. They tactfully referred to Wamalwa as a featherweight and a lightweight boxer who could not match Odinga, the heavyweight. However, in his defense, Wamalwa, an equally eloquent and tactful speaker, used the biblical parable of David and Goliath to dismiss his critics by positioning himself as David and Odinga as Goliath.

### The Tale of Odinga, the Son of Wanga

Besides what has already been discussed, another strategy that politicians use is identifying with their potential voters. It has already been made clear that in Kenya, politicians rely on voters of their own ethnicity to support them but must also portray a national outlook and embrace every Kenyan to form coalitions and win an election. A politician can manipulate any given story or situation to make political gains. While addressing Luhya supporters on several occasions, Odinga would identify himself with them to show that even though Kenyan politics were based in ethnicity, he too was a Luhya. Odinga did this knowing very well that the Luhya vote was crucial, and if he could have a unified Luhya vote, the presidency would be in sight. Unfortunately, several influential Luhya politicians had joined different parties, and some of them, such as Mudavadi, were even vying for the presidency. To gain the support of this group, he needed a very tactful strategy to persuade the voters that although he was not from Kakamega, he was still one of them.

At a political campaign in Kakamega, every speaker seemed to talk of their own "son" who would represent the Luhya community. When it came to his turn to speak, Odinga seized the moment and capitalized on the context to claim affiliation to the Luhya ethnic community. Here is how he recounted his case to validate his Luhya ethnic identity:

Kama ni mimi ninatoka hapa. Raila mwana wa Oginga, Oginga mwana wa
Odinga, Odinga mwana wa Raila, Raila mwana wa Rapondi, Rapondi mwana
wa Wenwa, Wenwa mwana wa Omolo, Omolo mwana wa Migono, Migono
mwana wa Ogola, Ogola wa Ogola mwana wa Nyibina, Nyibina mwana wa
Matara, Matara mwana wa Wanga. [If it is about me, I come from here. Raila
. . . the son/child of Rapondi, Rapondi the son of Wenwa, Wenwa the son of
Omolo, Omolo the son of Migono, Migono the son of Ogola, Ogola the son
of Nyibina, Nyibina the son of Matara, Matara the son of Wanga.] (*Bull's Eye*,
NTV Kenya, www.ntv.co.ke, January 22, 2011)

This led to applause and a standing ovation from the audience, and he connected with the crowd, which saw a clear connection with him because Wanga is
a subgroup of the Luhya people of western Kenya. Certainly not every politician
can do this, but when the context was right, Odinga did not only entertain and persuade but he also convinced his audience that, as a member of the family, his
thinking was right (Charteris-Black 2011) and he could be trusted. He presented
his case with the oral strategies used by many African communities to connect
with the crowd and make their credentials credible. The griots of West Africa,
who were viewed as entertainers as well as chroniclers of their societies, used
such strategies to justify and validate their stories and facts. Pedigree is important.
Odinga tactfully seized the moment and reconnected with his base, the second-
largest ethnic group in Kenya, in a very emotional way, for the crucial presidential
vote that he needed.

## Conclusion

In the foregoing discussion, it has emerged very clearly that political success and
survival depend on the power of words and how persuasive politicians can be when
they are talking to the electorate. The Kenyan political scene is similar to a theatri-
cal stage, where politicians use their strengths to outmaneuver their political opponents and at the same time woo and persuade voters to vote them in. This chapter
has focused on the presidential strategies of two crucial multiparty elections that
took place in 2007 and more recently in 2013. One political figure who took the
center stage was Raila Odinga, who has been described as an enigma in African
politics but remains popular among his supporters, at least in part based on his ability to talk in parables and metaphors. Although he initiates such talk, the (mis)inter-
pretations that emerge from his campaign rallies often trigger more discussions
among his political supporters and opponents.

This chapter has also claimed that the success of political discourse depends not
only on shared background knowledge between the speaker and the audience but
also on the right context for the two parties involved to connect. What is therefore
critical to the understanding of Kenya's political discourse is that the rhetorical
strategies used by seasoned politicians are embedded in African oral traditions and
their cultural experiences. Politicians who take advantage of this rich tradition are
likely to get more support at the grassroots level. The challenge that these politicians

face is how they can connect the oratory skills they possess with real issues that face their people and those issues that concern a different category of voters—those in the middle class whose major concern is the creation of a less corrupt nation that is focused on agendas that will propel their nation to higher heights economically, politically, and socially.

It has also emerged that on the Kenyan political scene, politicians constantly form and break alliances. Unlike in some countries, where politicians maintain their membership in the same political parties, in Kenyan politics there is no permanency in party affiliations. Such trends make politicians vulnerable to easy attacks, because any disagreements lead to accusations and counterattacks. Although this chapter has shown how witty Odinga is with words, his opponents have delegitimized him using his own strategy, the power of words, to portray him as a nonperformer. They have challenged him to move beyond riddles and metaphors and deal with real issues facing his people. The frameworks used in this study bring to the fore the deeper meanings that are made accessible to the audience through the use of metaphors that participants connect with cognitively, culturally, and experientially. The synergy between political rhetoric and pragmatic leadership is likely to emerge.

## References

Bakhtin, M. M. 1981. *The Dialogic Imagination: Four Essays*. Austin: University of Texas Press.

Charteris-Black, Jonathan. 2004. *Corpus Approaches to Critical Metaphor Analysis*. New York: Palgrave Macmillan.

———. 2011. *Politicians and Rhetoric: The Persuasive Power of Metaphor*, 2nd ed. New York: Palgrave Macmillan.

Chilton, Paul. 2004. *Analysing Political Discourse: Theory and Practice*. London: Routledge.

Chilton, Paul, and Mikhail Ilyin. 1993. "Metaphor in Political Discourse: The Case of the Common European House." *Discourse & Society* 4:7–31.

Fairclough, Norman. 1992. *Discourse and Social Change*. London: Polity.

Jones, Rodney H. 2012. *Discourse Analysis*. London: Routledge.

Jowett, Garth, and Victoria O'Donnell. 1992. *Propaganda and Persuasion*. London: Sage.

Kenya Citizen TV. 2009. *Heka Heka Za Kisiasa* Uploaded to YouTube on December 18.

Lakoff, George, and Mark Johnson. 1980. *Metaphors We Live By*. Chicago: University of Chicago Press.

Mooney, Annabelle, Jean Stilwell Peccei, Suzanne LaBelle, Berit Engøy Henriksen, Eva Eppler, Anthea Irwin, Pia Pichler, Siân Preece, and Satori Soden. 2011. *Language, Society and Power: An Introduction*. Hoboken NJ: Taylor & Francis.

Mueller, Susanne D. 2009. "Raila Odinga: An Enigma in Kenyan Politics." *International Journal of African Historical Studies* 42:134–36.

Nabea, Wendo. 2010. "Media Argumentation in the Kenyan 2007 Political Elections: Manufacturing of Ethnic Hate." In *Language and Politics in Africa: Contemporary Issues and Critical Perspectives*, edited by Daniel Ochieng Orwenjo and John Obiero Ogone. Newcastle upon Tyne: Cambridge Scholars.

Obeng, Samuel Gyasi. 2003. *Language in African Social Interaction: Indirectness in Akan Communication*. New York: Nova Science.

Orwenjo, Daniel Ochieng. 2010. "Of Shifting Goal-Posts and Scoring Own Goals: Patterns of Metaphorical Language Use in Kenya's Political Discourse." In *Language and Politics in Africa: Contemporary Issues and Critical Perspectives*, edited by Daniel Ochieng Orwenjo and John Obiero Ogone. Newcastle upon Tyne: Cambridge Scholars.

Paltridge, Brian. 2013. "Critical Discourse Analysis." In *Discourse Studies Reader: Essential Excerpts*, edited by Ken Hyland. New York: Bloomsbury Academic.

Ungerer, Friedrich, and Hans-Jörg Schmid. 2006. *An Introduction to Cognitive Linguistics*, 2nd ed. New York: Longman.
Van Dijk, Teun. 1993. "Principles of Critical Discourse Analysis." *Discourse & Society* 4:249–83.
———. 1997. *Discourse Studies: A Multidisciplinary Introduction*. London: Sage.
Zinken, Jörg. 2003. "Ideological Imagination: Intertextual and Correlational Metaphors in Political Discourse." *Discourse & Society* 14:507–23.

# 14

# African Languages on Film: Visualizations of Pathologized Polyglossia

ANJALI PANDEY
*Salisbury University*

## Rendering Africa's Linguistic Diversity in the Twenty-First Century

**THIS CHAPTER PRESENTS** generous visual evidence of the extent to which cinematic accounts persist in conflating African polyglossia with pathologized indecipherability, linguistic cacophony, and unintelligibility in twenty-first-century transnational encounters keen on privileging linguistic homogeneity. Such linguistic juxtapositions reflect the astute marketing strategies of accrued linguistic capital—a hierarchy of linguistic potential emerging in the world's linguistic resources (Pandey 2015). In such constructed clines of linguistic "portability" (Canagarajah 2013, 2), African languages remain relegated to scales of mitigated linguistic worth in comparison, for example, with the saliency accorded other spotlighted languages of transactional power and influence.

The noted hyperpolyglot Helen Abadzi (2011, 499), in a recent book review, notes that "African multilingualism is most definitely an advantage," both regionally for the continent's countries and personally for its speakers—via what she deems to be an accrual of cognitive advantage (see, e.g., Adesope et al. 2010). However, for whom is this polyglossia an advantage? Canagarajah (2013, 1–2) argues that the linguistic "portability" of African languages relative to languages like English and other megalanguages is increasingly in need of scrutiny, especially in an interconnected world of outward migration trajectories to receiving nations—from the so-called developing South to the developed North. For Canagarajah (2013) such multilingual repertoires afford opportunities for inter-African communication, even in Diaspora communities. The more important question, however, is why usage, particularly in twenty-first-century transnational encounters, persists in remaining confined to endocentric rather than exocentric domains of usage—that is, spoken by Africans to fellow Africans only—rather than, say, exported globally like other competitor world languages. This is a point in need of scrutiny and interrogation.

Is it merely on the global stage that the constructed status of Africa's languages is losing ground, or is this diminishing linguistic capital also apparent within national boundaries? Emerging accounts in the domain of education point to the diminishing role that African languages are assuming for example, in the current schooling practices of children across the continent. Desai (2001, 326) reports on the increasing lack of pride and "low status" accorded South Africa's nine official African languages, which contrasts sharply with "a growing trend toward English, and toward official monolingualism in practice." Could such linguistic attitudes explain the increasing policies of subtractive over additive multilingualism as the preferred route of educational access for rich and poor alike across the African continent and, specifically, in trail-blazing countries such as South Africa, the continent's richest nation (Skutnabb-Kangas and Heugh 2012, 16)?

The effects of linguistic policies that devalue multilingualism reflect what Pym (2013, 90) describes as "an asymmetry of opportunities between languages and leaving the main lingua franca as the only language that is learned, and thus the only one suitable for participation." More troubling, however, is the implicit double standard—an asymmetry of linguistic value—emerging regarding mother-tongue language education in the West versus the rest of the world. Desai (2001, 328) calls for an interrogation of such normative views: "As far as mother-tongue education is concerned, it is interesting to note that in the literature on mother-tongue education a case is never made for the importance of mother-tongue education for the majority populations of countries like the United Kingdom, the United States of America, France, Germany, and the Netherlands, to name but a few examples. In these contexts it is taken for granted that learners from the majority populations will learn best through their primary languages. Why is it then so problematic for the majority of learners in African countries?"

It is this last interrogative on which this chapter aims to shed light. Pym (2013, 90) argues that mother-tongue retention in smaller, emerging European geospheres such as Catalonia is easier in comparison with what he describes as "a much larger multilingual democracy like South Africa, with 11 official languages but a lack of resources for many aspects of public education." Though size is no doubt a factor, this still does not account for why a language such as Afrikaans, rather than say Xhosa or Zulu, shares visual spotlighting in the media space of South Africa. Sebba (2010) chronicles the invisibilization of African languages in the linguistic landscape in apartheid South Africa. Not much seems to have changed. Currently, English and Afrikaans—two languages originating in the West—"dominate South African television" (Pym 2013, 95). Outside South Africa, Afrikaans, like the other nine official African languages, lacks transnational currency; yet this particular language (with its implication in a history of human violence) continues to share screen space with English. Could repeated exposures to the media be one reason why Africa's linguistic richness—one of its greatest assets—remains underused? Why is the continent's multilinguality systematically devalued by outsiders in particular?

The persistent metaphorization or seeming cacophony conflated with African languages on the silver screen only serves to further iterate commonsensical notions of African multilingualness as valueless—as lacking in linguistic capital. Even more troubling is a systematic attempt at reifying what Weber and Horner (2012, 171) label the "pathologizing" of such multilingual use; in semiotic outputs, the result of carefully construed media reports, African multilingualism remains predictably conflated with "social disorder and street violence." In his analysis of newspaper accounts, Blackledge (2000, 38) reveals convincing evidence of conflations of

African multilingualness with even more sinister overtones of "evil"—a resuscitation of a seemingly bygone colonial-era perspective of language hierarchies (Norton 2013, 125). Interestingly, we encounter similar discoursal synergy at work in film. A few visualizations are examined in the sections that follow.

## Visual Semiotics: Pathologizing Polyglossia

Why does this chapter focus on visual media? Part of the reason could be that with growing technologies accessible everywhere, we are indeed witnessing what van Eeden and du Preez (2010, 4) label a "visual turn" in semiotic representations worldwide. The heightened potency of filmic imagery in shaping perceptions in our era of transnational encounters is becoming increasingly apparent (Blommaert 2010). Particularly in the current era of mass interconnectivity, "a major source of information about other people is through the media rather than personal contact" (Harding 2003, 69). Few would contest the claim that part of both the appeal and the potency of filmic media lies in what van Eeden and du Preez (2010, 33) describe as the "resignification potential of film"—scenarios in which images and signs become significant in maintaining dominant world views. Media representations of Africa on television, in film, and in journalistic accounts recenter and recycle a singular imagery of "need" in a continent that is consistently and constantly "crisis ridden" (Harding 2003, 72, 69). This visual framing of both country and continent is replicated with fervency, even in newer, online media channels hosted by respected news outlets such as the BBC and, more recently, Al Jazeera English. These latter two online channels consistently embody "text-image consonance patterns" in which the crisis frame and "negative news" predominate (Mellese and Müller 2012, 200). In a content analysis of 311 news stories collected over a three-month period, Mellese and Müller (2012, 191) show that "negatively toned reporting, both textually and visually, was even more dominant on the Al Jazeera website"—a finding they noted to be particularly troubling for a news channel priding itself on offering a Global South point of view. This latter finding should not be surprising, however, considering that the maiden launch of Al Jazeera English in fact began with an active recruitment and hiring of top celebrity journalists from the BBC (Seib 2012). Unsurprisingly, then, text-image conflations about Africa—even in static, newer online media formats—remain intent on recycling old negative tropes about the continent and some of its countries.

Few studies have examined how language representations fit into such portrayals—the subject of focus in this chapter. A thematic constant is the presentation of the entire continent as a monolithic mass. This description is uttered with frequency in film after film, and remains a characterization rampant in news stories (Mellese and Müller 2012). As an example, consider the offhanded remark uttered by of one of the actors in the Oscar-winning *Atonement*, as shown in figure 14.1. In this comment, the juxtaposition of India (a country) with Africa (a continent) is one all too commonly found in film. Aside from geographical ignorance, such descriptions result in the "invisibilizing" of Africa's inner linguistic diversity.

The popular view of African languages as a chaotic mass of exotic, indecipherable tongues with unique click sounds and tonal systems has been and continues to be hyperfetishized in the popular media and in film (Pandey 2011, 2012).

Figure 14.1 An Offhanded Remark Uttered by One of the Actors in the Film *Atonement,* 2007 (Courtesy Focus Features)

This linguistic devaluation of Africa's multilingualism is systematic and often occurs in the form of filmic remarks, levied under the guise of humor. These seemingly innocuous remarks aim to delegitimize the actual linguistic structure of sub-Saharan languages. As an example, consider the seemingly offhanded comment (followed up by a clumsy mimicry) on the phonetic patterns of an unnamed African language made by a lead character, played by Robin Williams, in the blockbuster *Night at the Museum,* shown in figure 14.2.

Here, as in countless other films, laughter is used to denigrate a unique feature of an unnamed Khoisan language in a monolithic "Africa." Of particular significance is the fact that this denigration occurs in collusion with another historical character—Sacagawea. The synthesizing of historical imagery by juxtaposing early twentieth-century, "Scramble for Africa" conquests of discovery with centuries-prior, geographical depredations (symbolized by Sacagawea and her role in charting a path for the further annihilation of Native American languages) in the "westward" expansion of American "exceptionalism" cannot be missed. What makes comedy such a particularly insidious strategy of linguistic denigration is that it has contradictory effects. As Oh and Banjo (2012, 456) note, "Because humor is not meant to be taken seriously, comedy works to minimize serious or critical readings." It makes sense, then, that humor remains a favorite linguistic invisibilizing strategy in film. Witness, for example, the opening scene from the comedy *He's Just Not That into You* (figure 14.3), where earlier-delineated languages, such as Japanese and French—a chorus of translated languages that see identification—occur in careful

Figure 14.2 A Seemingly Offhanded Comment on the Phonetic Patterns of an Unnamed African Language in the Film *Night at the Museum*, 2006 (Courtesy Twentieth-Century Fox)

juxtaposition with the subsequent split-second scene in which village women—somewhere in Africa—speaking an unintelligible language supposedly wonder why a "date" does not show up. The scene additionally manages to superimpose a Western-derived, urban-numbering-grid onto an African village.

Figure 14.3 The Opening Scene of the Film *He's Just Not That into You*, 2009 (Courtesy New Line Cinema)

Such acts of linguistic denigration are dovetailed with overt acts of linguistic exoticization—filmic scenes in which African languages are neither translated nor identified, as in the scene shown in figure 14.4 from another acclaimed film, *Paris je t'aime*, which aimed to sell a multicultural Paris to the world. In this scene, we witness how films subversively manage to marginalize Africa's linguistic diversity while simultaneously spotlighting it as "other."

The lack of identification of linguistic particulars is a consistent peripherizing strategy deployed in Hollywood. As another example, consider the two scenes from the well-publicized film *Invictus* shown in figures 14.5 and 14.6. *Invictus* aimed to reveal the significance of the first days in office of Nelson Mandela, the first black president of postapartheid South Africa. The first scene (figure 14.5) involves the use of Afrikaans, which sees filmic identification. In a juxtaposed scene involving Xhosa (figure 14.6), we see no such linguistic labeling. When the team decides to sing in Xhosa, the language remains unidentified. Examples such as these confirm the credibility of earlier observations about the asymmetrical valence of Afrikaans relative to South Africa's nine other African languages in current media representations.

A consistent strategy is one of the pathologization of African multilinguality— a thematic favorite that emerges in consonance with graphically rendered violence. Such an "abnormalization of multilingualism" (Blommaert, Leppänen, and Spotti 2012, 1) is observed in contrived filmic scenes where African languages are repeat-

Figure 14.4 Linguistic Exoticization, whereby African Languages Are neither Translated nor Identified, as Shown in This Scene from the Film *Paris je t'aime*, 2006 (Courtesy First Look International)

Figure 14.5 An Example of the Lack of Identification of Linguistic Particulars: Afrikaans Is Identified in This Scene from the Film *Invictus*, 2009 (Courtesy Warner Brothers Pictures)

edly presented as indecipherable acts of "shouting." An impressive number of highly regarded award-winning films, such as *The Constant Gardener*, keenly deploy such strategies. Often, African multilingualism is presented as cacophonous, undefined background noise—which is visually conflated with "tribal" violence, as in the scene shown in figure 14.7.

What makes such visual portrayals doubly potent is that the "comprehensibility" of English receives an exaggerated focus. A similar strategy of spotlighting "shouting" in African languages emerges in more current films, such as the Oscar-nominated *Captain Philips*, which focused on Somalian piracy. In effect viewers witness a diametric contrast between the intelligibility of screen-uttered English in its juxtaposition with the seeming unintelligibility of carefully presented "tribal" codes, which remain astutely conflated with cinematic backdrops and soundtracks of "extreme imagery" and "scenes of brutality" (Harding 2003, 74).

Figure 14.6 An Example of the Lack of Identification of Linguistic Particulars: Xhosa Is *Not* Identified in This Scene from the Film *Invictus*, 2009 (Courtesy Warner Brothers Pictures)

Figure 14.7 An Example of the Pathologization of African Multilinguality, whereby African Languages Are Repeatedly Presented as Indecipherable Acts of "Shouting," in a Scene from the Film *The Constant Gardener,* 2005 (Courtesy Focus Features)

This image of "lawlessness" in the land of Africa is another common photographic image seen in Hollywood's films. The effects seem to justify a racial and linguistic meritocracy (Oh and Banjo 2012). Consider the unfolding scene shown in figure 14.8 from the global blockbuster *Lord of War.* In figure 14.8 the "primitive" use of cutlasses to decapitate and maim young innocents occurs within a cacophony of "unknown" languages—barely heard and barely unintelligible. Here we see an extended filmic moment of African violence meted out to Africans by Africans.

As could be predicted, African violence remains conflated against a cacophony of indistinguishable, untranslated, and seemingly unintelligible background noise—continent-wide chaos. Note the consistent use of "shouting in African language," which appears in telecaptioned decoder mode. Such witnessed acts of foregrounded violence are presented in carefully rendered, distal terms—camera angles in which Western actors, and viewers alike, watch these pathologies unfold from afar, and often from "above." Such filmic moments unfold against equally distal aural backdrops—unintelligible backgrounded linguistic soundtracks—occurring as "undifferentiated backdrops" (Harding 2003, 70). We see the use of this strategy emerging in a slew of recent films, such as *Winnie Mandela,* a film that manages to show graphic scenes of "tribally triggered" "necklacing" enforced on the part of native South

Figure 14.8 An Example of the Common Photographic Image of "Lawlessness" in Africa, That Seems to Justify a Racial and Linguistic Meritocracy by Showing "Primitive" Violence within a Cacophony of "Unknown" Languages, from the Film *Lord of War*, 2005 (Courtesy Lions Gate Films)

Africans on fellow Africans, yet fails to photograph complementary graphic details of the murder of hundreds of Soweto's children at the hands of apartheid-regime policemen. The meticulous detailing of such acts of African-instigated violence is a semantic point in need of a more detailed analysis than space constraints permit.

The repeated trope of "tribal warfare" sees predictable recycling, even in films that are not about Africa. Consider, for example, the offhanded remark about Somalian immigrants in Great Britain made by a bigoted police officer in the film *Breaking and Entering* (a title of semantic import), as shown in figure 14.9. Such comments effectively normalize the "mass" anonymity of Africans as a "bunch" of people wielding "primitive" weapons in Global North nations. Interestingly, this film aimed to spotlight immigration issues in the United Kingdom in the era of the euro zone.

Figure 14.9 An Example of an Offhanded Remark about Somalian Immigrants in Great Britain, Normalizing the "Mass" Anonymity of Africans as People Wielding "Primitive" Weapons, Made by a Bigoted Police Officer in the Film *Breaking and Entering*, 2006 (Courtesy MGM and the Weinstein Company)

Blackledge (2000, 40) reiterates the prevalence of such perspectives and provides a variegated content analysis of accounts in the British press keen on presenting the African multilingualism of African immigrants as "retrograde and tribal" in comparison, for example, with the seeming orderliness and civility assumed of "intelligible" monolingual English users. Fear of linguistic indecipherability is similarly conflated for African immigrants in the Diaspora communities of North America, as can be witnessed in the scene from another acclaimed Hollywood film, *Gone Baby Gone*, in which an unidentified language is effectively conflated with a forefronted weapon—a gun—shown in figure 14.10.

Iterations of similar linguistic valuation predominate in other noteworthy films set on the African continent. Consider, for instance, the scene from another award winner, *The Last King of Scotland*, in which an African pleads for mercy amid cries uttered in an unidentified, indecipherable language, shown in figure 14.11.

In films, Africa's languages, unlike counterpart Western languages, are rarely identified in subtitling. Instead, as part of the trope of pathology, we witness overtones of animalism carefully synchronized with lead characters, as in the scene from *The Last King of Scotland* shown in figure 14.12. Here, pathology is delivered in and through an unidentified "African language" in a film keenly photographing the "wildness" indeed the "otherness" of the continent in the form of countless close-up scenes of Africa's insects.

To take *The Last King of Scotland* as a microexample, viewer and lead character soon move from "lighter" to "darker" portrayals within the span of the film itself. Thus we witness in *The Last King of Scotland* the refolding and recycling of a distal, Western point of view on the most infamous of Africa's presidents, Idi Amin. Viewers watch the unfolding of an extended, gruesome scene carefully por-

Figure 14.10 An Example of How the Fear of Linguistic Indecipherability Is Conflated for African Immigrants in Diaspora Communities of North America, as Shown in This Scene Where an Unidentified Language Is Conflated with a Forefronted Weapon, a Gun, from the Film *Gone Baby Gone*, 2007 (Courtesy Miramax)

Figure 14.11 Another Example of the Conflation of Violence and Linguistic Indecipherability, in This Scene Where an African Pleads for Mercy amid Cries Uttered in an Unidentified, Indecipherable Language, from the Film *The Last King of Scotland*, 2006 (Courtesy Fox Searchlight Pictures)

traying the dismemberment of one of Idi Amin's wives. This is a filmic concoction (too graphic to reproduce here) that is offered up to audiences under the guise of fact. After all, this is a story "based in truth," as viewers are reminded in its opening credits. African pathology is carefully conflated with an equally pathologized view of Africa's languages, as we see in figure 14.13, also from *The Last King of Scotland*. This conflation of violence with African language comes through in other award-winning films, such as *Hotel Rwanda*, where viewers are confronted by a crowd of thugs brandishing their violence in potent visual terms—in the form of machetes and spears—as in the scene shown in figure 14.14. In films such as the Oscar-nominated *Blood Diamond*, we witness the outcome of such pathology in the form of close-up camera shots of fear-inducing villains scarred by machete wounds and wielding them as well, as shown in figure 14.15.

A similar spotlighting of violence with African languages occurs in the opening scene of *Lord of War* (figure 14.16), where audiences cannot miss the foregrounding of weapons in the "hands" of Africans in the opening credits. This perception of Africa still persists a decade later, even in films presented as "more in-depth documentaries" (Harding 2003, 73). When languages are translated, the semantic content in itself is heavy with themes of violence. Consider the two scenes from

Figure 14.12 An Example of How Africa's Languages, Unlike Western Languages, Are Rarely Identified in Subtitling, in This Scene from *The Last King of Scotland*, 2006 (Courtesy Fox Searchlight Pictures)

another award-winning docudrama, *War/Dance*, shown in figure 14.17, in which translated soundtracks manage to zoom in on weapons in a carefully contrived opening scene. Viewers are then given details about such violent acts in the form of translated subtitles.

Docudramas such as *War/Dance* are particularly disturbing because they serve to "perpetuate a familiar image of a violent Africa"—"a land of chaos and decline, . . . a continent in crisis" (Harding 2003, 74, 75). In such filmic accounts we witness a strategic use of sensationalized imagery delivered in and through the conduit of "truth"—concocted "facticity." Docudramas are particularly effective media tools because in "presenting accounts of Africa which seek to be accurate, this often means that even as the stereotype is challenged, it is also perpetuated" (Harding 2003, 74). One of the most chilling scenes in this carefully concocted docudrama is of a girl speaking Acholi—carefully translated for audiences to "see"—which recounts a re-created scene of a recollected memory. Via a slowly unfolding and haltingly delivered narrative with an eerie soundtrack to match, viewers are told of her encountering a cooking pot on a fire—full of human body parts. Scenes such as this form the textual and filmic apex of the linguistic pathology being investigated in this chapter.

Figure 14.13 An Example of How "African Pathology," as Exemplified by a Supposedly Factual Portrayal of Idi Amin, Is Conflated with an Equally Pathologized View of Africa's Languages, in This Shot from *The Last King of Scotland*, 2006 (Courtesy Fox Searchlight Pictures)

Figure 14.14 Another Example of the Conflation of Visual Violence with African Languages in This Scene Where Viewers Are Confronted by Thugs Brandishing Machetes and Spears from *Hotel Rwanda*, 2004 (Courtesy Lions Gate Films and United Artists)

Figure 14.15 How the Audience Witnesses the Outcome of African Pathology, in the Form of Close-up Shots of Villains Scarred by Machete Wounds in the Film *Blood Diamond*, 2006 (Courtesy Warner Brothers Pictures)

Figure 14.16 An Example of How Violence Is Spotlighted with African Languages, whereby Audiences Cannot Miss the Foregrounding of Weapons in the "Hands" of Africans, in the Opening Credits of the Film *Lord of War*, 2005 (Courtesy Lions Gate Films)

Figure 14.17 An Example of How, When Languages Are Translated, the Semantic Content Can Be Heavy with Themes of Violence. Left: The Opening Scene Zooms in on Weapons. Right: The Translated Subtitles Then Give Details of Violent Acts. From the Documentary Film *War/Dance*, 2007 (Courtesy Thinkfilm)

When languages are identified and translated, then, their conflation with pathologized acts of violence is carefully transcribed for viewers to see. Consider the scene from the controversial film *District 9*, shown in figures 14.18 and 14.19, in which a guide takes care to identify these "foreigners" in a restricted zone of a segregated city. Though the film no doubt serves as a filmic metaphor for South Africa's segregated townships, words uttered to a white officer take special care to identify the languages spoken by these peripherized minority populations. Such linguistic identification is followed by a mythologizing of action in the form of pathologies difficult to watch (figure 14.18). In a scene reminiscent of *War/Dance*, we find a comment attesting to the "cannibalism" of Nigerians (figure 14.19).

Figure 14.18 An Example of a Case Where African Languages *Are* Identified but Are Then Conflated with Pathologized Acts of Violence, as in This Scene Where a Guide Identifies "Foreigners" in a Restricted Zone of a Segregated City, from the Film *District 9* 2009 (Courtesy TriStar Pictures)

The Nigerians were consuming alien body parts.

Figure 14.19 Another Example of an African Language Being Identified and Then Conflated with a Pathologized Act of Violence, in This Case Cannibalism, from the Film *District 9*, 2009 (Courtesy TriStar Pictures)

Interestingly, it is Nigeria, the producer of Nollywood films—a burgeoning DVD-based industry (Harding 2003) and ideological counterweight to Hollywood-based film production—that sees some of the most focused negative media attention. A three-month study by Mellese and Müller (2012) reports that the BBC devoted 14.7 percent of its stories to Nigeria and Al Jazeera English devoted 21 percent. Both news streams had coverage of Nigeria as their top focus. Nigeria, also coincidentally, is home to "514 languages" (Skutnabb-Kangas and Heugh 2012, 17). The emerging continent-wide appeal of Nollywood films, which are now being distributed all over Africa, is also worth pointing out (Allington 2012). Given the facts that Nigeria is prominently represented in the media and that it is pervasively multilingual, is it any accident, then, that Nigeria sees overt demonization in films such as *District 9*?

"More than any other medium," argue Oh and Banjo (2012, 454), "televisual media amplify neoliberal ideologies via repetition and familiarity." Visual images are doubly powerful in that they remain indelibly stored in long-term memory (Pandey 2012). Such scenes, analyzed not in isolation but rather taken together as a visual corpus, point to convincing evidence for the systematic use of multimodal media being used for the "racialization of linguistic encounters" (Norton 2013, 123, 126)—celluloid scenes keen on rechanneling bygone, colonial-era portrayals of a "pernicious paternalism which relegates Africans to a lower level of human development."

Inevitably, African multilinguality acquires "weak tender" status. In filmic scenes native speakers are exhorted into changing their linguistic practices. Consider, for example, countless filmic imperatives, such as that shown in figure 14.20; in another award winner *Nowhere in Africa*, a "native" cook, who is eagerly trying to teach the new owner of a house some words in Swahili, meets a harsh imperative.

Figure 14.20 An Example of a Native Speaker Being Exhorted into Changing His Linguistic Practices: A "Native" Cook Eagerly Trying to Teach the New Owner of a House Some Swahili Words Meets a Harsh Imperative, in the Film *Nowhere in Africa*, 2002 (Courtesy Zeitgeist Films)

In such filmic scenes, it is "longing" for access to megalanguages like English that is thematicized in films. Consider for example, the scenes shown in figures 14.21 and 14.22 from *Blood Diamond*, where intelligible English is presented as a linguistic ticket out of such mass pathology.

Therefore, Hollywood's eventual thesis, particularly for "natives" of the continent, is that languages such as English must be persued and acquired. Such exhortations form the subject of many a filmic moment. A "yearning" for English education, as voiced by a lead character in *Blood Diamond*, tells actor and audience alike why, inevitably, his efforts to learn English, such as taking his son to school every morning so that he can learn it, serve as the ultimate linguistic passport out of Africa's current pathology—indeed, from its linguistic incomprehensibility.

In rendering a hierarchy of linguistic worth then, such contrived filmic moments manage to reify the "oligolingualism" of English (Blommaert, Leppänen, and Spotti 2012, 6). Filmmaking is an expensive enterprise with every millisecond of action the consequence of deliberate orchestration (Pandey 2012). No filmic moment is accidental. It is such intentionality inherent in film that makes this visual channel one that demands closer linguistic scrutiny. In neoliberal-oriented market economies keen on enhancing linguistic exports—often effectuated under the guise of the benefits of standardization and regularization, and marketed under the auspices of "enhanced intelligibility" in transnational encounters (Park and Wee 2012)—such media efforts at lowering the tender status of Africa's multilingualism make economic sense. After all, Africa is home to approximately a third of the globe's current linguistic diversity (Skutnabb-Kangas and Heugh 2012).

■ Figure 14.21 An Example of How English Is Presented as a Linguistic Ticket out of Mass Pathology, in a Scene from the Film *Blood Diamond,* 2006 (Courtesy Warner Brothers Pictures)

Visualizations—such as those in figures 14.20, 14.21, and 14.22—instigate what West (2004, 258) labels the "homogenizing impulse." In such filmic scenes, then, we witness how in and through linguistic choices more insidious monolithizing linguistic processes are set in action. Via carefully contrived scenes that effectively lionize some languages while demonizing others—unsurprisingly, the continent's languages—we begin to understand how linguistic taste and distaste are in fact created. Homogenizing efforts are presented as having positive outcomes. Countless filmic scenes underscore feelings of linguistic "gratitude" for language abandonment. Consider a final example from another biographically inspired, acclaimed film, *I Dreamed of Africa,* shown in figure 14.23, in which we witness a speech act of "thanking" for this "gift of English" (Mukherjee 2009).

The mimetic effect cannot be ignored, in both the short and long terms. Inevitably, then, "we construct what we see, just as we are constructed by what we see" (van Eeden and du Preez 2010, 6). As demonstrable proof, consider the Western media's "crucial role in shaping perceptions of and knowledge about the continent" of Africa, as recounted by Mellese and Müller (2012, 194), who list the following effects: "One US study reveals common beliefs held among US students about Africans as wild natives living in primitive huts, still stuck in the hunting and gathering era. . . . Moreover in the same study, respondents exhibited common usage of terms such as tribes, primitive, cannibals, and savages."

Figure 14.22 An Example of a "Yearning" for English Education as the Ultimate Linguistic Passport, Voiced by a Lead Character in the Film *Blood Diamond*, 2006 (Courtesy Warner Brothers Pictures)

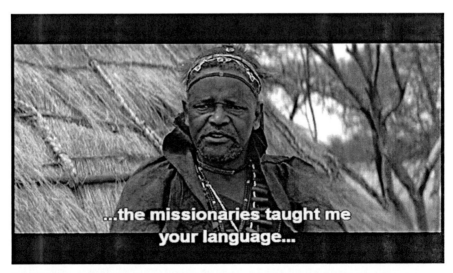

Figure 14.23 An Example of How Homogenizing Efforts Can Be Presented as Positive Outcomes, as the Speech Act of "Thanking" for the "Gift of English" Underscores Feelings of Linguistic "Gratitude" for Language Abandonment, in This Scene from the Film *I Dreamed of Africa*, 2000 (Courtesy Columbia Pictures)

These examples confirm what Harding (2003, 80) notes to be a metaphoric deployment of Africa for stories "*set* in Africa but not *about* Africa" in current Hollywood productions. Do such scenes of pathology have any real effects, one wonders? Is there any outcome of self-loathing emanating from such portrayals? Besha (2009, 9) notes one such effect: "But if nothing else, it has led the African elite to despise everything African, their languages being the clearest example."

What are some possible solutions? Increasing access to filmmaking potential, as in the burgeoning Nollywood film industry stemming from Nigeria, can counteract such hegemonic imagery about Africa. Localized productions of films by Africans, for Africans, and about Africa—presented either in local languages (Şaul and Austen 2010) or via the use of pidgin English, so that "the tales can be understood almost anywhere on the continent" (Harding 2003, 81)—form an exciting potential counterforce from within the continent and are bound to lead to the persistence of local linguistic diversity in spite of potent efforts keen on pushing for a paradigm of linguistic abandonment from outside the continent.

## Conclusion: Where Do We Go from Here?

This chapter has presented copious evidence for the overt and covert discoursal and visual strategies deployed in popular media streams poised to reduce and devalue Africa's multilingual capital. Such outcomes are accomplished via a thematic subverting of African multilingualism to Western-oriented monolingualism—scenarios in which real native-speaker multilingual knowledge is invisibilized and relegated to peripheral filmic space. Such synergized thematicizations of African multilinguality in twenty-first-century media accounts both showcase and aim to reaffirm the so-called diminishing and diminished transactional value of the continent's multilingualness. Multimodal data from such media streams are used to make a case for why the ideology of so-called low linguistic tender status—overt and covert deprecations, including the thematicized and real marginalization of the linguistic worth of Africa's diverse linguistic currencies—continues to persist. This is the case in spite of global interconnectedness, transnationalization, and deterritorialization, and in spite of increasing evidence of geoscapes worldwide, keenly pursuing nationally oriented acts of linguistic protectionism in education (Weber and Horner 2012), particularly in what have been dubbed the Global North nations.

Increasing numbers of accounts point to the actual value that African multilingualism accords skilled African workers from a plethora of nations in the Global North, in "translingual encounters" (Canagarajah 2013,15)—scenarios in which multiplex proficiencies in a multiplicity of codes form an asset rather than a liability, especially in participatory encounters in neoliberal economies. Why, then, do such commonsensical notions of the linguistic valuelessness of these languages persist? Can the media be implicated in such linguistic dispositions?

After all, renditions of linguistic value have long-term effects, both personally and societally and both within and across national borders (Weber and Horner 2012). In countries like South Africa, for example, even with official multilingual policies in place, learners with rich, local linguistic repertoires increasingly have "become mesmerized and paralyzed by English" (Desai 2001, 331). Even more troubling, schools—in a bid to join in the race toward the macro-imposed, market-driven forces of globalization (Park and Wee 2012)—increasingly seem eager to abandon mother-tongue learning in favor of English education. English is now often being introduced in earlier elementary grades and, as most teachers can safely attest, to the detriment of actual student academic performance. Desai (2001, 326) presents poignant ethnographic evidence of the educational effects of such choices. She chronicles in detail the remarkable contrasts in fluency levels in Xhosa versus English in her study of the linguistic output of fourth and fifth graders in a township school in Cape Town. Her findings contrast the richness of these elementary school-children's narrative performance in Xhosa with their paucity of performance in English on the very same tasks—scenarios that transform rich storytellers of Xhosa into semilingual, almost illiterate speakers of English. Such educational policies, she argues, inevitably "result in marginalizing the majority of its citizens" and, furthermore, sustain a cycle of linguistic powerlessness and the perpetuation of poverty—"a double divide" (Mohanty 2012, 139) between the elite and the poor not just nationally but also transnationally.

Desai (2001, 338) cautions about the need to develop "a healthy language industry that would benefit the speakers of African languages" and stresses that such solutions can only be accomplished if "ordinary speakers of African languages assert their language rights and agitate for greater currency of their languages." The mother-tongue-based, multilingual paradigms of education that are already in place in countries such as Ethiopia and Burkina Faso optimistically point to the feasibility of continent-derived educational models aimed at the maintenance of Africa's linguistic resources—in spite of the macro forces pushing toward the "mirage of a homogenous globalized world." As the analysis in this chapter has demonstrated, "formal education is, together with media, decisive for the future of the world's languages" (Skutnabb-Kangas and Heugh 2012, 1, 15). Understanding the historicization of linguistic devaluation, and thus how the ideology of linguistic denigration and invisibilization has been constructed and continues to be construed in and through the media, is one step in the right direction.

## References

Abadzi, Helen. 2011. "Multilingualism: An African Advantage—a Paradigm Shift in African Languages of Instruction Policies; a Review." *International Review of Education* 57:499–500.

Adesope, Olusola, Tracy Lavin, Terri Thompson, and Charles Ungerlider. 2010. "A Systematic Review and Meta-Analysis of the Cognitive Correlates of Bilingualism." *Review of Educational Research* 80, no. 2: 207–45.

Allington, Daniel. 2012. "English and Global Media." In *The Politics of English: Conflict, Competition, Co-existence*, edited by Ann Hewings and Caroline Tagg. New York and Oxford: Routledge and Open University.

Besha, Ruth. 2009. "Regional and Local Languages as Resources of Human Development in the Age of Globalization." In *African Languages in Global Society*, edited by Thomas Bearth, Jasmina Bonato, Karin Geitlinger, Lorenza Coray-Dapretto, Wilhelm J. G. Möhlig, and Thomas Olver. Cologne: Rüdiger Köppe Verlag.

Blackledge, Adrian. 2000. "Monolingual Ideologies in Multilingual States: Language, Hegemony, and Social Justice in Western Liberal Democracies." *Estudios de Sociolinguistica* 1:25–45.

Blommaert, Jan. 2010. *The Sociolinguistics of Globalization*. Cambridge: Cambridge University Press.

Blommaert, Jan, Sirpa Leppänen, and Massimiliano Spotti. 2012. "Endangering Multilingualism." In *Dangerous Multilingualism: Northern Perspectives on Order, Purity, and Normality*, edited by Jan Blommaert, Sirpa Leppänen, Päivi Pahta, and Tina Räisänen. Basingstoke, UK: Palgrave Macmillan.

Canagarajah, Suresh. 2013. "Skilled Migration and Development: Portable Communicative Resources from Transnational Work." *Multilingual Education*, 3, no. 8: 1–19.

Desai, Zubeida. 2001. "Multilingualism in South Africa with Particular Reference to the Role of African Languages in Education." *International Review of Education* 47, nos. 3–4: 323–39.

Harding, Frances. 2003. "Africa and the Moving Image: Television, Film, and Video." *Journal of African Cultural Studies* 16, no. 1: 69–84.

Mellese, Matewal Adane, and Marion G. Müller. 2012. "Mapping Test-Visual Frames of Sub-Saharan Africa in the News: A Comparison of Online News Reports from Al Jazeera and British Broadcasting Corporation Websites." *Communication, Culture and Critique* 5:191–229.

Mohanty, Ajit. 2012. "Mother Tongue Language Education and the Double Divide in Multilingual Societies: Comparing Policy and Practice in India and Ethiopia." In *Multilingual Education and Sustainable Diversity Work*, edited by Tove Skutnabb-Kangas and Kathleen Huegh. New York: Routledge.

Mukherjee, Alok K. 2009. *This Gift of English: English Education and the Formation of Alternative Hegemonies in India*. Delhi: Orient BlackSwan.

Norton, Charles. 2013. "'Translating Africa': Review of *Africa in Translation: A History of Colonial Linguistics in Germany and Beyond, 1814–1945*, by Sara Pugach." *Critical Multilingualism Studies* 1, no. 2: 123–26.

Oh, David C., and Omotayo O. Banjo. 2012. "Outsourcing Postracialism: Voicing Neoliberal Multiculturalism in *Outsourced*." *Communication Theory* 22:449–70.

Pandey, Anjali. 2011. "Invisible Languages: 'Translating' African Multilingualness on the Silver Screen: A Semiotic Study." Paper presented at African Conference on Applied Linguistics, University of Maryland, College Park, June.

———. 2012. "'War on Terror' via a 'War of Words': Fear, Loathing and Name-Calling in Hollywood's Wars in Afghanistan and Iraq." *Alternate Routes: A Journal of Critical Social Research, 35th Anniversary Edition: Uniting Struggles: Critical Social Research in Critical Times* 23, no. 1: 11–58.

———. 2015. *Monolingualism and Linguistic Exhibitionism in Prize-Winning Fiction in a Flat World*. Basingstoke, UK: Palgrave Macmillan.

Park, Joseph S., and Lionel Wee. 2012. *Markets of English: Linguistic Capital and Language Policy in a Globalizing World*. New York: Routledge.

Pym, Anthony. 2013. "Translation as an Instrument for Multilingual Democracy." *Critical Multilingualism Studies* 1, no. 2: 78–95.

Şaul, Mahir, and Ralph A. Austen, eds. 2010. *Viewing African Cinema in the 21st Century: Art Films and the Nollywood Video Revolution*. Athens: Ohio University Press.

Sebba, Mark. 2010. "Discourses in Transit." In *Semiotic Landscapes: Language, Image, Space*, edited by Adam Jaworski and Crispin Thurlow. London: Continuum.

Seib, Philip. 2012. *Al Jazeera English: Global News in a Changing World*. New York: Palgrave Macmillan.

Skutnabb-Kangas, Tove, and Kathleen Huegh, eds. 2012. *Multilingual Education and Sustainable Diversity Work*. New York: Routledge.

Van Eeden, Jeannem, and Amanda du Preez, eds. 2010. *South African Visual Culture*. Pretoria: Van Schaik.

Weber, Jean-Jacques, and Kristine Horner. 2012. *Introducing Multilingualism: A Social Approach*. New York: Routledge.

West, Cornel. 2004. "The New Cultural Politics of Difference." In *The Cultural Studies Reader*, edited by Simon During. New York: Routledge.

# Contributors

**Carolyn Temple Adger** is a senior fellow at the Center for Applied Linguistics.

**Kingsley Arkorful** is a social development consultant affiliated with the School of Continuing and Distance Education, University of Ghana.

**Richard Beyogle** is a PhD student in the School of Foreign Languages and Linguistics at the University of Illinois at Urbana-Champaign.

**Eyamba G. Bokamba** is a professor of linguistics at the University of Illinois at Urbana-Champaign.

**One Tlale Boyer** is a postdoctoral researcher in the Department of Linguistics at Georgetown University.

**Lydiah Kananu Kiramba** is a PhD student in the School of Foreign Languages and Linguistics at the University of Illinois at Urbana-Champaign.

**Ruth Kramer** is an assistant professor of linguistics at Georgetown University.

**Leonard Muaka** is an assistant professor of English and foreign languages at Winston-Salem University.

**Eyovi Njwe** is a faculty member at the University of Bamenda.

**Tolulope Odebunmi** is a graduate student at the University of Ibadan.

**Anjali Pandey** is a professor of applied linguistics and teaching of English to speakers of other languages at Salisbury University.

**Samson Seid** is a faculty member in indigenous studies at Dilla University.

**Sheena Shah** is a postdoctoral fellow in the Centre for African Language Diversity at the University of Cape Town.

**Barbara Trudell** is a senior literacy and education consultant at SIL Africa.

**Stephen L. Walter** is an associate professor at the Graduate Institute of Applied Linguistics.

**Elizabeth C. Zsiga** is a professor of linguistics at Georgetown University.

# Index

Italic page numbers with a *t* appended indicate tables; *f* is for figures; and *i* is for photographic illustrations. Specific cities will be found under their countries.

CPSIA information can be obtained
at www.ICGtesting.com
Printed in the USA
FFOW04n1828270115
10653FF